Rockets and Rodeos

Books by Thomas Mallon

NONFICTION

Edmund Blunden

A Book of One's Own

Stolen Words

Rockets and Rodeos

FICTION

Arts and Sciences

Aurora 7

Rockets and Rodeos

and Other American Spectacles

THOMAS MALLON

TICKNOR & FIELDS
New York 1993

For information about permission to reproduce selections
from this book, write to Permissions, Ticknor & Fields,
215 Park Avenue South, New York, New York 10003.

Library of Congress Cataloging-in-Publication Data

Mallon, Thomas, date.
Rockets and rodeos and other American spectacles / Thomas Mallon.
p.   cm.
ISBN 0-89919-939-9
1. United States — Social life and customs — 1971–   I. Title.
E169.04M35   1993
973.928 — dc20   92-33189
CIP

Printed in the United States of America
BP 10 9 8 7 6 5 4 3 2 1

Some of these essays appeared in slightly different form in
The American Spectator, The Yale Review, Southwest Review,
and *The Best American Sports Writing 1992.*

Excerpt on pages 48 and 49 reprinted with permission
from the New York *Post,* June 14, 1990.

FOR BILL BODENSCHATZ

ACKNOWLEDGMENTS

Over the past four years I have been more grateful than I can say to Wladyslaw Pleszczynski, managing editor of *The American Spectator,* the magazine in which many of these pieces first appeared. Wlady gave instant and encouraging assent to whatever unlikely subject I proposed writing about, and he was always generous with space, deadlines, and expenses. Without his support I could not have begun or completed this book.

I am also indebted to *The Yale Review*'s Penelope Laurans and Wendy Wipprecht, and to Willard Spiegelman of *Southwest Review,* for opening long stretches of their journals' pages to the atypical material I presented.

In traveling around the country, I have been more than usually dependent on the kindness of strangers, who provided me with rides, directions, and conversation. I am grateful to every person who allowed me to thrust a tape recorder or notepad at him, and to the full-time journalists in whose company I often found myself: they were unfailingly patient in answering questions from the novelist-critic blundering along behind. To all of these people and to everyone listed below, for myriad reasons, my thanks: David Beckwith, Martin Beiser, Elmer and Sophia

Acknowledgments

Blistein, Nan Chalat, Art Cooper, Laurence Cooper, Dayna Cravens, Charles Deehr, Jack Dillard, Mary Evans, Mary Farrell, Jay Geary, Ned Hamlin, John Herman, Frances Kiernan, Michael Kroll, Liz Smitten, Nancy Willard.

Thanks to Teddy, too.

CONTENTS

Contents

INTRODUCTION

In the fall of 1988 I asked *The American Spectator* if I could cover the launch of the space shuttle *Discovery,* the first one since the *Challenger* disaster thirty-two months before. I was in the middle of writing a novel set on the day of Scott Carpenter's Project Mercury flight, and all the research I'd done for that — plus the fact that I'd taken the *Challenger* accident hard — made me want to be at Cape Canaveral to see the space program get off the ground once more. "By the Late Morning's Light" was the piece that resulted, and I soon found myself embarked on a whole book of "spectacles," a word I defined loosely enough to result in the rest of the essays here: reports on the launching of a Black Brant XII rocket into the aurora borealis from Alaska's Poker Flat Research Range; the attempted-murder trial of a bank robber in Manhattan criminal court; the hours at San Quentin before Robert Alton Harris's execution would either be carried out or stayed; the senatorial campaigns of Rhode Island's patrician Claiborne Pell and his young opponent, Claudine Schneider; some political barnstorming with Dan Quayle; the fiftieth-anniversary commemorations at Pearl Harbor; a summer at the United Nations; Owosso, Michigan's annual Curwood Festival; the International Finals Rodeo championships in Oklahoma; the 1992 Sundance Film Festival; and the auction of Rex Harrison's personal effects at the William Doyle Galleries in New York.

I came to some of the subjects out of lifelong interest (the rocketry pieces) or curiosity (the rodeo), whereas others simply arose from circumstance (the death of Rex Harrison, the arrival of the Pearl Harbor anniversary). Some brought me back to places I knew (Rhode Island, where I'd gone to college; Manhattan criminal court, where I'd done jury duty), but most of them took me to locations I'd only heard of (San Quentin) or never knew existed (Owosso). In gathering them into this book, it seemed to me that each of the twelve pieces could, with a bit of stretching here and there, be paired with another, and that's how I've presented them, with six short postscripts spaced throughout the book.

A critic typically has to circle his subject, contemplating its various aspects as he might a sculpture's, whereas a novelist, confronted with a similar mass, looks for a narrative line, the rope that will help him up and over it. I was used to the different trajectories from books I'd written before this one, and as *Rockets and Rodeos* accrued, I realized that the reason the whole thing felt like none of those other books was that it was a little bit like all of them. Some of the events described here had narrative lines running straight toward climax and resolution (the rocket goes up, the election is held), while others could only be circled (going from booth to booth at the Curwood Festival, from meeting to meeting at the United Nations).

Travel has almost always been beyond my capacities for enjoyment. I used to ascribe my disappointments with it to loneliness, but even now, when I'm not traveling alone, a certain absence will sadden me. What will be missing is work, that endlessly reliable companion from whom I can't stand being away more than half a day at a time. The self-improving or "broadening" function of travel is too vague and long-term to vanquish a sense of purposelessness that befalls the workaholic wayfarer. But making these trips was different. They didn't mix business and pleasure; they were a pleasure *because* they were business. Though I made them alone, I felt fine because I was functional. The sight of my own pen and pad domesticated whatever hotel room I stayed in, like the family photos or good-luck knickknack one takes along to set out on the hotel dresser, whose fast-sliding empty drawers sound the same wherever you go.

I approached these dozen spectacles in an attitude of active passivity — not so much busy-bee reporter as fly on the wall. I wasn't trying to "dig out" anything so much as get buried — or, let's say, immersed — in the events I was watching, and was watching others watch. For however many days I was in the grandstand or on the campaign trail or wandering the fairgrounds, I was doing what Hazlitt called "living to one's-self" — that is, "living in the world, as in it, not of it: it is as if no one knew there was such a person, and you wished no one to know it: it is to be a silent spectator of the mighty scene of things, not an object of attention or curiosity in it; to take a thoughtful, anxious interest in what is passing in the world, but not to feel the slightest inclination to make or meddle with it." I suppose I still have a few dormant fantasies about being an astronaut, but I haven't the slightest inclination to ride a Brahma bull or be vice president of the United States. Wherever I went, I was glad to consider myself what the Victorian parent told the Victorian child to see himself as: the least important person in the room. During each trip my own narrative — my regular life back home — stopped for several days, and my irrelevance to what was in front of my face left me, I hope, more percipient than participation would have.

Despite the above, many of these pieces make use of the first person, since they are, after all, personal reflections, and since any writer's character will eventually bob to the surface no matter how many anonymous, third-person pronouns he weights it with. Readers will quickly detect a sensibility that is, politically and otherwise, fairly conservative, and certain peculiarities will be evident as the book goes on. I am, for instance, phobic about driving, and although I am frequently in someone else's passenger seat in the course of these pages, I am never behind the wheel. This made for a number of practical difficulties: cabs will take you to the gate of the Kennedy Space Center but no farther, and you have many miles more to go once you're inside. At the opposite end of the country, for the other rocket launch, I felt pleased to be booked into a lodge just one mile from Alaska's Poker Flat Research Range, until I learned that walking to the range was inadvisable: the moose were weary of the winter's heavy snowfalls and disinclined to share the road.

After watching Dan Quayle and his family parade through Huntington, Indiana, on July 4, 1991, I got ready to hop down from the back of the press pickup truck that had been riding in front of them, and experienced a twinge of realization: I had the knees of a middle-aged man, and what's more, I had them because I *was* a middle-aged man. So I'm glad I took my housebound nature on the road during the past few years, because I don't think I'm likely to write a book like this a decade from now: I'll be back to composing belletristic ones at home in my slippers.

I never came back from any of these places sorry I went, but it was only after writing about them that I knew for sure whether or not I'd really been present.

NEW YORK CITY
JULY 17, 1992

Rockets

By the Late Morning's Light

Late Tuesday night, September 27, at the Holiday Inn on Merritt Island, Florida, about ten miles south of Cape Canaveral, the moon, like a neglected mistress, was looking down on the outdoor pool, the floodlit palm trees, and the porno-receptive satellite dishes. Throughout the hotel and all over the island, people were thinking about the relaunching of the space shuttle, only thirty-six hours away. The mood officially declared by local chambers of commerce was resolute enthusiasm: GO DISCOVERY! read the fast-food marquees along Route 520 and State Road 3.

But the native boosterism, like the space program itself, was tinged with nostalgia. "Back to the Future," one popular button said, leaving its observer to realize that a successful launch could only put us where we had been three years ago, before *Challenger*. A big press-kit button (made in Canada) showed the phone number for more information about Florida's Space Coast: 1-800-USA-1969, the last four digits inviting one to think, What a falling off was there. Down the road from the hotel, one could enter a small establishment called Apollo Hair Systems, a baldness clinic. Perhaps the least onward-and-upward signs were the green ribbons hung all over town: meant to convey

3

faith that everything was "go for launch," they instead gave subliminal stimulus to memories of hostages, terror, and Carter-like malaise.

There was, however, another sight to be seen Tuesday night, a light, one that could, if we wanted it to, be pointing unequivocally into the future. In the southeastern sky, only about 36 million miles above the pool, it was shining much more invitingly than usual. It was Mars, closer this month to Earth than at any time since 1971, the year before we abandoned the Moon.

On July 7, the Soviet Union launched *Phobos 1,* an unmanned probe, to the Martian moon. "Sometimes we surprise ourselves with how bold we are becoming," Dr. Roald Z. Sagdeyev, head of the Space Research Institute, was quoted as saying of the glasnost with which the phases and technologies of the Soviets' thirty-year program of Mars exploration are now being debated. As it happens, *Phobos 1* began spinning uselessly out of control late in August, but that wasn't as big a setback as one might think: a *Phobos 2* had already gone up on July 12.

A police state, a plan, a probe, a planet. The Soviets are committed to going. By contrast NASA has a whole palette of splashy ideas — they've looked great in the newsmagazines these past few months — and a firm commitment to none of them. At the rate we are going, the Soviets won't bury us; they'll just pass us in the cosmos's left lane. We can even give them the maps, which we've had for more than a decade: 97 percent of Mars was charted by the barely remembered *Viking* probes of the seventies.

But late on L-2 (Tuesday, two days before launch) there was no time to think about these things. However unsure of its destination, America was once more ready, in the words of Chuck Yeager and Alan Shepard, to "light the candle."

The networks and wire services have permanent quarters at the Kennedy Space Center press site, small structures with bright logos that look like beachfront condos. At certain moments on

L-1, Wednesday, one can see condensation on their big picture windows: the NASA habit is to air-condition facilities to the point where the agency's real business seems to be not space research but cryogenics. Most outfits smaller than the networks make do with trailers, and there are at least four times as many reporters here now than were present on January 28, 1986, for *Challenger.* Even that launch had attracted more than what was, by then, usual. That morning there had been the human-interest angle: the teacher going up.

At 8:30 A.M. today the white press dome serving all the media is filled with reporters trying to find out if they're sheep or goats. For this launch NASA has adopted a two-tier system of access. A card with a mere orange stripe will allow you on the press site only until midnight. After that you're to be cleared out of the KSC and made to watch the lift-off from the causeway. What you want instead, like an immigrant, is the "green card" — a badge that, after midnight, will allow you back onto the press site for a view from the bleachers in front of the huge digital countdown clock. There's a lot of resentment and perplexity about the restrictions. Are they trying to limit the number of pictures of another accident to, say, one thousand instead of five thousand? What's the point?

The dome tries to maintain the same sunniness of the local merchants. It's ringed with an assortment of foreign flags (there's China's, but where's the USSR's?), and the walls are decorated with spectacular photos of past lift-offs that have been signed and donated by press regulars. A banner sounding like a TV network's fall-season promo declares: "America's Pride: The Journey Continues." And there are more green ribbons. Behind the foreign reporters' assistance desk is a small sketch of the seven *Challenger* astronauts, bordered in black. Elsewhere there's a small, almost cheerful needlepoint memorial to them.

Little green countdown clocks say −11:00:00. We're in a prolonged, built-in hold that allows the ground crews to catch up on their work. Lists of "Photo Opportunities" and "Bus

Departures" are posted, as is "Shuttle Weather," updates of conditions at the Cape and the various landing sites, scheduled and emergency. The latest information is marked in black wax pencil, an anachronistic touch, as if everyone were keeping an eye out for Lindbergh or Amelia Earhart.

I overhear one reporter telling another: "If you want to see the rock fall, you gotta be there." This seems a bit much in the hard-boiled-humor line, until I realize he's saying that on Monday he plans to be in California, at Edwards Air Force Base, for the landing.

At 9 A.M. there is a press briefing from Frank Merlino, NASA test director at the KSC. You can attend it in the auditorium or watch it on NASA Select Satellite SATCOM F-2R, Transponder 13 — which is to say, the TV monitors in front of the press bleachers and inside the dome. There is standing room only inside the auditorium, and a row of video cameras on tripods, like a firing squad, at the back; but the questions are mild and predictable, as if the reporters don't want further to worry a man who's already got so much on his mind. What is the mood of the launch team? "I think they're excited and looking forward to tomorrow," says Merlino. Can he elaborate on "the abrasion on the forward thruster"? It's not a problem. Is there "more attention to duty" now? Well, yes. That much he has to say. Like most NASA officials he has the job of assuring the public that everyone's being super-careful this time even though they were never really sloppy before. There is little inclination on the press's part to pursue this into the realm of contradiction.

A reporter asks about the "AFE" problem — Acronyms For Everything — the briefing's laugh line, a preface to a real question about the FSS, the Fixed Service Structure at the pad. The woman next to Merlino reminds us that there is an acronym dictionary available in the dome. An alumna of the Phyllis Oakley Spokesperson School of Imperturbability, she weeds out questions not dealing strictly with the "launch process," saving Mr. Merlino from any heavy going, however unlikely, and re-

minding the press that they can ask anything they like at the
1 P.M. briefing from higher-ups.

"I like the process," Merlino says when he's asked about the
new leadership role the astronauts have been given since *Challenger.* The final decision on whether to launch will come tomorrow from Captain Robert L. Crippen, who flew the first
shuttle with John Young back in 1981. Minutes before lift-off,
he's supposed to poll a twenty-one-member management team
— engineers, contractors, a weatherman, a safety expert — before he himself says, finally, yes or no. With this life-and-death
power, he is in some ways the big story here, the emotional
focus, almost as a single Mercury astronaut would have been a
quarter century ago. From the moment Project Gemini began
sending two men into space instead of one, the mythic lone-
eagle aspect of launching was lost. The truth is that if two men
— or seven — blow up, those witnessing the catastrophe will
feel less anguish than if it's only one. Circuses shoot one man
out of a cannon, instead of five, not for cost-effectiveness but
because the single death is a fate, a destiny; the multiple one,
like an Asian earthquake, seems too haphazard to engage our
imaginations in the same way. If *Discovery* blows up tomorrow,
five stories will be too many to absorb. In a day or two, boyish
Pinky Nelson, the most colorful of the crew, will get mixed up
in our minds with Colonel Covey and Commander Hauck. But
people here will remember Captain Crippen as the man whose
life was shattered by saying yes.

The purpose of STS-26 (the twenty-sixth flight of the Space
Transportation System) is to test out the hundreds of changes
made to equipment and procedures since *Challenger* and the
Rogers Commission, and to launch, from the shuttle's cargo
bay, TDRS-C, Tracking and Data Relay Satellite C, into a geo-
synchronous orbit of the earth. Pushed up to 22,300 miles, it
will be on a sort of celestial treadmill, flying at the same speed
the planet does, and therefore, more or less, standing still. Co-
operating with TDRS-A, it will eliminate the need for the neck-

lace of tracking stations NASA has had to maintain for three decades in intermittently friendly countries around the globe. TDRS-A has been in the skies since 1983; TDRS-B blew up with *Challenger.*

Aside from releasing TDRS-C, the *Discovery* crew will do the usual array (or at least four days' worth) of onboard experiments and broadcast a tribute to the crew of STS-25 (*Challenger*). But there is really only one purpose to this mission and everybody knows it: STS-26 is about finding the nerve, once more, to get up on the high wire.

The real problem of the shuttle is that, like TDRS-C, it is essentially going nowhere. In his book *Entering Space,* STS-14 astronaut Joseph P. Allen, intending not irony but enthusiasm, wrote that the "astronauts aboard each shuttle mission are no longer simply space explorers but, rather, a collection of skilled space workers." *Simply* explorers! There are those who argue that man is unnecessary in space, that all these satellites can be as easily launched and manipulated by remote control. (The air force, in particular, is not happy with the shuttle and would rather send up some of its payloads on refurbished Titan boosters.) In rebuttal, NASA continues to talk of how there are certain quick-decision contingencies to which man's nifty brain responds better than a computer. These statements usually suffer from sounding defensive and sentimental, but the truth is that they're not sentimental enough. If man isn't good enough to go into space for his own sake, for his own willful pleasure and assertion, then what's a rocket for?

At 10 A.M. on L-1 a press bus drives out to the ghost-town portions of the KSC, the places where, twenty-five years ago and more, not hand-wringing but chest-thumping was the order of the day. First we pass the inhumanly scaled Vehicle Assembly Building; then a white sphere, looking like the Montgolfier brothers' balloon and holding liquid nitrogen; then the parked crawler that gets eighteen feet to the gallon when it takes the shuttle from the VAB to the pad; and then pad 39-B, where the shuttle itself, still scaffolded by both the Rotating Service Structure (RSS) and FSS, points the dull reddish head of its liquid fuel tank toward tomorrow morning.

After a stop there, the pad numbers drop and the years fall away. Past 34, site of the 1967 Apollo fire that killed Gus Grissom, Ed White, and Roger Chaffee; past 19, off which Geminis flew; and on to the most audacious one of all, 14, from which Glenn, Carpenter, Schirra, and Cooper rose, an eerie silver 7, entwined with the symbol of Mercury, now standing on the spot, celebrating the first group of astronauts. Beyond that lie the covered silos of an abandoned missile site, grass coming up through the bricks as if they made up city sidewalks instead of lids on Armageddon. And then we reach an early Redstone rocket, looking like a smaller version of the black and white Cape Canaveral lighthouse, built in 1868.

Inside the musty blockhouse of launch complex 26 one can touch the toggle switch that sent *Explorer 1* into orbit, a few months behind *Sputnik,* and look at a roomful of huge Univac-style equipment, all of the information it held now stowable in a single desktop computer.

That was then, this is now — a time when we know more than we know what to do with.

At 1 P.M. most of the press are in the bleachers, cans of diet soda and mosquito repellent beside their keyboards, for a briefing from five officials, including Rear Admiral Richard H. Truly, the former shuttle astronaut who is now associate administrator for space flight, and Dale D. Myers, NASA deputy administrator. Truly and Myers and the three others sit between the bleachers and the countdown clock at a dais made of crudely smoothed concrete; it evokes *The Flintstones,* though one supposes the designer was striving for something lunar.

Once again, the adversarial mood is decidedly muted. Before the gentle questions begin, there's even an isolated "hear, hear" from the bleachers when the weather is said to be looking good for tomorrow morning. Someone from *Aviation Week* asks Myers, who wears a black eye patch like Wiley Post, to contrast the current mood with that immediately after *Challenger*. He compares the change to the recovery of spirit that took place after the 1967 Apollo fire. Lynn Sherr of ABC asks if there isn't perhaps too *much* caution this time. Truly says that maybe there's some paperwork they could "tease out of the system" — but, of course, "You can't have too much safety," and space flight will never be without risk. It will also never be cheap, he tells the BBC man who inquires about all the boats and planes that will be deployed in the area tomorrow.

Can the space program survive another disaster? Myers says yes: "The issue of continuity is to me inevitable . . . Americans want to explore." But continuity won't extend to every office. Asked whether, since the astronauts will have their lives on the line tomorrow, they think their own jobs should be on the line, too, one of the men says: "I think I do."

Truly says, just before a good wind blows into the reporters' sunburning faces, that they're not going to push the weather "one iota."

Looking beyond tomorrow morning, Myers notes that a space station will take us "either to the Moon or Mars," putting them, at least, into a climactic sequence. The rest of his forecast is less than ringing. He reminds us that building a space station is administration policy — we're signing a treaty with our allies tomorrow in Washington; they're going to be helping us — but he can't tell us that going to Mars is official policy, because it isn't. The shuttle is "the key for support for the space station," he says; it's "still a vital part" of the program — which makes it sound more like Old Paint than a snorting charger.

But the "future of the program" isn't the story right now. The only story is whether or not the astronauts will survive the flight. As if to underline this, a fire truck and ambulance can suddenly be heard racing in the distance. The five officials, in an act of collective will, decide it's not worth turning around to watch.

Questioned about press restrictions, Truly says that they are the result not of *Challenger* but of other recent findings — like the "dispersal" problem noted after the recent accident with a Titan 34-D. He seems to be talking about a wider distribution of missile shrapnel than was once thought to occur. Oh.

But enough of that. "The American space program is not going to stop, manned or unmanned," says Truly; a hundred years from now, reporters will be questioning people sitting where he now sits about trips to Mars and other outposts. Still, the cheerful ex-astronaut adds, as if to appease the gods, another accident is "inevitable . . . in the cards."

The afternoon passes lazily. The RSS has been rolled back, and reporters sitting in the bleachers gaze across the grass and water at the *Discovery*'s three conical boosters like tourists who've decided to rest their feet in front of the Taj Mahal. At 5 P.M. all the local TV newscasters sent down here come out to do "stand-ups" near the countdown clocks. They wear great-looking blazers and blouses and, male or female, have hair sprayed to withstand winds stronger than ones it would take to scrub tomorrow's launch. Telegenic and underinformed, these video visitors are the androids of the whole business, made, it seems, of Velcro and Naugahyde. The print press in the bleachers, who have been living on Cremora and doughnuts for the last couple of days, pay them little mind.

At 6 P.M. everyone boards buses for the sunset photo op. First there's the chance to take several thousand stills and miles of videotape of the shuttle from about 2,500 feet. "Can anybody watch it from here?" someone asks a NASA rep, meaning can they watch it from here tomorrow morning. "If you want to die," she cheerfully replies. The pad is fringed with thin poles, which hold the remote-operated cameras that will film the launch and keep the press photographers from incineration.

NASA, despite its fixed smiles and uninflected voices, is quite mindful of theatricality, and it saves the best for last. By 7:30 the sky is purple, and the press are taken to a second stop, probably no more than a thousand feet from the pad. As evening begins to fall, the floodlights on the shuttle are incrementally brightened, prompting a restrained version of the *oohs* that come on summer nights between the flare and boom of really good fireworks. Several thousand more pictures; more miles of videotape, all of it of an empty, motionless rocket. The clicking and the whirring, weird and worshipful, goes on and on in the dark, and nobody cares about the mosquitoes and the sandspurs because nobody wants to leave. It's suddenly clear that this is not Old Paint. It *is* a charger, the night before the race of its life, and no one wants to say good night to it, no one wants to stop stroking its beautiful mane with his lens.

But eventually the buses back to the press dome must be boarded, and when you get there you notice that the countdown clock, frozen all day at T minus 11:00:00, has started to move. The floodlit shuttle, now more like Rockefeller Center than the Taj Mahal, can be seen in the distance, or you can watch a continuous live shot of it on the TV monitors in the dome. The NASA reps remind everyone that the site will be cleared by midnight. If you've got a green card you can come back; and if you're wise, you'll be back inside the KSC gates well before 4 A.M. A million and a half people are thought to be coming to watch the launch, most of them from campers and RVs they've already started parking on the roadsides.

Having secured a green card and cleared four checkpoints with it, I am back at the KSC before two in the morning, and an hour and a half later I am in Multifunction Facility K6-1145, the cafeteria and gift shop. It's near the corner of Saturn Causeway and Instrumentation Road, just down from the old moon rocket that lies like an immense beached hypodermic, thrown away after injecting the species into its first extraterrestrial home. At 3:30 the place is pretty crowded. Still, I'm having trouble staying awake and warm, so I decide to cross the road to the KSC fire station and ask if I can talk to some of the people on duty tonight.

Jerry Angel and Bill Meeks have been at the Cape for more than twenty years each. Both of them were off the day *Chal-*

lenger blew up, but Angel, who was out in the woods forty-five miles away, could tell even from that distance that something had gone wrong: "You couldn't have felt any worse if you'd been right there."

He says, "We're supposed to save lives and put out fires, but that's just in between." Their real business is preparing for launches. How do they feel tonight? "I'm a little bit apprehensive," allows Meeks. They agree that people at the Cape are especially serious now — not that things were ever really sloppy. But they can recall how before *Challenger* the occasional standby (having a fire truck around while something like welding went on) was eliminated. Not anymore.

Jerry Angel and Bill Meeks remember Apollo, and they agree things were more exciting then. Meeks says he felt "a part of history." But Angel guesses that the novelty wears off anything, and you've got to remember he was twenty-five when he started here. Still, there is something special about the morning that's only a couple of hours away. Angel's wife and seventy-five-year-old father-in-law are coming, and Meeks's wife recently told him to try to get her a pass, one of seven allotted to the fire station. She hadn't asked for one in years.

There is great American enthusiasm for space — only 18 percent in one recent poll would trim the NASA budget — but neither side in the vacuous 1988 presidential campaign really bothered to tap it. The Republican platform urged a Mars mission around the year 2000, and Bush supported the space station. Dukakis, after having wanted to pull back on that during the primary season (when liberal voters show their greatest strength), showed up at the Marshall Space Flight Center in Huntsville, Alabama, in August, during the general campaign, to say he was all for it. The Democrats' platform had no space plank, but their candidate said we should talk to the Soviets, and just about everyone else, about going to Mars.

The fact is that no one spoke with real specificity, or much interest. So where does that leave us? There's no point in dreaming about private enterprise and Mars. Only government will get us there. The appropriations are simply too massive and, even more to the point, only government can provide the inspiration. One more thing Jerry Angel and Bill Meeks agree on is that people at NASA do feel as if they're working for their country, not just punching some multinational's clock. I ask Angel if he thinks we ought to go to Mars, and he says, "That's all beyond me," but it's plain that if his country would only sound the call, he and Bill Meeks would gladly put their shoulders to the gyroscope.

By seven o'clock the sun and the astronauts are up, but there is a problem with the weather: it's lovely. The onboard computers are programmed for stronger, autumn winds, and the ones now in the upper altitudes are officially described as "springlike." The computers can't cope. You can feel everyone in the press dome getting ready to write the afternoon headline: GOOD WEATHER SCRUBS LAUNCH. Things proceed pessimistically, though at 7:20 Frank Merlino says the crew can suit up, and fifteen minutes later he tells them to go to the pad. All sorts of preparations and problem-solvings continue — the balky fan in Colonel Covey's suit; a bad fuse; garbled voice checks — yet they seem to be going on just in case there's a change in the weather.

But hours pass and the issue seems forgotten. Around 11:00 word comes that the latest weather balloon shows wind conditions are better — that is, worse. Nothing definitive gets said, but now the assumption is that it will go. The "window" lasts until 1:30 today; there are still more than two hours available, except for the six minutes from 12:13 to 12:19 during which a collision with the Soviet space station would be possible. Nervous laughter in the bleachers: STAR WARS. (Actually, the best indication of how behind we are in this whole business.)

And yet, it all suddenly seems to be moving too fast. At 11:15 Captain Crippen is taking his poll. At 11:25 he says it's going to go, and cheers go up. The count resumes, after the last built-in hold, at T minus 9 minutes.

One looks out across the grass, across the water, and thinks: it can't possibly make it. It's too big, too ugly, asymmetrical, not a flying thing at all. But the flames have begun to force their way out of it, and it lifts. At first one hears only the still-even voice of the Shuttle Launch Controller, and the applause, and the screams, but then it's past the tower and going faster, rolling, as it's supposed to, like a great whale, and an immense crackling forest-fire roar washes toward the bleachers, vibrating them and the ribs of everyone standing and crying.

After a minute it is gone, into a fluff of cumulus. But gone safely? Beyond T plus 73 seconds? The jinxed moment everyone wants to get past? Can you trust your ears, knowing how long the crackle probably took to get across the water and grass? But your ears don't matter, because the rocket's just been spotted, between two clouds, higher still, in a patch of wild blue yonder, and now you know that it's going to make it, and you search your mind for the first descriptive words it can think of, and they come, feeble and appropriate: like nothing on God's earth.

Later, you realize that the camera lies after all. It isn't really a visual experience. What you remember is the sound, the feel of your hands on the plank of wood in front of you. It isn't even a technological experience. It's too primitive — more like a volcano, something erupting amidst, because of, prayer and fear. Something that will have meaning only if the tribe gives it meaning.

Forty minutes later I'm sitting in the auditorium watching instant replay after instant replay of the launch, taken from various remote cameras and a helicopter, and available for use by the TV news people. The *Discovery*'s crew are already sailing over Madagascar, and outside, over pad 39-B, dark clouds are gathering and rain is ready to fall. There's a strange, Good Friday feeling. Even stranger is the sight of the FSS without the rocket. How can it be gone? It's as if one were crossing Lexington Avenue and looked up to see that the Chrysler Building, which was there just a minute ago, had somehow disappeared. The explanation that the *Discovery* isn't there *because it's flown away* seems implausible.

The event, however, is established. It's also over. The TV and newspaper people are making for Houston. The parking lot is emptying with no more trouble than if a concert or ball game had just gotten out.

At 11:30 I fall asleep with *Nightline* going at the foot of the bed. Thomas Paine, former head of NASA, is having a split-screen debate with former NASA historian Alex Roland. Paine is saying we need to go to Mars now, and Roland, echoing something Senator Proxmire has said ("Space is going to be there for a long time"), insists that the heavens can wait. Paine, who favors colonization (as opposed to the mine-and-run moon missions), declares his confidence that the first generation of Martians is already toddling around down here on Earth. Roland doesn't see the point of trying to do something before the technology is really ready.

Paine is the one making, if you will, common sense. You can apologize and justify and rationalize why we've been doing this for thirty years. You can read U.S. GPO pamphlet 1986-0-730-017/41011, "Space Program Spinoffs," and nod approvingly at news of new flame-resistant materials, the REDOX battery, dental arch wire, and Thermaflex ("being used in the development of a 'stay-dry' bicycle seat"), but you will be avoiding the truth that, from the beginning, this has all been directed toward saying goodbye. As Michael Collins, the real writer who's come out of the astronaut corps, puts it in his book *Liftoff:* "In a fundamental way Project Apollo was about leaving, the first move outward . . . I don't want to feel a lid over my head, or the heads of my children." Let's try to go with the Russians, he says, but let's be prepared to go by ourselves "if the promised collaboration does not materialize." It won't, of course. Two countries that can't keep ballet dancers, wheat, and Olympic athletes flowing reliably between them from year to year will not find a way to hold hands for thirty years and 75 million miles.

If we go, we will go alone. President Reagan, whose only memorable contribution to space exploration will remain the words he spoke the day of the *Challenger* accident, was, nonetheless, in September, given enough wing by his lame-duck status to revive a nineteenth-century imperial cry, declaring: "It is mankind's manifest destiny to bring our humanity into space, to colonize this galaxy. And as a nation we have the power to determine whether America will lead or follow." If we go, we should go now, rather than wait for the more comfortable technology or for the depleted ozone layer to evict us. Ego and nationalism are not unworthy propellants, and in any case they will burn away to nothing in the first wholly alien atmosphere we reach, where everything will be unrecognizable and where, reinvented, we may somehow at last know ourselves for what we are.

George Will has observed that "we haven't had a space policy since May 25, 1961." He was referring to President Kennedy's declaration, made that day to Congress, that we should pursue the "exciting adventure of space" and reach the Moon "before this decade is out." There are two other Kennedy quotations we ought to be keeping in mind now. One of them isn't really his but Robert Frost's (from "The Gift Outright") and was recited at the inauguration: "The land was ours before we were the land's." Which is to say, it was our fate to seize it; only having done that were we free to surrender to it, to sink roots, to be possessed by it, addicted to it as to home, the eventual absence from which makes one sick. But if we are afraid to seize the next place, it will no doubt be our fate to die from a graver sickness, failure of nerve. As a nation we will shrink to Holland, and as a species we will be the passenger pigeon.

The second Kennedy quotation is his peroration, in which he said that "here on earth, God's work must truly be our own." Those words were reduced to a half-truth eighty-two days later, on April 12, 1961, when Yuri Gagarin went into orbit around the planet, a day we will eventually recognize as the one on which our ticket was punched. From then on, we have had the chance to do God's work in the heavens, and a motive for leaving far stronger, finally, than any to do with science or adventure. Having been granted outright a second gift, the know-how, we should be mindful that God is not likely to forgive us if we fail to use it in order to repay whatever visits He may have made here.

The Last Rocket Club

FEBRUARY 1991

The heights by great men reached and kept
Were not attained by sudden flight,
But they, while their companions slept,
Were toiling upward in the night.

— HENRY WADSWORTH LONGFELLOW
"The Ladder of St. Augustine"

At five o'clock on weekday nights, workers leaving the University of Alaska's Geophysical Institute walk to their cars under the watchful eyes on a totem pole standing between the institute and the university museum, and at this hour, on Friday, February 8, 1991, thirty miles to the north, men at the institute's Poker Flat Research Range are struggling, at pad 3, with a Nike-Orion rocket whose thirteen sections of booster and payload, measuring 11.193 meters, look like a modern, faceless version of the totem pole back in Fairbanks.

But if the Indian carvers of the pole meant to fix the faces of their tribe's protectors, to make them permanently available for reverence, the men on pad 3 have only one goal for the Nike-Orion tonight, and that is to get rid of it: to fire Professor E. A. Bering III's experiment into an arc of the aurora borealis, which, with any luck, will be strong enough and directly over-head. The rocket's chief mission, to test and recover an x-ray pinhole scintillation camera, has already flopped once, last March, and there are only ten more days to get this refly off the ground during the current launch window. After February 19 the solar depression will be wrong. Unless the weather and the aurora and the payload's electronics bring themselves into a triangle of cooperation before then, the rocket will have to come down and all the NASA support personnel from Wallops Island, Virginia, and all the scientists from the University of Houston will have to pack up and go home and reassemble during some other window.

There's a second rocket ready to go on another pad close by, a Black Brant XII that will be one of the biggest missiles ever launched off the range. Its mission, according to the Flight Requirements Plan, is to study "the interaction of fields and particles in the auroral acceleration regime," by obtaining data "above a bright, active, auroral arc during a magnetic sub-storm." Unlike the Nike, the Black Brant is heading for an arc far to the north, not directly overhead, and after it's come down no one will go searching for its payload. The principal investigator on this project is Dr. Paul M. Kintner of Cornell, but his wife is ill and he isn't here, so the decision to launch, to bet on the right momentary conjunction of a volatile game-board of conditions, will be made instead by Dr. Roger Arnoldy of the University of New Hampshire. Payload components from the investigators' two universities — different experiments packed onto the same rocket — are combined like some joint program for study abroad.

Ray ("Marty") Martinez, a retired air force man still in his forties, has recently come to Poker Flat as the new launch officer. You go where the jobs are, he says — even if they bring you to a place so cold you can sometimes fling your hot coffee into the air without ever seeing any liquid come back down. Whichever rocket goes first, this will be his first launch. He explains to me the vagaries of weather and auroral light, variables on which tonight, he hopes, his grasp will change from the theoretical to the practical. So far things look promising; the sky is just a light overcast. But if the rockets don't go up tonight, we'll just keep coming back and staying each night from about 5 P.M. to 3 A.M. until they do. The scientists, says Marty, are choosy about their conditions, but by the end of a window they're more willing to settle, to shave some degrees off the desired auroral arc. Think of the expense involved: if they don't make it during their window, the rocket's batteries will have to be removed and all those visiting NASA personnel will have to go home, only to be brought back up later; and since there are already projects on for next month, the launch schedule will back up — just as it does in the space shuttle program all those time zones and latitudinal lines to the south.

What can be done on the cheap at Poker Flat generally gets done just that way. "The truck you're sitting in is retired military equipment," Marty tells me, and in this respect the beat-up old vehicle is like most of the rockets that rise off the range. People here get on with the job from an un-unionized willingness to improvise and pitch in. Marty was involved with the safe storage of munitions during his air force days, so there's a logical connection between his old job and this new one. But "just about everybody here is a jack of all trades," he says, as the men we look at through the truck windows pack the Nike in Styrofoam insulation. (When they're through, only the fins near the tail will stick out. The Styrofoam casing and the yellow wadding that fills in the cracks will remain on the rocket even as it's fired. The fins will just slice their way through it, from end to end.) The same men tend to the portable heaters around the launcher. Up here, where there's steam, there's life: the exhaust plumes seem less like pollution than breath, akin to the umbilical electric cables one sees attaching parked cars to outlets everywhere in Fairbanks.

Interiors, whether of buildings on the range or of the Chatanika Lodge just down the road, are toastily warm. No one worries about conservation when the oil pipeline that still pays

annual dividends of about $900 per person is visible from a
nearby stretch of the highway. Even in the sludgy wake of the
Exxon Valdez, Alaska remains a land where man feels rather
tickled by his success in placing himself. By mid-February a
traveler finds that his midnight-sun expectations are long since
obsolete: Poker Flat gains seven minutes of sunlight every day
after the winter solstice, and by now it doesn't get dark much
earlier here than it does in New York. The cold, however, lives
up to imaginings. Within seconds of leaving one of those toasty
interiors, a rainbow of ice crystals forms on the eyelashes. And
it's not a good idea to go walking on the road: both Marty and
Shirley Franklin, who with her husband, Ron, runs the lodge,
advise against it. The moose are aggressive right now. It's been
a snowy winter and they are tired of trudging in the woods:
they're likely to charge if they think you mean for them to give
up the plowed road.

At 6 P.M. both the Black Brant and the Nike are armed —
their safety restraints have been removed and they're ready to
have their solid-fuel propellants lit, ready to head toward two
different theaters of the same vast illuminated spectacle.

It is hard to keep lyricism out of even the most basic scientific
descriptions of the aurora. The Geophysical Institute's brochure
describes it as "the beautiful, visible evidence of the interaction
between the solar wind, the magnetosphere, and the upper atmosphere; a natural neon sign." Thomas A. Poterma, writing in
Smithsonian, uses awesome comparisons to summarize interest
in it: "Today, scientists are trying to find out what happens when
up to a trillion watts of power are injected into the upper atmosphere, producing heat, x rays, ionized particles and, when
viewed from space, more light than all the cities of North
America." The aurora sometimes surges alarmingly (in 1989
one could be seen as far south as Mexico), and it does a surprising amount of earthly damage: "serious interference to radio
communications, radio navigation, some defense-related radar
systems, and power transmission lines," according to the insti-

tute. Even the oil pipeline has been corroded by the "current created by changing magnetic fields accompanying the aurora."

Beyond these defensive reasons for studying it are some visionary ones: orbiting power stations might someday harvest the aurora's energy, and beyond even that, it might explain to us our origins. There are scientists who believe that using rocket-flown instruments to study the aurora's plasma gases can tell us something about the solar system's development from a contracting cloud of such material.

About 60 percent of Poker Flat's launches relate to the aurora. Since 1969 the site has been, as a sign on the wall of its office proclaims, "The Only Non-Government Rocket Range In the World Dedicated to Supporting Investigations of the Aurora Borealis and the Earth's Atmosphere." It got its name from the Bret Harte story as well as a Poker Creek that's in the area. Dotted with plain wooden structures, like a colonial settlement, the range has a handful of humble buildings housing workshops — carpentry, electrical, and so forth — that support its more exotic edifices, like the Telemetry and Optics domes up the hill. Near the range office is the NASA radar "tower," which is actually squat and gurgling, like an old washing machine. Like the rockets, the big Payload Assembly Building was made, in part, from scrap — materials left over from the demolition of the range's early A-frame launcher.

The Blockhouse, to which Marty returns me a little before 6:30, is the site of Operations and Payload Control. The latter is the place in which the visiting NASA guys, most of them from Wallops Island, keep the rocket and its cargo ready for launch. The Payload Assembly Building may boast a "class-100 clean room for assembling dust-sensitive payloads," but this control room is a grungy, junk-food paradise for tinkerers. Along with computers and countdown clocks are a TV, a microwave, a toaster oven, and a popcorn maker. Strewn amidst the parkas and paperback novels are bags of tortilla chips, Hostess doughnuts, Gatorade, Nutter Butter cookies, and raisins. Here the support team of engineers and technicians wait and eat and talk. Now they're watching the local news and weather, discussing the local Sizzler steak house down in Fairbanks, and arguing about a missing pair of pants.

The pants are significant, because a group has been told to go out to pad 4 and disarm the Black Brant, which is thought to be suffering from a self-discharging — that is, leaky — battery. The payload has got to be taken off the rocket and pulled apart. So the men are slowly putting on leggings, boots, and scarves. One of them says he'd rather work at Burger King — fewer problems — though somebody else reminds him, during this fourth week of the Gulf War: "At least we're not getting shot at." "Don't get hypertension or nothing, Al," one guy jokes to another who's not bothering to look up from his Joseph Wambaugh novel. "This shit don't bother me at all," says Al, reminding everybody that he spent fourteen years on one shuttle experiment. "I guess I'll eat dinner while you guys are gone."

If Poker Flat were the setting for a science fiction novel by Allen Steele, the technicians in Payload Control would be the "beamjacks," those orbital hardhats charged with the scut work of building man's future in the heavens. Or, to exchange space slang for military argot, these guys in Control are the grunts, the footsoldiery of above-the-atmosphere flight. With their gimme caps and scraggly hair, a lot of them look more like a heavy-metal audience than a careful assemblage of NASA nerds.

As *MacGyver* plays on the TV across from the popcorn popper, Wayne Ramer, a mechanical technician up here to work on the Nike's payload, describes himself to me as a wandering construction worker ("I torque bolts"). If the favorite rocket range for a lot of his Wallops colleagues is the one at White Sands, New Mexico, his own favorite location is probably in Sweden, where in the summer "they" (the scientists) study cloud formations. Alas, this year's trip there will probably be postponed for fear of terrorism.

"It's a pain in the ass with two rockets, isn't it?" asks Stuart MacKellar, the tattooed electronics technician working with Wayne on the Nike. Their payload is okay, but it can't get off the ground while people out on pad 4 are nursing the Black Brant. Geoff Bland, the Nike's project manager from Wallops, a preppy black man who is calmer, less profane, and more given to resigned smiles than the rest of the guys in the room, has been with NASA for nine years. (He was up at Poker Flat last March for the failed Nike mission of which this current one is a refly.) He tells me that Wallops supports thirty to forty rockets a year. A different team is put together for each launch, but he's worked with most of these guys before. The way it works is this: professors like Kintner and Bering apply to Wallops for grants and materials for their experiments. After that it takes six to eighteen months to design the payload, and another six to eighteen to build and test it. Most of the Nike payload now on pad 3 was built in-house at Wallops.

If a rocket doesn't get launched before the scientists run out of window, the payload is sent home: you never leave one on a launcher, because motors have to be attended to twenty-four hours a day. The assumption this time is that Kintner, whose Black Brant is ailing, won't have a window in March. If he doesn't get off the ground in the next eleven days, he'll have to wait until October or even next year. Sometimes, if there's a window and funding available within the next month, the same whole team can be brought back to the launch site, like a class that had dispersed for a vacation. During the design and testing phases, Geoff says, he's "communicating quite a lot" with the experimenters, but once everybody is in the field, they're functioning as separate teams.

Operations, across the Blockhouse's cinderblock corridor, owes its more homelike and mannerly feeling to its being staffed by permanent range personnel. Mike Cogan, the safety officer, is a lanky, soft-spoken fellow, just right for a small good-guy part in a western. He's been here for eleven years and says that when launch season is over, people like himself turn into "sweepers and carpenters," doing all sorts of jobs all over the range. Mike is the man who's slated to turn the key and fire the Black Brant: it's really Marty's job, as the launch officer, but since this is his first time, he's going to watch Mike. In years past, Mike was the "windweighter," a job Clif Moore now holds: "I point the rocket" is his economical description of what he does in a little room off the main one of Operations. Ed Heath, a bearded native-born Alaskan (the only one around here), has been on the range for nine years and is now in charge of Communications; Ralph New, who's been here for twenty, is Poker Flat's red-headed radarman. He sits at his scanner, munching popcorn, reading books, chuckling over his own stories about trapping and the early days of the range, and making sure some independent-minded bush pilot doesn't sneak in under the radar.

Chief credit for Operations' merry civility belongs to Mary Farrell, the "voice of Poker Flat," a grown-up version of the girl boys let into their tree houses, a lithe, friendly, alert young woman who sits behind her console in a cowboy hat. One suspects she had a lot of brothers: throughout each long night she manages to get everyone where he's supposed to be, and away from where he isn't, with a minimum of fuss. She's been at Poker Flat for four years, through fourteen launches, and lives in a little house right on the range. Usually, she says, you just "launch 'em and never hear any more about 'em," so not long ago she decided to go to a professor's lecture on the results of TOPAZ II (Topside Probe of the Auroral Zone), the predecessor of TOPAZ III, what's now on pad 4. As it turned out, most of what he said was so technical that, unless it was about the rocket and the payload, even Mary's quick mind couldn't grasp it. The experience only further demonstrates the peculiar disconnectedness of this coordinated undertaking.

Geoff Bland says it's been a "crazy/relaxed few days," and Mary, who never gets a vacation during launch season, tells someone on the phone: "We're trying to launch a rocket, and it's just not working out." She remarks to Geoff that Dr. Bering "doesn't look like a very happy camper this year." Geoff mentions that the professor was recently in Antarctica, and offers a kind of humorous sigh about "fame and fortune," burdens not borne by the Blockhouse grunts. But Mary points out that you can't get any fame if you can't get any data — and that could be Bering's fate, at least tonight.

"It hasn't been a great night, no," says Marty. In fact, he and Mike Cogan and Jack Dillard, the range manager, are on their way out, in heavy coveralls and fur-trimmed hoods, to help take the Black Brant's payload off the pad. A voice over the speaker says that the weather is all right, though "unfortunately the spacecraft is pretty sick."

By 8:20 P.M., back in Payload Control, someone is already giving an ululating Tarzan yawn. The smells of popcorn and cigarette smoke are mingling, pervading an operation that now, at least in the Blockhouse, seems listless and overmanned.

The Black Brant is "prime" tonight — first on the vertical runway, with priority over the Nike. When it gets its payload back, it will need a strong auroral arc to form over Kaktovik, also known as Barter Island, way up on the northern coast. The watch, over many hours, ranges from negligence to boredom to intensity. If an arc is forming, it will be noticed by the "all-sky" cameras, scanners of the heavens that are monitored on little black-and-white screens in Operations, Payload Control, and Optics. Like the beginning of a perfect wave or the distant shape of a white whale, an arc will start to coalesce and provoke hopeful mutters, ones meant to encourage both the sky and the watchers without tempting what Mike Cogan calls "the aurora gods." A strong arc will come to look like a stream of squeezed toothpaste against the grayish screen. There are many false alarms, and the first thing an all-sky-cam watcher has to learn is that the tantalizing white band at the top of the screen is only the lights of Fairbanks, thirty miles southwest, reflecting off the clouds.

As a watch drags into the early morning, Mike Cogan and Mary Farrell will play cribbage, a game in which one can overplay one's hand. With the arc it's the same. The scientists may find something terrific building up on the screen, but they must remember that it will take their rocket six minutes to reach the aurora; by the time it arrives the arc that looked so promising may have, in Mike Cogan's phrase, "mushed out." Prime time on the all-sky cam occurs around midnight. The odds of anything really good forming drop dramatically as the early morning wears on. At 3 A.M. it's easy to be tricked by "pulsating aurora," great patches of white on the screen that prove on closer inspection to be thin luminescent gruel.

At 8:45 on Friday, when the night and watch are young, I take a walk outside the Blockhouse. The winking red lights atop the radio towers seem to beckon the aurora, and in the darkness and quiet (broken only once in a while by Mary's announcements crackling out of speakers all over the range) Mike Cogan's talk of the aurora gods seems plausible, even pertinent. Surely the light can be coaxed down.

Its divine properties have been credited by any number of earthly hyperboreans. As Dorothy Jean Ray writes, Eskimos widely believed the lights to come from "spirits of the dead playing ball with a walrus head or skull" — rather as thunder over New York was once said to be the sound of Henry Hudson's ghost playing ninepins. During a nineteenth-century trek of Inuit from Baffin Island to Greenland, the migrants believed that the aurora was emanating from the head of their shaman, "a sign from the spirits and sure proof of his infallibility," according to Sam Hall in his book *The Fourth World*. And there were gold miners — Robert Service joked about them in verse — who thought the lights were caused by vapors from a fabulous secret lode. Even today, those gold miners still around here remain estranged from scientific explanations. Jack Dillard, the range manager, tells me that before launch season the Geophysical Institute advertises in the local papers, warning the miners that they're in an impact zone. Pilots of helicopters and fixed-wing planes also fly over the area to drop warning leaflets and to get an idea of who's out there. But Dillard says the miners are often more skeptical than grateful: they think someone's just trying to get them off their claims.

On suborbital, unmanned missions like tonight's, launchers can "jump the count" — just skip some of the prescribed countdown — when opportune circumstances present themselves. But by 9:00 it's clear that only the other kind are in effect for the Black Brant. Its payload is now off the pad, and unlikely to be fixed before the night's window for launching it closes at 3 A.M. In the Blockhouse eating has become a substitute for any kind of useful engineering activity. As the McLaughlin Group scream at one another on the TV, people move on from sandwiches to cookies and popcorn. Marty says it's the cold that does it to you; he's never eaten as much as he has since moving up here, and he's still losing weight. At 9:05 he struggles with an unmicrowavable pizza and suggests we give the Domino's down in Fairbanks a good laugh by asking them to deliver up here.

A half hour later Al Richardson, the altitude control man from Wallops, asks if I'd like to ride over to the Assembly Building and watch them work on the Black Brant's cranky payload. "No wonder we can't launch this goddamn rocket," he tells Phil Eberspeaker, the project manager, joking about the way Phil drives the short distance along the snow-covered road.

It is inside Payload Assembly, a big shed of a building full of machine tools and NASA shipping crates, that the scientists, come down from their Optics dome on the hill, and the Wallops guys, away from the junk-food-happy Blockhouse, manage to join forces. The Black Brant's nose cone, silver and golden and slim, like the steeple of a postmodern church, has been lifted off the man-and-a-half-tall payload; it now hangs from a hook. The trouble was indeed a wet-cell battery, which leaked down onto a sensor: rockets don't like to be left horizontal on their launchers for too long.

The Wallops guys do their work, and the young professors are left with time to stand around on the concrete floor. Steve Powell, of Cornell, and the University of New Hampshire's Mark Widholm and Marc Lessard explain to me that they are the "experimenters." Their senior colleagues (Kintner and Arnoldy) are, in the academic chain of command, the "investigators." The numerical data yielded by the experiment will be crunched, unsurprisingly, by graduate students.

Powell, Lessard, and Widholm have been up here for weeks, but right now they're only a distraction to the Wallops engineers, nervous horse owners getting in the way of trainers and grooms. Widholm and Powell get a telephone report that there's a beautiful arc building up south of Kaktovik, and they can only laugh regretfully that they won't be ready for it in ten minutes. Wayne Ramer, the mechanical technician for the Nike-Orion, comes over from the Blockhouse with the same news. "Rub it in," says Widholm. The nose cone has been dropped back over the payload to keep it clean and out of harm's way as the repairs proceed. It's pretty clear tonight is a scrub for the Black Brant; Phil Eberspeaker and the experimenters, talking among themselves, look discouraged. Tonight, like the neck of Ariel, Sylvia Plath's horse, the lights over Kaktovik will be the "arc . . . [they] cannot catch."

Of course the other rocket, the Nike, can still go, so back in the Blockhouse, the watch on the sky directly overhead continues. By 11:00 Geoff Bland is ready to remove the Nike's cargo strap, a twenty-minute operation. The experiment is go and he's waiting on the winds. But a report comes over the speaker that there is only a soft, fading aurora, a 30° arc, and it's in the region of Fort Yukon. "Can we fire for effect?" asks Mary. It's one of her standard jokes as a launch night drags on. "If you have a hundred-fifty millimeter howitzer, go and fire it," comes the reply, "but don't fire the rocket." By 11:10 the sillies are setting in. Marty calls in over the speaker to ask if anything interesting is going on. "Zip," responds Mary. He says in that case he'll just show a couple of visiting air force guys around. She says, "Roger," and he says, "No. Marty." Ed Heath comes in, and somebody says, "Hi, Ed." "Yeah," he replies, "I'm high." Then Jack Dillard comes in to say it's warming up. The temperature is –25°F, and this is *not* a joke.

Phil Eberspeaker convenes a little conference that eventually includes Dillard, Geoff Bland, and Mary Farrell. He says the Black Brant group is thinking of taking tomorrow off: they won't have the battery ready until late in the day, and the weather is supposed to be bad. So they'll just come in on Sunday. He and Geoff proceed to coordinate schedules for that day in case the Nike hasn't gone up by then either.

A report comes over the speaker that Marty and the air force visitors, driving up to Optics, are waiting for a moose to get out of their way. (Driving up to Optics is always a tricky business at night. At a certain point on the hill you've got to kill your headlights lest they disrupt the monitoring equipment in the dome you're heading toward.) Mike Cogan and Mary bring out the cribbage board. People talk about stories in the local paper concerning satanic cults. Marty reports that nothing is going on up the hill other than a heavy card game at Telemetry. The moose, after a long staring match, got out of the way.

The Nike watch goes on for hours, but the sky is dead. Jack Dillard, who's got less patience, or fatalism, than the rest, looks at the all-sky cam and says, "Come on. Something *happen* there." Eventually I doze off, awaking only at 3 A.M. to the news that the Nike mission has been scrubbed for tonight. Auroral activity has been detected, but it's behind too much cloud cover, and the winds aren't right either. The weather for tomorrow looks generally unfavorable, and the decision is made to forget about both missions until Sunday. Tomorrow (today) will be the first day off in nineteen, and Mary is thinking of going skiing.

The Blockhouse is abandoned for the night, and everybody drives off the range, past the old missile at an 80° angle that mimics a railroad scissor gate.

Jack Dillard is Poker Flat's new broom. A burly man with pleasant corporate manners, he arrived here last July after five years working on the air force shuttle program at Vandenberg and a stretch as vice president of an aerospace company that outfitted planes for customers like the Sultan of Brunei. (The *interior* of the Sultan's jet cost more than a 747.) On Sunday afternoon, in the last available daylight, he gives me a tour of the range. Driving his pickup past the rocket storage building and on up to Optics and Telemetry, he explains Poker Flat's peculiar organization with the exactness of someone who had to memorize it just recently. The range is really a joint operation: the university owns the land and NASA has title to most of the buildings — or at least the U.S. government does. When not long ago a state OSHA inspector came around, he found the range in violation of "probably every code ever written," and fixing things involved untangling as many jurisdictional questions as wires.

Confident that he was brought up here to make Poker Flat a "world-class facility," Dillard says that for a long time this place was like a "rocket club," run practically on scrap. He concedes the justice of its can-do reputation — a 97 percent success rate with launchings, and 83 percent with payloads — but says that the place he found last summer left a lot to be desired. When it wasn't launch season, the eight or nine guys working here were not exactly used to working hard. Since he arrived, he's had them "building buildings, cleaning things, and chopping trees," and they haven't liked it all that much. He talks about an upcoming meeting with the chancellor of the university, mentions Senator Ted Stevens, and says he hopes to meet with Governor Hickel, too. If this really is going to be a world-class operation, they're going to have to upgrade the launchers and everything else; if they can develop an orbital capacity, they'll be able to launch commercial satellites, not just these up-and-down experimental payloads.

Up at Optics (which, like the Blockhouse, has its own kitchen), Jack puts his hand into a cookie tin and comes up empty. But there will be plenty of food for tonight's watch. Jack's plump, vivacious wife, Glenda, is helping prepare a big taco supper. At 5:35, over the speakers, I can hear Marty giving someone instructions about how to shred the lettuce. "Roger" comes the can-do response. There's a feeling of optimism, and not just about the tacos. "It's not even jacket weather out there," somebody says — it's 20° above — and the sky above the launchers, which are pointing up with payloads attached, looks nice and clear.

A little before 6:00 Ralph New is reading a book behind his radar console, Al Richardson is playing video golf in Payload Control, and somebody else in the Blockhouse is snoring. But as the evening progresses, one can sense amidst the good spirits a certain tension between the rocket-club atmosphere and Jack Dillard's plans, which seem part of the ever-more-regulated world outside. At Mary's console, Mike Cogan and Clif, the winds man, talk with her about a recent memo from the wetlands administration; it's made them realize the range has been violating regulations by just going ahead and clearing trees around the launch sites whenever it wants. The three of them speculate that someday soon they won't even be allowed to use Styrofoam covers to keep the rockets warm on the pads, since they're not biodegradable and range personnel can never recover all the pieces that blow away after a launch.

At 7:30 we're finishing up the taco and chili party. Glenda Dillard has brought over chocolate cake, too. She is a sparkler, warm and perky in false eyelashes and leather pants — a woman who enjoys being the boss's wife. A report of a faint arc to the north, this early in the evening, is bringing Geoff Bland to life. Mary reports that Roger Arnoldy would like to be ready to go by 8:00. The FAA called a little while ago to say a plane would be in the launch area within about an hour and wanted to know if that would be a problem. Mary was happy to tell them it might. "Things are gettin' head up," Jack Dillard tells me. At 7:44 Marty, at his console behind Mary's, is adjusting the launch angle of the Black Brant on pad 4. On the little monitor you can see the rocket straighten up from 73.5° to 83.5°. And then, over the speaker, in keeping with the look-alive attitude of the moment — and the new era — Mary reminds all range personnel that they need to have their time sheets in to Jack Dillard right away.

A little after eight o'clock I drive up to Optics with the Dillards, all of us watching out, even after we douse the headlights, for the mother moose and her baby that were on the road Friday night.

It's from up here in Optics that Roger Arnoldy has been seeing the "arcs and sparks" over Kaktovik. He's a bit nervous, not terribly eager to have more people under the dome. A couple of video journalists from Italy are already here, as well as Neal Brown, the still-youthful man who directed the range for fifteen years (the road in from the gate is named for him) and is now pursuing his own research. Things are not quite as cheerful up here as down in the Blockhouse. The launch prospects don't seem so rosy either: as it turns out, there's still a fair amount of cloud cover.

Also present are Dr. Syun-Ichi Akasofu, the director of the Geophysical Institute, and his wife. Jack Dillard seems surprised to see his boss's boss and decides he should hang around a bit longer. He explains to Dr. Akasofu that, since conditions are better at Kaktovik than they are overhead, we may wind up shooting the Nike before the Black Brant. And he gives him the shipshape piece of news that, because of this afternoon's warm weather, it took only forty-three minutes to reattach the rocket's payload.

Dr. Akasofu has been in Alaska for over thirty years, since he was a graduate student of the great aurora expert Dr. Sydney Chapman, who headed the International Geophysical Year projects in 1958. Quiet and authoritative, Akasofu is clearly the man who handed Jack Dillard his new broom. He tells me that orbital launches of commercial satellites (Motorola is interested) are only three years away, even though the building we're in isn't good enough for the equipment it houses now. He points to the exposed wires near the ceiling and says that this is no good. He wants to build a new facility at a higher altitude. Around a quarter after nine I can hear Jack Dillard telling him not to "lose faith," because he, Dillard, "will get the right team assembled." As if to marry short- and long-range optimism, he points to the all-sky cam with the view over Kaktovik. One can now see stars and a faint auroral arc. "It's lookin' good," says Jack.

Dr. Akasofu tells me that in a few years this is going to be "a very busy place, maybe too busy." At Vandenberg and White Sands scientists have about six hours to get their experiments off the ground. Here they can wait and wait for their ideal conditions. He recalls one scientist who wouldn't shoot for ninety days and drove everybody crazy: "We nearly had a riot." He insists, though, that once those orbital, Motorola-monied launches are under way, the commercial people will be told they can't get in the way of the science.

It's a worthy sentiment, though one doesn't really believe it. The likelihood that Motorola will brake for the humble grant-funded experiment of a couple of university scientists isn't very great. Over the next ten years at Poker Flat, commerce will no doubt overwhelm science, just as five thousand miles to the southeast, the space shuttle has driven adventure off Cape Canaveral. In fact, one can more confidently predict the situation here a decade hence than an hour from now: at 9:30 the arc over Kaktovik keeps coming and going, and no one can tell if it will fatten or fade.

Attractive and hospitable as the Dillards are, it's hard not to hope, as one drives back down the hill from Optics with them, that Jack doesn't get his wish. Georges Pompidou once declared that Paris is not a museum, and the same should probably be true of the Poker Flat Research Range, but in a world that already has too many orbiting telecommunications, what is really so bad about a snow-covered rocket club?

Before we started down the road in the pickup, just after exiting the dome, I wondered if I was seeing an aurora. No, just scattered wisps of cloud with the lights of Fairbanks reflecting off them — real life playing the same trick as the all-sky cam. Now, as we stop at a shed painted the range's standard blue-gray, another sight seems as if it, too, must be *trompe l'oeil:* through the doorway one can see five white balloons, fully inflated, trapped under a net near the ceiling. This is, in fact, the Balloon Inflation Building, and Jack Mahoney, on orders from Clif back in the Blockhouse, is about to launch one of them to test the winds. The Dillards and I wait in the pickup for a couple of minutes until Mahoney, after lighting the pink flair attached to its tail, lets the big balloon go, like a bird being freed from a barn. It's a lovely sight, and the three of us in the truck smile and decide that if nothing else happens tonight, we will have seen at least one launch. Now that the balloon is up, unless it passes through or near a cloud, Mary Farrell should be seeing a little white dot on her all-sky cam down in Operations.

As soon as we're back in the Blockhouse, I can see it's going to take more than one of Jack Mahoney's launches to bring the place to life. The watch is dragging on. After 11:00 Mary and Ed Heath start a game of cribbage. "I could use a little false alarm here to get my adrenaline going," she says. "I'm having trouble staying awake." Geoff Bland asks her to get an update from the scientists on the hill. The two of them joke about the mushrooms down here needing to be fed. But Roger Arnoldy can only tell her they're still waiting on the aurora. "Roger, Roger," is her response. A big cheer goes up: the sillies are setting in early. "Hark, an arc!" exclaims Geoff over some weak display on the all-sky cam. Payload Control and Operations begin exchanging tape-recorded insults over the speakers, and Mike Cogan says he thinks we may be here until 5 A.M.

Then, suddenly, at 11:25 the cinderblock joint is jumping. Optics instructs Operations to pick up the count, and Mary's voice starts ringing out over the range: "All stations are go. The range is go. The pad is clear." The clock is moving down toward six minutes, when there will be an automatic hold. At 11:47 Mary tells Arnoldy that we can stay at this status for only thirty minutes, by which point, without a further request to the FAA, clear airspace will run out. And we still need the arc to move farther north.

Eight minutes later the edge is off. The guys in Payload Control have begun to watch a half-clad girl dancing on TV ("There's some activity *there!* Let's have a look at *those* arcs!"), and Optics reports that, while it isn't breaking up, the arc just isn't bright enough. By 12:08 we're recycling the count to T minus 10 minutes and letting the air traffic through.

Over the next hour everyone will watch and wait. An arc will build, the count will pick up, and the airspace will be cleared — and then, when the arc fades again, we'll go back to T minus 10. Somebody theorizes that whenever Ed Heath puts his dinner in the microwave, things start to jump. Since it's past midnight, we can now wish Ralph New a happy fifty-eighth birthday. Just before 2 A.M., when Arnoldy's Black Brant team will finally scrub, Jack Mahoney comes into the Blockhouse saying there was so much excitement at the Balloon Inflation Building he could hardly stand it. But even the scrub does not mean the night is over. It's Turnaround time, the thirty-five minutes it will take to reconfigure the telemetry station and make the Nike "prime," and Bering and his people are still interested in seeing if *they* can launch tonight.

As Turnaround proceeds, Mike Cogan asks Mary if she ever knew a scientist to have much sense; they begin to play crib-bage. Someone comes in from the parking lot to report that he's accidentally hit a moose and crumpled a piece of his fender.

It gets close to three o'clock, and the Nike's turn seems to be coming. A bright squiggle of an aurora has suddenly formed on the all-sky cam. The launcher is adjusted to jibe with current wind conditions, and we wait for the arc to position itself directly overhead. But before we can get past T minus 4, it has fled too far north — toward the spot we needed for the other rocket. By 3:18 we are into pulsating aurora, the light on the all-sky cam quivering like the hind legs of a tired moose. The pulsations indicate a weakening of the light, and we can expect them to continue, without a clear arc, until morning. There's always the hope that the trend will reverse itself, but each passing minute of watchfulness is like another attempt to strike a wet match: the potential for success only diminishes. "Oh, let's go home," says Mary, after we've gone back to T minus 10. And at 4:30 A.M. we do.

Station time on Monday, February 11, is 4 P.M., and with Ed Heath and Ralph New I make the quick ride from the lodge to the range (delayed by a moose, who eventually yields the right of way). The sky is overcast, and Jack Dillard thinks we may quit early on the Nike, whose tricky airspring is now being worked on by Marty and some others. In any case, the Black Brant is prime tonight.

At 7:00 Geoff Bland is sleeping in front of his console, and an hour later, when the launch window actually opens, the boredom in Payload Control is truly severe. No one has anything to do but eat, watch the Gulf War news coming in poorly from a fuzzy-faced Peter Jennings, and torture everybody else with snatches of songs like "All My Exes Live in Texas." Across the hall, Mary calls up to Arnoldy, asking about some FAA information that a Lufthansa plane is going to be in our airspace for the next hour. The professor says to let them have it, because there's no way we're going to launch in that time.

It's a dull, desultory evening until a little before 11:00, when a strong arc begins to build and hold in the north. Marty is soon optimistic enough to ask Mary who will eat all of tomorrow night's planned pea-soup supper if we launch tonight. She reminds him that we've got two rockets on the pads. At 11:20 the count is holding at T minus 2, as we wait for the arc to move where we want it. Jack Dillard is blocking off the road outside the entrance to the range. "Come on! Go north! Go north!" Mary shouts at the arc, before it weakens and we cycle back, yet again, to T minus 10. "Yeah, you can have your airspace back," she tells the FAA over the phone. And the automobile traffic, if there is any, can reclaim the Chatanika Highway.

But then midnight arrives, like a fairy tale in reverse: the dull pumpkin overhead is turning into a coach. The count is going back down to T minus 2, and the roadblock is going back up, because a beautiful, thick white band is visible on the all-sky cam watching Kaktovik. We're going to launch; everyone knows it now. "Got any airplanes, Ralph?" No, he tells Mary, there are none on his radar screen. The single strong arc has been joined by other ones: the all-sky cam is now a celestial aquarium swimming with life. "I'd shoot right now," says Mike Cogan, just before changing his mind. Mary says she sure wouldn't want to be in Roger Arnoldy's shoes, calling this launch for the absent Professor Kintner, taking his shot, his one swing, for him.

But that's what is happening. Mary's voice goes out over the whole range: "*Stay under cover until launch.*" She asks everyone for a last-minute confirmation of status, and "Go" is the answer that comes back through the speaker every time. The clock reaches T minus 1.

The scientists up the hill under the Optics dome will actually see the rocket to which they've pinned their payload, and hopes, rise from the snow-covered ground and fly to the aurora. But down here in the Blockhouse it is the fate of the "mushrooms" to see what is being accomplished in the way most of life's important events are witnessed: on television. The count reaches zero, the key in the launcher is turned, and a great swallowing roar slams the walls outside. One of the little monitors shows a black-and-white flame engulfing the pad; another shows the area being showered with Styrofoam trash. After all the preparation, it is over, like a toboggan run or a parachute jump, the principal difference being that this was accomplished *against* gravity's will.

The rocket is gone, on its way toward an apogee of 3 million feet. Ralph New has lit a cigarette, and across the hall in Payload Control, Phil Eberspeaker is shaking hands with his team. I step outside the Blockhouse, newly appreciating its igloo-like protectiveness. The smell of combusted rocket fuel hangs in the night air, and above that, in the dark unoxygenated sky, a green-ish-white arc, the overhead aurora the Nike would still like to hit, reminds you the night isn't necessarily over. Ed Heath, for one, is charged up with optimism. "One down, one to go," he declares, after returning from one of the roadblocks.

The flight, after only fifteen minutes, is judged a success. "Mary," says Clif, coming in from the windweighting room with a piece of paper, "we flew within 1.1 kilometers of projected apogee." Jack Dillard arrives back from a roadblock and I shake his hand; the first launch of his era is a success, and he must be feeling at home. (As newcomers, he and Marty are now supposed to have their shirttails cut off and marked with the date.) He does a comic imitation of Ron Franklin, the Chatanika Lodge owner, coming out on the road to ask, "What's goin' on? What's goin' on?" At 12:35 Mary, after thanking Roger Arnoldy for launching on her young son's birthday, tells the FAA that all pieces of the rocket are now down and they can have their airspace back. The ever-cheerful Geoff comes across the hall and says, "We're next," a remark upon which Brent Weisiger, another Wallops guy, throws some friendly cold water: "It would simplify your life too much. You'd be bored." Mike Cogan says he should speak for himself: he could stand some life-simplification, what with a new baby at home.

Weisiger gives Mary a congratulatory kiss, and she and Ed Heath complain that the Black Brant team is going to be party-ing without them. Sure enough, some of Eberspeaker's men are already leaving for the Westwood Lodge, and a number of them will be catching a morning flight out of Alaska. Mary tells one of the guys to look her up when he's back in town.

At 1:10 A.M. Jack Dillard says that Arnoldy has obtained armloads of excellent data. Marty reports that up on the hill everyone is happy, and the expression on Steve Powell, once he enters the Blockhouse, confirms it. It will take three months to sort out all the information they've harvested. The Black Brant has become science, history, and attention in the Blockhouse is shifting to pad 3, where the Nike is still a matter of imminent adventure.

Actually, it will not fly tonight. In fact, the whole season's window will close without its being fired; the Bering team will have to reassemble themselves and the rocket sometime in 1992. Still, as the morning approaches, we will come close once more to the requisite perfect moment, the optimal split-second conjunction of a thousand circumstances that is a launch. The count will get far down, all personnel will be ordered into the Blockhouse, and the highway will be sealed off. The aurora will never position itself quite where it's needed, but in the judgment of naked eyes there will be moments when it is not only over-head, but nearly frightening in its proximity and beauty. At 1:50 A.M. I go outside to stand under a grand greenish-white swath that's been paintbrushed, practically rollered, onto the night sky above, and an hour after that Stuart MacKellar and I are looking at a gorgeous forest fire of shaking northern light. Racing to-ward it is one of Jack Mahoney's balloons, carrying its small pink flare, testing the winds.

But things will still not be right for the rocket. The last beautiful buildup of light comes around 3 A.M., a spectacular arc, a frosted emerald comb raking the tresses of winter sky, so forceful in its animation, in its appeal to the eye and spirit, that one cannot avoid the thought that it is surely somehow alive, that this is that rare thing: a scientific phenomenon about which scientists themselves would like to be proved wrong. Most auroral legends associate it with spirits and the afterlife, but now, after a long night, it seems as if the sight of the aurora is carrying you not forward to whatever lies beyond this life, but backward, toward a world you remember from thirty years ago, when every Friday night there was another searchlight waving in the skies of the brave new modular suburbs, those lunar Levittowns powered by nuclear families. Alas, you knew even then that by getting on your bicycle and chasing the beam to its origin, you would only succeed in running it to earth — the parking lot of whatever new supermarket whose opening it heralded.

Like the explanations one preferred to imagine for the searchlight, these nights at pre-Motorola, un-upgraded Poker Flat have been a boy's fantasy: loads of junk food, lots of television, the chance to joke with a girl who can throw switches like a boy — and on top of that, getting to launch a rocket. Launching two in one night would be overdoing it, but for the next forty minutes or so, before scrubbing on the Nike, we all watch a wild swirl of diffuse, pulsating aurora that keeps changing shape and starts looking, on the all-sky cam, like everything from the *2001* embryo to the left and right sides of the brain. The principal investigator, Dr. Bering, calls down from his Optics dome to tell us we are in the paradoxical situation of having, however diffuse it may be, "too much aurora." On Mary's last call about airspace, the FAA rep on the other end of the line wonders idly if the sky isn't somehow responding to the first rocket we surprised it with tonight.

POSTSCRIPT

The shuttle has been launched with repeated success over the past four years, but the country remains without anything like a coherent, let alone visionary, space policy. Richard Truly was forced out as the head of NASA in February 1992 because his plans for the agency were in one respect too timid and in another too ambitious. As the *New York Times* put it: "The White House opposed building more shuttles, wanted to entertain radical ideas for space exploration and sought to scale back plans for huge science projects meant to expand the frontiers of knowledge. These and other initiatives were generally resisted by Mr. Truly and the space agency."

Scott Carpenter tells me that within its limited budget the space program is doing all right, but "there are so many more important things to do than what we're doing." Going to Mars is one of them, and despite a presidential promise to do that, made less than a year after the *Discovery* launch, we've traveled no discernible distance outward. On the question of cooperation with the Soviets, I was, I think, both right and wrong in what I wrote in 1988. I thought a joint venture with them was inadvisable because of the ups and downs of U.S.-Soviet relations; I didn't anticipate that the USSR, like little *Phobos 1,* would just shut down and disappear. A few months before the official dissolution of the Soviet Union, its space officials were reduced to taking money from Coca-Cola to raise funds for their program. ("The liquid goes very smoothly," said flight commander Anatoly Arsebarsky after drinking some Coke as part of an experiment for the manufacturer.) As of this writing, Boris Yeltsin is trying to sell the Mir space station.

I'm delighted by the demise of the USSR, but take no joy in the collapse of its space program. Its misfortunes only contribute to the weird retreat of the human race during the past twenty years. On the morning of the *Discovery* launch there were twelve extraterrestrials living among us. Since then, one of these American astronauts who walked on the Moon (James Irwin, Apollo 15) has died. It seems likely that this small species will age its way into extinction long before the spotted owl does. Whether it will ever be succeeded by Martians — that is, transported Earthlings — is a matter of considerable doubt.

The Kennedy Space Center should be a wildly romantic place, but it isn't, and I realize, rereading these pieces, that on starry nights since I've written them, I've never really fantasized about being back there. But I have thought of ad hoc, can-do little Poker Flat and wondered what might be going on inside the Blockhouse tonight.

Crime and Punishment

Bank Bandit Dies
in Wild Shootout

AUTUMN 1991

"Jimmy, can you hold us a panel?" asks Paul Odems, courtroom clerk to Judge Martin Rettinger. "This looks like a go." If Odems is right, and *People of the State of New York v. Fred Batson* gets under way this morning, then Part 41, on the twelfth floor of Manhattan criminal court, will be needing a load of prospective jurors. When Odems has finished putting in his order and is off the phone, one of the guards asks him about the defendant: "Is that the guy that was putting shotguns to people's heads?"

His facts are mixed up, but he has the right case in mind. The immediate problem with defendant Fred Batson, however, is that he isn't here. At 10:20 A.M. his lawyer and the prosecutor and Judge Rettinger are all present and ready to go, but no one is sure of the accused's whereabouts. It's not only Part 41 that's having trouble this morning; a lot of other judges haven't gotten their defendants from Rikers Island either. Inquiries by Odems produce the assurance that Batson is in transit, but so is the morning, and the judge is impatient. He has Odems call the case anyway.

"I heard you had an accident, hurt your leg," says Rettinger to Steven Goldstein, the young assistant district attorney.

"Not that I'm aware of," Goldstein replies.

"Then stand up!" screams the judge, before smiling. The sudden shift in volume and expression is typical of Rettinger, a juicy, mercurial New York character given to sentiment, autobiographical reference, shtick, indignation (feigned and genuine), and a palpable desire to be loved.

But even with Goldstein on his feet there's little to do but wait. By 11:50 there's still no sign of Batson, and the judge, who's been reduced to reading the paper, lets the jurors go until 2:00. As the day wears on, the attorneys find time to talk to me at the back of the courtroom. Goldstein explains that Batson's trial, for attempted murder during the robbery of an automatic-teller location, is really the last case growing out of this crime that he's had to deal with: one of the conspirators was killed during the robbery; two pleaded guilty; and one fled the country.

"And one," says a smiling Michael Hardy, lawyer for Fred Batson, "had nothing to do with it." Mr. Batson's defense will be that he wasn't even there.

That's not what the papers said sixteen months ago. On June 14, 1990, the *New York Post* carried the story of the robbery on its Metro page: BANK BANDIT DIES IN WILD SHOOTOUT:

A bandit was fatally shot and a guard critically wounded in a blazing gun battle in a back room of a Manhattan bank yesterday.

Police said two holdup men and two guards traded at least 15 shots while standing at little more than arm's length from each other in a 4-foot wide office.

"With that many shots fired in that small a room, it's lucky anyone got out alive," said Lt. Ray O'Donnell, a police spokesman.

One holdup man staggered out of the Citibank branch at 481 First Ave., and managed to turn the corner on East 28th Street before collapsing to the pavement.

He was identified as Carlton Julian [*sic*], 20, of 310 Schenectady Avenue in Brooklyn.

He had bullet wounds in the temple and neck and was dead on arrival at Bellevue Hospital, across the street from the bank.

His suspected accomplice, Fred Batson, 31, of 321 Eastern Parkway, Brooklyn, was chased and captured by private security guards a short time later. . . .

Batson faced charges of attempted murder, first-degree robbery and weapons possession.

The indictment from the Manhattan D.A.'s office would finally run to nine counts, with burglary, assault, and conspiracy added to the charges predicted by the *Post* reporters.

The defense has asked for its share of postponements, though last week it was Goldstein who requested more time. He was having trouble finding an important witness, the off-duty security guard who was doing his banking at the teller machine when the robbers fled past him. But Rettinger said a reading of the grand jury minutes convinced him that no witness was key to the case, and he gave the assistant D.A. only one more week. Expressing distaste for the task before him ("I wish all of us were able to find some other way to make a living") and despairing over the way the news has lately left him too stressed out to enjoy simple pleasures ("When I turned on the Giants game Monday night, it looked like sandlot football"), he also ruled that the trial would stand in recess each Friday, out of respect for Mr. Batson's religion: "I will never direct a Muslim to be here on Friday. That I will not do." It may seem an act of considerable religious devotion for the presumptively innocent Batson, who wears dreadlocks and a beard and the sort of eyeglasses once favored by Malcolm X, to lengthen his sixteen-month incarceration by choosing not to proceed with his case each Friday. But his piety may be prudent, considering what Rettinger, after reading one third of the grand jury transcript, told the defendant's lawyer last week: "I respectfully submit to you that if you're looking for help, you'd better look skyward."

The Citibank robbery took place on the day jury selection began for the Central Park jogger trial, and today, sixteen months later, the papers are full of a debate over whether prospective jurors for a gay-bias murder can legitimately be asked if they themselves are gay. In the tribal warfare of New York life in the 1990s, disruption of one's ordinary routine can be the least of the anxieties arising from a jury summons. Nonetheless, at about 3 P.M. on October 24, 1991, by which time all the principals, including Fred Batson, are present, Judge Rettinger tells the large pool of jurors secured by Paul Odems that they're "going to find this a very rewarding experience."

Batson rises so that all can attest they have never met him. Then Rettinger reads the indictment, emphasizing that it is only a piece of paper, not evidence. Still, its enormities go on long enough, count after count, that the judge has to stop for a drink of water and then ask, confused, if he's already read the seventh count.

"You don't want to get me in trouble with the governor, do you?" he jokes to an Italian man, asking him to remain among the prospective jurors once he's demonstrated that his English is sufficient for him to follow the trial. Throughout these preliminaries Rettinger keeps everyone awake with little jokes and small explosions, alternately relaxing the people in the pool and keeping them in line. He stresses the presumption of innocence, even though he finds it fair to say Batson isn't here "waiting for a bus." But most important: "Is there anything about this gentleman that would undermine your ability to be impartial?" Batson stands again to face them. "Take your time," says Rettinger.

Time is what the jurors will be giving up — ultimately quite a bit more of it than anyone now thinks. Rettinger lists his acceptable excuses: somebody bedridden at home ("even a good friend"); a little store (say a tailor shop: your partner's sick, and if you're not there, somebody can't get his outfit for the prom); a child in a special school for the handicapped ("they still use that word"). Nervous smiles cross the prospectives' faces when he mentions the possibility of sequestration, but nobody raises a hand in protest. "You're leading me to believe you want to stay here, Part 41 with Rettinger. You must have heard of me, right?"

It turns out to be abstractions, not the prospects of practical hardship, that bring on cold feet. After the judge explains the difference between civil and criminal proceedings, one woman says she'd have a "philosophical" problem judging another human being. A second juror expresses psychological and religious reservations, and a third doubts her ability to reach a verdict. They're let go, but "That's it!" shouts Rettinger. "I went to Brooklyn Law School," he says, offering this as *prima facie* evidence of common sense; we're not going to have a "stampede." Anybody else with objections can put them on the record during a sidebar conference with him.

While the rest of the pool remains on the benches in the rear, a smaller group is put into the jury box. They include: a housewife; an associate buyer for a catalogue company; a postal driver who serves as a church deacon in his spare time; an accountant/student from Harlem who also serves as a junior deacon; a legal secretary; an insurance company employee from the fancy Sutton Place area; an amateur musician from Greenwich Village who's the mother of small children; a food-service worker from Inwood who also does some church work; a student; a secretary who mentions, once again, church work as a spare-time activity; an investment banker from the Upper East Side; a violinist; a woman in publishing who is now in the process of changing jobs; and the chairman of the Columbia University economics department. "Is the recession over?" asks Rettinger. "I don't do that kind of economics" is the reply.

If a hometown observer is surprised by the incidence of church volunteerism on Manhattan island, he is hardly unprepared for one other statistic he can assemble from the responses of those in the box: eight of the sixteen have been victims of a crime. Three have had cars stolen, two their apartments burglarized; a woman has been mugged; another has an eleven-year-old son who was attacked by nine boys (she is excused); and another woman has been the victim of a crime she will discuss only after approaching the bench.

The attorneys conduct their questioning in an almost apologetic manner. Goldstein, who would of course like law-and-order jurors, asks the group to think about their experiences with the New York City police department. (One black woman asks to approach the bench, and after a sidebar conference she is excused.) Then there are questions about any involvement jurors may have had with the criminal justice system. A woman asks for a sidebar with the judge; then another does; and then a young man does, too. The rest of the prospectives are already sighing and smiling and whispering with impatience at how long this is going to take: for each little moment of drama there is a longer stretch reminiscent of homeroom or Motor Vehicles.

"Is there anyone," asks Michael Hardy, "who believes that because Mr. Batson has been indicted he must be guilty of something?" One woman honestly admits that she can't presume he's innocent, but when Rettinger talks to her about the law, she declares she can be open-minded. Hardy reminds the group of a judge who once said a grand jury can "indict a ham sandwich" if it wants to, before asking if they have relatives and acquaintances in law enforcement, and if any of them have been witnesses in court proceedings. The secretarial student says yes, she once had to fill out some papers because "they" thought she had witnessed a crime. And what was that? she's asked. "Attempted murder," she responds, before being excused to resume daily life in the city of New York.

"Everybody will have their lunch," assures Rettinger. "Don't even worry about it." At 1:15 P.M. on Monday, October 28, he and the lawyers are completing the selection of twelve regular and four alternate jurors, playing what looks like a game of solitaire with little square slips of paper tucked into a blotter, keeping track of places filled and ones still vacant. When the chosen sixteen are sworn in, Rettinger warns them all not to visit any of the premises connected with the case, lets them go for lunch, and tells them to be back here on the twelfth floor by three o'clock.

On a breezy fall day a juror from criminal court can head into

Chinatown for lunch or eat at one of the outdoor stands all around the miniature city that is Foley Square. There may be a demonstration in progress outside one of the courthouses, and a glimpse of the mayor could be available a few blocks away at City Hall. The area offers abundant architectural curiosities, too. Family Court is a great black cube of a modern building with irregularly placed windows that open outward, like an Advent calendar's. Inside, forlorn adults, the remnants of exploded and never-formed families, wait on line in sneakers, jeans, and caps, weary of the whole antonymic place. Just outside its doors stands the inevitable life-hating abstract municipal sculpture, near which someone sells children's books from a folding table, hoping to take advantage of an exiting person's parental feelings, just after they've been rubbed back to raw life by whatever proceeding he had to face inside.

Lunchtime usually lasts longer than the judge allots, since lawyers from other cases will seek his ear before the trial at hand resumes, and Fridays are not the only days that *People of the State of New York v. Fred Batson* must be recessed: each Tuesday is Judge Rettinger's "calendar day," hour after hour of crowded, controlled chaos when the court seems like the floor of a commodities exchange — lawyers, defendants, Spanish-language interpreters, and clerks, all of them negotiating, accepting and protesting an assembly line of judicial postponements. On this Monday afternoon three o'clock passes without the case resuming, leaving me enough time to ask Michael Hardy if he's satisfied with the jury he got. "I think so," he says. "I'll know when I see the twelve together." What he worries about most is prejudice against black male defendants, and he admits that the dreadlocks complicate matters in this case. To evaluate a prospective juror's openness to a black male client, he tries to see how open that juror seems to *him,* a black lawyer. He supposes the sixteen people just chosen form an acceptable mixture of age, race, and sex, though the slight preponderance of males may be cause for worry: he thinks men may actually feel more threatened by this crime than women, since women don't typically work as bank security guards and therefore won't as easily imagine themselves in the position of the man who was shot.

When the proceedings at last begin, there is a full cast of participating characters — judge, jury, law clerks, defendant — in front of the courtroom, but most of the time, on the benches in back, no more than a handful of spectators. Steven Goldstein begins his opening statement by reading selections from the indictment in a much louder voice than the one he used while questioning the jurors. "Everything [in the indictment] relates to one transaction, one event," he says, seemingly unaware of his choice of a banking term to describe the violent occurrence at the "off-site ATM" (only machines, not an actual Citibank branch with tellers) at 481 First Avenue, within the Phipps housing complex. It was "a very large gun battle" that took place there sixteen months ago, during which Citibank guard Daniel Cherizol was shot three times. It was an inside job, planned by one Carlton Julien Jerrome, Jr., and some Citibank employees — that's how the robbers had the keys. One of those employees was Michael Callender, the defendant's cousin.

On a typical day, Goldstein explains, guards arrive around 3:45 P.M. to pick up the deposits; after they deactivate the alarms, anyone with keys can get in. Daniel Cherizol and Curtis Jones were both "armed chauffeurs," partners, on June 13, 1990. While they were in the CAT (Citibank Automated Teller) room behind the machines, Jones heard someone at the door who he thought was a maintenance worker. In fact, it was Carlton Julien Jerrome with a machine pistol and Fred Batson with a revolver. Jerrome started firing and Daniel Cherizol began shooting back. Batson remained in the doorway and fired at Cherizol at least twice before he and Jerrome fled, the latter holding his head and bleeding profusely. Curtis Jones fired at them as they ran away; the next time he would see Batson was in a police lineup. Cherizol, who was shot three times, will testify, even though he didn't see the defendant's face.

Outside the automated bank, Goldstein continues, Jerrome

collapsed and died on the sidewalk, and Phipps housing security men, having received a radio report from an off-duty colleague (the missing witness) who happened to be at the ATM doing his personal banking, began chasing Fred Batson, who was wearing a construction helmet and work boots and trying to escape in a classic zigzag run. They spotted him on East 25th Street, by which time the helmet was gone. Then Derrick Harrison, one of the guards, saw him take off his gloves and green T-shirt and stick the shirt into his pants. By the time Steven Moses and Harrison caught him, he was walking — after having stopped to talk to a street peddler. Harrison flagged down police patrol cars that were on the way to the scene. The arresting officers brought Batson back to the bank before taking him to the 13th precinct station. Later, police officer Jesus Rivera, upon searching the patrol car in which Batson had been transported (a routine procedure against the planting of contraband), found a set of keys that, it was discovered, could open the doors at the Citibank ATM.

The police, Goldstein went on, were unaware that Batson needed medical attention. Only later in the day, at central booking, would they find out that he had sustained a gunshot wound during the battle. A bullet, Goldstein argues (promising the testimony of a doctor to back this up), had grazed the defendant, and its own heat had cauterized the ditchlike wound it dug into his skin; that's why he hadn't bled noticeably. The reason Batson did not want to bring his injury to the attention of police is obvious.

Thus went the People's theory of the case. Goldstein's presentation was organized and compelling, if somewhat adenoidal. A thin, handsome young man, he is fairly humorless and tightly wound, a natural but unwilling foil for the Runyonesque Rettinger, who will get his goat, intentionally and otherwise, at least twice an hour throughout the trial.

Shortly before four o'clock Michael Hardy rises to open the defense. A good-sized, well-spoken man who favors stylishly conservative suits, he is connected to a firm of activist lawyers whose clients include the Reverend Al Sharpton. Given Hardy's easy charm, one can imagine being outside the courtroom with him, having a beer and retelling one of Rettinger's jokes, a picture into which it is hard to insert the uptight Goldstein.

Mr. Batson is sitting at the defense table, Hardy tells the jurors, only because somebody pointed a finger at him. "We are not contending that a bank was not robbed," he says, which seems only a concession of the incontrovertible until you couple it with his reference to "possible victims" in this case. Throughout the trial Hardy will try to suggest that Curtis Jones, the Citibank guard who identified Batson, was a participant in the robbery, and he now guarantees the jurors that when Mr. Jones leaves the stand, they will have doubts about whether the police arrested the right man. Batson was first stopped by two "civilians," the Phipps housing guards. When they ran up to him, Batson was talking to a black peddler, and the guards held *both* Batson and the peddler at bay. Curtis Price, one of the five alleged conspirators, is "nowhere to be found," while Mr. Batson sits here ready to confront the witnesses and face the jury. Mr. Batson, says Hardy, has made that choice and is confident that the jurors won't be swayed by "hype" and "hysteria." What Hardy expects to hear from them is "Not guilty," and he actually pronounces the phrase twelve times, once for everyone in the box but the alternates.

As Rettinger put it last Thursday, Batson isn't here because he's waiting for a bus, but Hardy made it sound as if he'd RSVP'd to an invitation, and after the opening arguments, when the jury is out of the room for a five-minute recess, Goldstein explodes: Batson has been "in remand since day one!"

Rettinger, calmly: "I think Mr. Goldstein has a point."

Goldstein (who shares with Hardy an inability to quit when he's ahead) to defense counsel: "You compared a defendant in remand [Batson] to a fleeing felon [Price]!" — if only for purposes of contrast.

Rettinger, still calm and philosophical ("I've got a lot of years in this business"), requesting that Hardy stay away from further suggestion that Mr. Batson is here voluntarily: "You would make my judicial life a little easier and more bearable." Hardy, politely: "I have no reason to address it again." Which is true enough, since he's already succeeded with it.

When Rettinger asks the assistant D.A. if he's satisfied, Goldstein responds, "Momentarily," and sure enough, when the byplay turns to the question of the missing witness (the off-duty security guard), Goldstein finds the chance to make another sarcastic reference to Hardy's ploy. Rettinger, off the record and almost fatherly now, reminds Goldstein (who will never during the trial figure out that the judge actually likes him) of the much bigger Hardy: "You know where this is going to wind up. He's going to wind up inviting you to step out behind the courthouse."

Part 41 is recessed until Wednesday at 9:30 A.M.

It's past 10:30 that morning before things can get going. A missing juror has called in to say she overslept after being out last night at a charity benefit. Rettinger growls (unconvincingly) that this affair may prove to be more expensive than she thought. An alternate is sat in her place.

Darlene Smith, the trial's first witness, is an Olive Oyl–like figure who keeps her Reebok knapsack on while being sworn in. An operations supervisor for Citibank, she is the boss of those employees servicing off-site ATMs. She describes the routine of an "armed chauffeur" — filling the machines with cash, taking out deposits, checking to see if the pens are working, and so forth.

Yes, she tells Goldstein, Michael Callender and Roderick Harrigain, now convicted felons, were armed chauffeurs employed by Citibank until June 15, 1990, and Curtis Price had been their colleague until about December of the previous year.

Goldstein now tries to establish that Colin Forbes, the missing witness, had an account at Citibank, thus making it plausible for him to have been doing his banking at the off-site ATM at the time of the robbery. Rettinger barks at the prosecutor over the poor photocopy quality of the document verifying Forbes's account, only to apologize a second later ("I say that respectfully. After thirty-five years I become a little impatient sometimes"). When the jurors are excused from the room, Hardy makes a strong, impressive objection to what Goldstein is trying to do — namely, establish in the jurors' minds that Forbes was in the bank, whereas if Forbes doesn't show up to testify, only the hearsay testimony of Derrick Harrison (one of the Phipps security guards) will establish that it was Forbes's voice on the walkie-talkie report back to headquarters. "Mr. Forbes did not participate in the robbery, I don't think," says Hardy. "But who knows?" (Given what Darlene Smith had to say about Harrigain, Callender, and Price, all private security guards for Citibank, Hardy may be plowing suggestive ground with insinuations like these, if he can continue to make them in front of the jurors.)

But Goldstein is successful, and when the jury returns, Darlene Smith testifies that the poorly Xeroxed record shows that Colin Forbes opened his Citibank account in May 1987 and closed it in October 1991.

"What do you think jurors are, potted plants?" Rettinger asks Goldstein when he blocks their view of an easel display of police photographs. But this latest scolding is soon irrelevant, since an objection by Hardy sends the jurors out of the courtroom once again. Defense counsel complains that the color pictures, which show a lot of blood, are inflammatory. Indeed, Darlene Smith, who was at the crime scene fifteen minutes after the shooting, and who even appears in one of the photographs, is looking at these reminders of what must have been the worst day of her working life with visible distress. But Rettinger allows the pictures to go into evidence, and after the jury returns to see so much fumbling over the easel that even Batson smiles about it, Darlene Smith tells of the phone call she got from Curtis Jones saying that his partner, Daniel Cherizol, had been shot. She jumped into a cab with some coworkers and went down to the bank, where police showed her three or four keys they had recovered. The one she tested in the door worked.

Given to old-fashioned figures of speech ("not much rhyme or reason," "on a wing and a prayer"), Smith explains to Hardy, during cross-examination, just how the alarms and keys work at the off-site locations. The testimony he elicits becomes sufficiently prolonged and technical to prompt objections from Goldstein and to put the court security officer sitting behind Batson to sleep. Rettinger annoys Hardy by asking his own questions of the witness, and makes the defense lawyer explode when he refuses to let him inquire about the turnover rate among armed chauffeurs. Rettinger won't even let him approach the bench, leaving Hardy to ask if he's facing *two* prosecutors now. Goldstein objects to Hardy's "antics," but Rettinger overrules this rare bit of solidarity from the D.A. and says he can take care of himself.

When Darlene Smith steps down from the stand, one suspects that the only lasting impression her complicated testimony made on the jurors came when Hardy asked her if there are cameras at 481 First Avenue, and she replied that, while none were there on June 13, 1990, "There are at this point."

Curtis Jones is thirty-four years old and has the compact build of a college wrestler. Still employed as an armed chauffeur by Citibank, he also continues the years of night classes he's been taking toward a degree in sociology. Married for about a month, he makes a gentle, appealing impression throughout his soft-spoken testimony on Wednesday afternoon.

Yes, he knew Callender, Harrigain, and Price. (Goldstein gets this out of the way at the start, so whatever inside-job insinuations Hardy makes won't sneak up on the jury.) On the afternoon of June 13, 1990, while he was working in the CAT room with Daniel Cherizol, sorting the deposits, he heard keys being used. Two men came in; one entered all the way and the other stayed at the door. They "announced a holdup." One of them grabbed him, and "about that time shooting started." He was against the counter, trying to get his weapon out. After five or ten seconds the two men bolted, and he fired one round after them. His partner, Daniel, had been shot in the stomach, so he, Jones, called 911.

Asked if he recognizes anybody from that afternoon in court today, he says yes, "the gentleman with glasses" at the defense table — the one he identified in a police lineup two summers ago.

"Who came in first?" asks Goldstein.

"The man that got killed," answers Jones, meaning Carlton Julien Jerrome, who said "Freeze!" Cherizol went for his gun. Batson held the door open with his foot and shot at Cherizol two or three times from a distance of six to eight feet. Out of the corner of his eye, Jones could see the other man, Jerrome, firing a machine pistol: his arms were going up and down as the bullets kept pumping out, almost as if he couldn't control himself. Jones stands up and mimes a kind of Edward G. Robinson scene.

The other man, the defendant, had "locks," and was "kind of heavy, kind of big up top," and was wearing a green T-shirt and a hat. No, Jones assures Goldstein, he does not need glasses, and he had not taken any medication or drinks that day.

When the shooting was over and 911 had been called, Jones checked on Cherizol, called Citibank, and looked outside. He came back in and tried to call his partner's wife, but Cherizol, hit in both legs and the left side, was unable to give him her number. Jones says he also tried to give Cherizol first aid. When the police arrived, Cherizol — who had succeeded in killing Carlton Julien Jerrome, whose body lay on the sidewalk of 28th Street — was removing empty shells from his weapon and trying to reload. The police asked Cherizol to drop the gun, and Jones turned his .38 over to them, too.

Goldstein has the witness identify the green T-shirt that's been inside a plastic bag for sixteen months. Then he extracts Carlton Julien Jerrome's automatic weapon, which on June 13,

1990, before the shooting began, was briefly held to Curtis Jones's head. He brings it up to the witness box. "Keep that down," says Rettinger, theatrically disgusted by Goldstein's casual handling of the gun. Jones looks at it with a sort of mournful respect and then IDs it. He remembers the defendant's gun (which was never recovered) as being silver.

No further questions.

Rettinger grants a brief recess, telling the jury they can think about everything they've heard (as if they could help that) so long as they don't form any conclusions.

A little while later Hardy begins his cross-examination by asking Jones if he is aware that he was at one time a suspect in this case. Jones (after Goldstein's objection) says he was never informed of that, though he admits being given a Miranda warning: he was in the detectives' squad room of the 13th precinct until 1:30 or 2:00 the following morning. Hardy gets him to concede that he gave no physical description of the defendant during his call to 911, and that he originally told police the only man who fired a weapon was the man with the automatic.

HARDY: Would I be mistaken to say that you were very nervous [when the automatic was at your head]?
JONES: No, you wouldn't.

After the man put what Hardy starts calling "the Uzi" to Jones's head, he turned him around, pushing him against a counter. Batson, says Jones, was standing "half in and half out" of the CAT room, which Jones, in contrast to Darlene Smith, now says was equipped with cameras. He describes the man in the doorway as being brown-skinned "but not dark." " 'But not dark,' " Hardy repeats (Batson is considerably darker than Hardy himself), and when Hardy has Jones look at a police report of the lineup, he admits it shows that, when asked if the man he picked out looked like the man in the doorway, he answered, "Kind of." His explanation for the apparent equivocation is: "Sometimes I talk that way," an answer that brings sniggers from a few Batson partisans who've taken up places in the rear of the courtroom.

Rehabilitation is the name for a process undergone not only by convicted defendants but also shaky witnesses, upon "redirect" by the attorney who first called them to the stand. Goldstein tries it with Curtis Jones, who has been credible (Hardy's suggestions of an inside job never get anywhere) but hardly persuasive about his ability to remember the events of June 13, 1990, with any real precision. He looks again at the photos and tells the assistant D.A. that he can now see he was wrong to say there were cameras in the customer-service area of the ATM on the day of the shooting — a memory lapse for which Hardy will needle him on recross.

On the following day, Halloween, juror number three is missing, at home in bed with a 102° fever. Hardy wants to postpone everything until Monday rather than seat another alternate, but Rettinger tries to persuade him and "my friend Fred, Mr. Batson" to accept a substitute for the ailing Mr. Kaplan, an investment banker. Losing someone from that profession would be a big break, he tells Hardy: "They live in fear every time they go outside." Who wants a person like that deciding somebody's fate? Hardy is cheerfully unmoved, determined, he tells me later, to strike a balance between cooperation with the judge and aggressiveness in defending his client's prerogatives. On the other hand, he admits, by waiting for Kaplan he may be giving Goldstein enough time to find Forbes.

He also tells me he doesn't really believe that Curtis Jones was involved in the robbery, though he can't help wondering: why didn't they (Carlton Julien Jerrome and whoever was with him) shoot at Jones as well as Cherizol? And is it believable that, with a gun to his head, Jones would have done anything but close his eyes and pray, please God, don't let this thing go off?

The case is held over until Monday, but not before Part 41 loses another juror, who is excused, in tears, because she has to fly to Australia on the sixteenth of November and realizes the case will not be over by then. We're now down to two alternates, and Rettinger again mentions the possibility of a mistrial, with the defendant having to wait until after New Year's Day for a new one. "Of course, with bail," whispers Batson to Hardy, who repeats the joke for Rettinger.

"He's an investment banker!" shouts the judge. "He's not running this court! I'm running this court!"

Monday has come around and Mr. Kaplan is still creating problems. He's back, but he wants out. Standing before the bench, he complains (incorrectly) that Rettinger said the trial would last less than a week. His bonus from Morgan Stanley — "in a bad year" — depends on his making a meeting, a few days from now, in Orlando. Kaplan, who has no qualms about interrupting the outraged Rettinger, is a thoroughly disagreeable yuppie, and in the end no one is especially sorry to see him go. "These are the people that are running this country!" says Rettinger. "They make it up as they go along." So Kaplan is sprung, but not before being made to feel as wretched as possible. "Not another word!" says Rettinger, glaring at him as he skulks away. Batson smiles and the judge jokes that the defendant is the only one having a good time, a remark that has the two of them sharing a laugh.

But by now Rettinger is very concerned about the trial's viability. We're moving "at a snail's pace" and are down to one alternate. If the jury is "shaky," we really could be headed toward a mistrial. He asks Hardy if he now might want to negotiate a plea bargain, and he tells Batson to think about it: maybe this is the best way for him to serve some time and get back to his wife and family. The defense turns the offer down, knowing what the jury doesn't: that Batson's history as what the system calls a "persistent, violent felon," with previous convictions for crimes such as robbery, makes going for broke almost prudent. Any judgment of guilt, from either a plea or a verdict, will have to involve a long sentence.

The jury comes in and Rettinger gives them a pep talk. He tells them how important their service is to a system whose criminal trials cost $50,000 a day (probably more than the robbers could have expected from the ATMs). "So let's hang in there together," says the judge.

Derrick Harrison, a twenty-eight-year-old security guard from the Phipps Houses, is sworn in to testify that on June 13, 1990, he responded to a radio call about a robbery in progress. He ran out of the office and passed the defendant as he radioed back for more information. Goldstein cautions him not to tell the jury about the response he got over the radio, because that would be hearsay — prompting Rettinger to bark that it's not Goldstein's function to explain the law: "That's my job. You want my job? Earn it!" Regardless of prerogative, the restriction on Harrison's testimony makes it seem curiously incomplete. He can't tell exactly why he was chasing Batson, aside from the fact that he saw him running, because the physical description he had came from Colin Forbes, the still-missing witness.

During part of the chase Harrison was accompanied by his superior, Steven Moses; at other times they got separated. As he ran after the defendant, Harrison saw Batson drop a pair of gloves onto some garbage near a garage. The defendant took off his green T-shirt and tucked it into his waistband. Harrison called out, "Yo!" and Batson turned to look at him. It was on First Avenue, between 23rd and 24th streets, that Batson stopped to talk with the street vendor. "You have the wrong guy" is what Batson said when the two security guards caught up with him. Moses asked Batson to lie down, which he did, while Moses kept his gun on him. Harrison flagged down the police, who handcuffed Batson and put him in the patrol car. On his way back to the Phipps Houses Harrison looked for the gloves on the pile of garbage but couldn't find them.

Goldstein elicits this testimony through repetitious, leading questions. Harrison's answers are slow and somewhat mechanical, but his recollections are precise, in contrast to poor Curtis Jones's. Hardy seems to realize that he will have to be tough in cross-examination, and he tries to deck the witness in an opening exchange:

HARDY: Mr. Harrison, you came here today to help Mr. Goldstein?

HARRISON: I came here to tell the truth.

HARDY: You came here to tell the truth. When are you going to start?

Rettinger has to do what kills him: sustain an objection by Goldstein.

But Hardy has succeeded in turning Harrison into a surly, unappealing witness who needs to be reminded by the judge not to answer questions with other, sarcastic questions. Much of the cross-examination refers to the diagrammed chase route resting on the easel. There's a hard-to-follow who's-on-first quality to it, but if Hardy has gotten the jury to feel uneasy about the failure to recover the construction helmet and gloves Batson supposedly was wearing, let alone the gun he is accused of using, he may have made a profitable dent in the People's case.

Officer Jesus Rivera of the 13th precinct, a member of the force for seven years, gives his shield number and swears to tell the truth. In a voice whose last traces of a Spanish accent are being driven out by New Yawkese, he describes the arrest of Fred Batson and the way he later searched his own patrol car. After delivering a prisoner, he says, it is standard procedure to remove the back cushion and look for things. On this occasion he found a set of keys, which, when he brought them back to the bank, unlocked the door.

Whenever he's escorted into the courtroom, Batson's hands are always behind his back, in handcuffs, though he still manages to carry his Koran and some papers. The prejudicial cuffs are always removed before the jury enters, and that procedure is followed after lunch on Wednesday, when Officer Rivera retakes the stand to complete his testimony. During cross-examination Hardy gets him to say that he spoke to no peddler and that nobody mentioned one at the time of the arrest; he also saw no blood on Batson.

Now it is time, according to Hardy's plan, for a demonstration of the way Rivera handcuffed Batson. Hardy offers to serve as the defendant's stand-in. Goldstein objects, insisting that a court officer would be more appropriate, but Rettinger thinks defense counsel has a good idea. "You want the union up here?" he asks Goldstein. "What's wrong with you?"

So Hardy drops dramatically to the ground, and the jury is instructed to stand up so they can see him. He wants to plant the idea in the jurors' minds that Batson had no keys on him, and Rivera admits that his frisk of the defendant turned up no weapon and no bulge large enough to make him search further. Still, Rivera tells Goldstein on redirect, even in cuffs a man can extend his hands and move them about, so one can't say that Batson, while in the back seat, remained completely still. And yet, he admits during Hardy's recross, officers apply the adjustable cuffs to a suspect so that his hands will be fairly secure in them.

The afternoon continues with the testimony of a nurse, Danielle Greco, the first in a series of medical and forensic witnesses at whom Hardy will try to chip away. This is what Rettinger's assistant, Ned Hamlin, himself a former prosecutor, characterizes as a Fabian defense — avoiding the big, damaging, and obvious import of the state's case in favor of raising small qualms in the jurors' minds about sloppy procedures, incorrect reports, and so forth — things that to one temperament seem normal glitches but to another sinister contrivances.

From the defense point of view Danielle Greco, a head nurse in Bellevue's emergency room, is an unfortunate witness. She is a study in competence and good sense, and very pretty, too — the sort of presence a gunshot victim would consider a gift from God in any E.R., let alone the one in Bellevue, a place so vast and chaotic that Jimmy Breslin once said a cement mixer could get lost in it. While treating Daniel Cherizol just after the robbery, she recovered a bullet that appeared to have fallen from his left buttock, where there was an exit wound. At the crime scene Cherizol had been put into pressurized pants by emergency medical workers, "standard procedure with any gunshot victim" to control bleeding. She concedes to Hardy that it's possible the bullet she found had been swept up into the pants while they were being put on Mr. Cherizol, but she tells Goldstein that those pants are so highly pressurized (to force a victim's blood upward from the legs, where it's least needed, to the vital organs and brain) that a bullet lying between them and the wearer's skin would have left a bruise, and she didn't see any on Mr. Cherizol.

During a break in nurse Greco's testimony, with the jury gone, Rettinger jokes that he hopes Hardy won't be wanting the nurse to demonstrate anything on him. Maybe she could use him to show how the pressure pants are applied, the defense lawyer says with a smile. Poor Goldstein, who usually has to be dragged, like a scolded child, into any humorous exchange, is asked by Rettinger why he objected to Officer Rivera's demonstrating the frisk procedure on defense counsel. Goldstein smiles and says he respects Mr. Hardy so much, he couldn't bear to see him like that on the floor — a response that draws a laugh even from Batson.

The last witness on Monday afternoon is Officer William Hamilton, Rivera's partner for the past three years, since he was transferred from a "neighborhood stabilization unit" in the Bronx. He identifies Batson; says that he, too, saw a green T-shirt and black hat on the ground near the defendant at the time of the arrest; and testifies that he was with Rivera at the beginning of their tour that day, around 3:30, when Rivera checked the back seat of the patrol car and found nothing. This too was standard procedure, just like the other search, the one made after Batson was delivered to the 13th precinct.

Hardy's performance with Hamilton is weak, but he doesn't have much to work with. He tries to show that the "chain of custody" wasn't properly maintained: plastic bags, for example, may have been opened in the D.A.'s office without proper notations being made. But the shirt and hat are entered into evidence nonetheless. Hamilton testifies that only at 2 A.M. on June 14, while he was doing paperwork, was he told that Batson was injured. He left his desk to go down to see the prisoner, who had a gash in his left side. He then took Batson to Bellevue (where Daniel Cherizol was beginning a painful three-week stay).

At the 13th precinct Batson had told Hamilton his name was "James Jones" and his address "101 Lincoln Road, Brooklyn." This "pedigree" is on a page of the command log, which Goldstein wants to introduce as evidence of the defendant's untruthfulness, but the sheet of paper is full of superfluous information, and after the jury is excused from the warm, windowless courtroom, Rettinger erupts in the prosecutor's direction. It's "outrageous!" he says. "You're jamming this trial! That's what you're doing!" Goldstein protests that he never published the page to the jury and is willing to eliminate the extraneous portions. Moreover, Mr. Hardy can take care of himself. Hardy, with the goody-two-shoes composure of the kid who's not done anything wrong, says he hadn't even had a good look at the document before the judge handled the matter so eloquently. Rettinger objects to the term "eloquently" — he just tries to call them "down the middle," and when the jury is once more present, he sweetly tells Goldstein that his request to put the log sheet into evidence is denied, "albeit most respectfully."

The tired principals are getting touchy and silly. Hamilton's testimony resumes with a discussion of ballistics and the "twenty-two assorted bullets and shell casings" he received from the crime scene, but Rettinger decides to put off Hardy's cross-examination until the day after tomorrow, Election Day, when, Rettinger complains, he will be the only judge working arraignments.

As it is, Wednesday is a calendar day, during which the judge has to hear from 130 lawyers on 65 cases. But he's determined to take at least an hour or two of testimony before he turns to them. Back on the stand for cross-examination, Hamilton explains how he made a request (pursuant to one by Goldstein) that the police laboratory examine Batson's green T-shirt to see if the two holes in it were made by bullets. The results of the test, he tells Hardy, were negative. Hardy gets him to say this twice, despite Goldstein's sustained objections.

Margaret Radzieta now works in plainclothes in the 13th precinct, but on June 13, 1990, she was on radio patrol in a marked car with her partner. When she arrived at the off-site ATM, she saw the body of Carlton Julien Jerrome lying on the north sidewalk of 28th Street, approximately five car-lengths west of First Avenue. "The man was bleeding profusely from his head. There was no movement." She also recovered a large light-colored canvas bag containing some rope, metal tools, and duct tape, all of which she marked and vouchered. Hardy objects to every question and answer from this witness as being irrelevant to Mr. Batson's case, though as Goldstein points out, one of the things Mr. Batson is charged with is conspiracy, and the contents of the bag are certainly germane to that count of the indictment. (Had Daniel Cherizol not drawn his gun, but chosen instead to cooperate with the men who stormed the CAT room, the rope and tape would have been used to keep him and Curtis Jones tied up and quiet in the basement.) The contents of the bag go into evidence. As usual, Goldstein wins the important point, however joylessly the victory comes. As calendar day commences, one can overhear two other assistant district attorneys conversing in the elevator about "Steve's case." He's trying it before Rettinger, one tells the other, and he's having a terrible time.

With no testimony being taken on holidays (Veterans Day is next week), calendar days, and Mr. Batson's Friday sabbath, Thanksgiving is fast approaching, at which point the jurors will be sure to balk. On Thursday, November 7, Rettinger declares that we'll work through lunch today; the court officers are instructed to take sandwich orders from the jury, and if the appellate judges in Albany dislike this unusual arrangement so much that Rettinger winds up paying for the sandwiches himself, so be it. As it is, we're already losing time: one of Goldstein's police witnesses has neglected to bring his memo book, so Rettinger orders the officer to take the train back to his suburban Long Island home to get it and to be back here by three o'clock. Bringing your memo book when you testify? It's fundamental — "like putting on your shoes!" — for God's sake. We start instead with Dr. Eric Lazar, a young resident surgeon at NYU and Bellevue hospitals who treated Cherizol in the latter institution's trauma room on June 13, 1990. The armed chauffeur had three bullet wounds, one in the lower left abdomen and one in the upper part of each leg. All abdominal wounds are considered potentially fatal until they're determined to be otherwise, says Dr. Lazar. Mr. Cherizol was very lucky, though the muscle damage he sustained can make standing up and walking difficult.

The cross-examination of Dr. Lazar proves to be one of the weakest episodes of the trial for the defense. Nice young men like Dr. Lazar (and nice young women like nurse Greco) are the kind standing between New Yorkers and the city's constant threats of personal calamity; like middle-class taxpayers, these bulwarks aren't supposed to be hassled. But Hardy picks at the doctor's qualifications, getting him to admit he's not "board-certified." Does this mean he's some sad sawbones who barely got through med school in Grenada? No, the only reason the baby-faced doctor isn't board-certified is that he's been a resident surgeon for less than five years. Rettinger mischievously asks some questions of his own, establishing that Lazar got one of seven acceptances to a program that had four hundred applicants. "You brought it [the matter of qualifications] up," he tells Hardy with a smile.

The police lineup in which Curtis Jones made his nervous ("kind of") identification of Fred Batson was not conducted until August 2, 1990, by Detective David Argenzio, whose own mistakes in recollection — he refers to "Mr. Curtis" instead of Mr. Jones and calls the defendant "Mr. Baston" — give one a bit of pause about the whole business. He isn't on the stand long, since objections by Hardy make Rettinger order Goldstein to go back to his office (while the jurors have their sandwiches) to see if there were other Polaroids taken of the lineup besides the single one he's brought to show Argenzio this morning. The judge is also livid that the prosecutor may not have enough witnesses to fill up the day. Goldstein has miscalculated, since most of the witnesses taking the stand today have relatively brief testimony to give. He makes some calls trying to get additional ones on short notice, even asking Officer Daniel Taylor, Margaret Radzieta's partner, if he knows how they can get hold of some of the other cops on the list.

The big fight of Monday afternoon is over the testimony of Richard Lebowitz, the young doctor who treated Fred Batson at Bellevue early on the morning of June 14, after the gash "just above the hip on the left" was discovered. Hardy argues, fiercely, that anything the defendant told the physician is covered by doctor-patient privilege, whereas Goldstein reminds the court that the defendant gave inconsistent statements that night about how he was injured (climbing a fence, being knifed three days before). Hardy says that Goldstein is trying "to impeach the credibility of a witness who has not even taken the stand" — that is, Batson — and if the statements his client made to Lebowitz are allowed in as evidence, he will move for a mistrial. Rettinger seems to lean toward the prosecution, but he wants time to think about the issue and orders the two attorneys to draw up competing briefs for him over the weekend.

The cop who forgot his memo book has returned from Long Island, but there's no time left for him today.

On Tuesday morning (another calendar day when we'll put in a couple of hours) Rettinger announces that, on the basis of Ned Hamlin's research, he has reached a "preliminary decision" about what Dr. Lebowitz can and cannot say, but he still wants to read the briefs he's requested. Like candidates who can't stop campaigning, Hardy and Goldstein press on orally, the former reminding the judge that Batson's injury was never designated or reported as a bullet wound, the latter pointing out that in an earlier hearing Batson's first lawyer (not Hardy) waived doctor-patient privilege, and since a partial waiver is not permissible in New York State, the privilege cannot be "resurrected." Batson's side made the injury an issue during an earlier hearing, so it has to remain one.

Another medical matter also turns out to be at issue this morning: the juror who sits in the top row of the box, farthest from the judge, comes out of the jury room to discuss a scheduling problem. He has to go in for exploratory surgery on the twentieth of the month, but it will take only a day. He's retained, gratefully.

Detective Argenzio retakes the stand, but his testimony about the lineup and the confusion over the Polaroids proves anticlimactic, and the one thing anyone will remember from it is the information that sometimes the "fillers" for the lineups come from shelters for the homeless. Detective George Field from the 13th precinct's robbery unit follows. Fat and rumpled, with only a fancy print tie to remind one of the much more elegant Argenzio, he testifies that, in searching for Batson's weapon, he and five or six other officers spent between twenty and forty-five minutes covering the escape route. No, they did not look in any manholes or up on any scaffolding, he tells Goldstein, whose turn it is, for once, to have an interest in showing sloppy police work. Hardy's cross-examination creates more frustration, for himself, than anything else. He angrily questions Field about his description of one of the corner buildings in the area as a "drug-prone location," asking him to describe any location in the city that *isn't* drug-prone. "My home," answers Field. A heated, pointless discussion of "drug-prone locations" follows. "And Officer," asks defense counsel, "after conducting this thorough and professional search, did you find anything?" Hardy, whose devotion to the idea of Batson's innocence seems genuine, is let down in this instance by his sarcasm: if he wants the jury to believe that no weapon was found because Fred Batson wasn't carrying one, he should be doing what he can to make them think Detective Field's search *was* a thorough and professional one.

The calendar-day crowds will not wait any longer. Rettinger warns the jurors that he wants to work late on Wednesday and Thursday. Hardy doesn't object, but he reminds the court that Mr. Batson is awakened at 4 A.M. on Rikers, and even on a normal day doesn't get back there until about 9 P.M. The judge says he will try to relocate the defendant to the Tombs, just across the street, for the remainder of the trial. While Rettinger is still discussing Batson's schedule with a court officer, Goldstein comes up to the bench, thereby earning his daily swat: "What's wrong with you?" moans Rettinger. "Your youthful enthusiasm is gonna cause me nothing but grief."

Three witnesses during the trial bring everyone to hushed attention, and the first of them appears on Wednesday morning, November 13. Michael Callender has come down from the Fishkill correctional facility upstate, where he is serving 1-1/3 to 4 years for bank robbery.

"What robbery specifically?" asks Goldstein.

"Citibank," says Callender, who eventually pleaded guilty to an April 1990 theft carried out with some of the others, but not with his cousin, Fred Batson.

Callender, around whom two armed guards hover all the time he is on the stand, speaks in a soft Caribbean accent and pronounces his r's as w's. He says that he made no deals for his testimony today, which begins with an account of his five years' service as a Citibank armed chauffeur, during which time he worked with Roderick Harrigain and Curtis Price. Carlton Julien Jerrome, Jr., was someone he'd known "from on my block" for ten years. "Fwed," however, was someone he'd known even longer, "all my life," he says. Their mothers are sisters.

No, Curtis Jones and Daniel Cherizol had nothing to do with the robbery on June 13, 1990. It was Harrigain, Price, Fred, Carlton, and himself: all five met at Callender's apartment to plan it. Fred and Carlton were to tie up the two guards they knew they'd find servicing the machines, and put them down in the basement. After five minutes Curtis Price would come in and work the combinations, which he would have extracted from the guards' pockets. It was all Price's idea; the money from the April theft was running out and he wanted more. But he couldn't enter the bank with Fred and Carlton because his colleagues, Jones and Cherizol, would recognize him. Callender suggested Fred to Price; Carlton used to spend some time at Callender's apartment; "one thing led to another," and the conspiracy was formed. Batson ruled out someone else's participation because he didn't know him well; Carlton he knew.

After all the technical testimony that's preceded it, Michael Callender's story seems electrifying. A veil has been lifted, a clutch popped. Throughout the trial the telephone at Paul Odems's desk rings frequently, but today it gives the rapt listeners a start. Callender gets more nervous and depressed as his story goes on and cousin Fred keeps looking at him, calmly. He does not look back.

At the hour of the robbery, Callender and Harrigain were working at another Citibank location. Harrigain had given Batson the keys the night before. Fred and Carlton were supposed to dress in "construction clothes" in order to look like maintenance men, bringing along duct tape, rope, and a duffel bag. When it was over, that evening, they would return to Callender's apartment with the money. No, he doesn't know where Curtis Price is now; the last time he saw him was the day of the robbery.

Hardy finds himself able to object to little more than what he claims is the leading nature of the prosecutor's questions. He doesn't get far on a meandering cross-examination either. Callender admits detectives "intimidated" him and told him they knew Batson was involved, though he denies they made derogatory remarks about his "ethnicity."

"You look up to Mr. Batson, don't you?" asks Hardy.

"Yes, I do," replies Callender, probably meaning it, though he'll never again be able to look *at* him.

* * *

Certain New York crimes (the Marla Hanson slashing, the preppie murder) make wonderful tabloid stories because they can run day after day for weeks and be periodically revived as the legal system makes its slow turns. The Citibank robbery was a one-issue wonder. The *Daily News* gave it the entire front page on June 14, 1990 — WILD, WILD EAST SIDE SHOOTOUT, *Guards foil bank holdup; bandit killed* — but would never send a reporter to the trial. The one-day "heroes" it pictured on that June front page were Derrick Harrison and his superior, Steven Moses, the thirty-nine-year-old security manager of the Phipps project. Now an investigator for the Florida Department of Business Violations, he was, for twenty years before the Phipps job, a New York City transit policeman.

Flown up from Broward County to testify, he enjoys his time on the stand, and at first seems a more appealing witness than the easily angered Harrison, but the impression doesn't last. As Moses describes the chase, one notices a love of the spotlight, a nostalgia for his day on page one. His answers are flip or know-it-all, and Rettinger has to caution him against beginning them with phrases like "Believe me."

Batson calmly regards this man who once held a gun to his head, as Moses tells of receiving Colin Forbes's off-duty radio transmission and setting off in pursuit with Derrick Harrison. He identifies the green T-shirt, and talks about seeing the peddler, hearing the police car, drawing his gun. Batson "kind of hesitated for a short period of time," but he eventually got down without a fight. Hardy's cross is another search for graspable straws ("By the way, do you wear contact lenses?"). The best he can do is get Moses to state that, when "patting down" Batson, he did not go through his pockets — meaning, from Hardy's point of view, there were no bulge-producing keys. No, Moses never saw Batson in the bank, and when he stopped Batson he did tell him he would kill him if he moved. "And you said this to somebody whom you'd not seen do anything illegal?" asks Hardy. In describing how he restrained the defendant, Moses seems almost apologetic toward the man to whom he owes his status as hero-for-a-day: "He was not being combative. He was going with the program, so to speak. He acted like a gentleman."

Dr. Richard Lebowitz, a parents' dream, retakes the stand in the afternoon. Hardy once more places on the record a running objection to every question and answer involving this witness, whom Rettinger has decided to let testify about Batson's late-discovered injury.

The wound was "superficial, with a clean removal of a small amount of tissue" — about a half inch wide, says the doctor. It could have been made by something traveling at a high velocity, though not by a knife or razor, and it didn't bleed much because the projectile did not graze a particularly vascular area.

Hardy does score on cross when he pounds away at Lebowitz's failure, anywhere on the medical record, to indicate that what he called a "laceration" had been caused by a bullet. Still, the defense attorney overdoes his sarcasm — the chemistry between him and the young doctor is just no good — and Goldstein objects to the hectoring tone. Hardy even comes back to the business of board certification, the absence of which seems even more meaningless today than it did with Dr. Lazar, since young Dr. Lebowitz has just mentioned a particularly strong bit of on-the-job training afforded by medical residency in New York: in his brief career he has treated approximately forty gunshot wounds.

Goldstein can never be faulted for doggedness or grasp of detail. Only lately has he added Warren Gervais, a straight-arrow Citibank office manager, to his witness list. Mr. Gervais, who has been with the organization for twenty-two years, says that Citibank began to install cameras in thirteen "test" off-site ATMs in March 1990, and 481 First Avenue was *not* one of them. Cameras weren't installed there until March 5, 1991, nine months after the robbery, and were taken out this July 30 because of their incompatibility with the phone lines. With this testimony Goldstein succeeds in laying to rest any suspicion that there might be photographs of the robbery in progress that the prosecution is hiding, but what Mr. Gervais says still does not erase the mistake Curtis Jones made when he said there *were* cameras at the ATM on June 13, 1990. And it may even, in attentive jurors' minds, undercut the dramatic inference that could have been drawn from the testimony of Darlene Smith — namely, that Citibank finally installed cameras at 481 First Avenue because of the blood that was spilled there on that late spring afternoon.

For the first time in his fourteen years as a judge, Rettinger resumes taking testimony after a dinner break, during which Hardy comes in with a sandwich Fred Batson's wife has gotten for her husband. An officer has to open it up for inspection, a process over which Rettinger and Batson manage a laugh, though the instinct of most observers would be to lower their embarrassed eyes. After Hardy makes a polite objection to the nighttime proceedings, Rettinger and a court officer discuss arrangements for getting jurors home: some of them don't want to use the subway at the hour we'll be finishing up.

If Michael Callender was the first witness to consume everyone's attention, Daniel Cherizol is the second. The fifty-two-year-old Haitian immigrant, who has raised five children since coming to New York twenty years ago, approaches the stand with a slight limp and holds his right hand sky high while taking the oath. A tall, beefy man with a broad mustache and the suggestion of a sense of humor, he has been waiting all day to testify. Yes, he knew Callender, Price, and Harrigain from the time they worked at Citibank — where he still does, as an armed chauffeur. "Oh, I can't believe it!" is what he remembers Curtis Jones saying when the robbers came in. "This is serious business!" was the warning from the man in the doorway, whose face he never saw. He does, however, know that both robbers shot at him — the man in the doorway at least once, when he was about to flee. He doesn't know how many times he himself fired, but he points to each of the places he was shot, affirming that he still has pain in the stomach area and will have it for the rest of his life. His lower left leg is "dead."

Hardy again shows an inability to quit while he's ahead, or at least less far behind. What Cherizol says about the defendant at the table — "I never saw that face" — would be a good place for defense counsel to stop, but Hardy goes on cross-examining this big, dignified man, even asking him what the gunfire from Carlton Julien Jerrome's machine pistol sounded like. "*Da-da-da-da-da*," says Cherizol, miming the rapid fire as he goes. Rettinger asks the young court reporter, Mr. Berkowitz, to read that back, and Cherizol joins the jury in smiling.

It turns out to be a simple technical question, another Fabian feint, that delivers Hardy and Batson their worst moment of the trial. Asked by Hardy how long he remained standing, Cherizol says, with matter-of-fact pride: "Until the battle was over." Hardy wanted only to make a point about logistics and timing, but more than likely some of the jurors are restraining themselves from vaulting over the box to shake the witness's hand, which is what one of the court officers will ask to do when Cherizol gets into the elevator after his testimony.

The robbers met their match in Daniel Cherizol, who managed to draw his gun and kill one of his assailants while being sprayed with semiautomatic fire. Up until now the great presence of this trial was Batson himself, who had the allure of a silent film star; but after Cherizol he seems small, even pathetic. And if the defendant made an observer's less attractive fears itch over what "new elements" were doing to life in the city, the presence of Daniel Cherizol, formerly of Haiti, was a tonic to one's civic spirit. Who wouldn't want new neighbors like this?

Judge Rettinger does not mind taking the subway home to his wife (a banker) and young daughter. After the evening session I ride the number 6 with him and he gets off at Bleecker Street, only to tell me the following morning that this was one station too early: Astor Place is actually his stop, but he's so wrung out from these "volcanic" proceedings that he forgot what he was doing. The pressure is awful — every day making dozens of rulings that the appeals court judges can laugh at and overturn. Throughout the trial one can recognize moments when Rettinger is really talking to those judges in Albany, just as one notices how Hardy, whenever he stops to "make a record," is registering an observation not for the ears of Part 41's jurors but for the magistrates upstate, in case he and Batson have to fight another day.

On Thursday a police chemist testifies that when he examined Batson's green T-shirt he found traces of lead, though not the kind usually consistent with lead bullets. He couldn't test the shirt to see if it had been hit with copper-jacketed ones because the shirt had copper dye. (Goldstein will later argue that since Carlton Julien Jerrome was firing wildly, Batson was probably grazed by one of Jerrome's bullets.) Then Detective Robert Cotter, retired from the NYPD ballistics squad "as of today," takes the stand to speak of the test he performed on the guns involved in the case — all except Batson's, that is, which is still somewhere out in the city. Cotter's testimony is intricate, confusing, and finally numbing, ballistics being to murder what exegesis is to ecstasy. The chief implication of what Cotter says is that while the caliber of the bullet nurse Greco found cannot be precisely determined, it probably came from a .38. Since it did *not* come from a machine pistol, it probably came from Batson's gun — via Cherizol's body.

Cotter was once a member of the U.S. Rifle Team, has tested about twenty thousand guns, and testified in court 389 times. But he's not, Hardy establishes in his credentials-busting mode, a member of AFTE, the ballistics professional organization. Hardy also makes Cotter admit that he threw away the plastic cup in which the Bellevue bullet was given to him. But this apparent procedural sloppiness turns out to be just one more fact of New York life: the ballistics squad doesn't have room for all the plastic cups they're sent from the city's hospitals, so the bullets are transferred to envelopes.

The following Monday morning, November 18, there's a lot of waiting around before Batson is brought up. Goldstein isn't at his table either. Rettinger jokes that if a defendant tries to escape, it is his policy that everyone be shot, starting with him. A roly-poly guard replies that *his* policy is to shoot the defense attorney, but maybe in this case that should be changed to Goldstein. "He'd never notice — he wouldn't change his expression," Rettinger says, imitating the young prosecutor's Achilles-like pout.

The playing of 911 tapes, which by now have a ghastly familiarity from the local news, turns out to be the main business of the morning. Hardy would of course prefer the jurors not to hear the panicked voice of Curtis Jones, but Rettinger rules that it's proper to allow the tapes in for the purpose of establishing the time of crucial events. When the frustrated defense counsel chooses this moment to declare that the judge has not liked Batson's claim of innocence throughout the trial, Rettinger erupts, and Hardy quickly retreats, conceding that the judge has conducted a fair trial. The apology restores Goldstein to his habitual role as Rettinger's chief exasperator: "He catches me this way on a Monday morning," the judge complains about the tapes, which he didn't know were going to come up. "That's the way he works."

After testimony from two police witnesses — and as Elizabeth Lederer, the prosecutor in the Central Park jogger case, occupies a bench in the back of the courtroom — the tape of Curtis Jones's call to 911 is played. It plays so quickly (Jones, hysterical, talks about his partner being "shot up") that one realizes how the whole incident — entry, shooting, chase, and capture — which by now has grown to epic proportions in one's consideration, took less time than that spent on the stand by the most perfunctory witness.

"Mr. Goldstein, we're not deaf!" shouts Rettinger, telling him to turn down the volume on the tape of a call made at 3:59:52 by Officer Kennedy, the console operator at the Phipps project's security office. "There's a dead body over there," Kennedy tells the 911 operator, who seems, as they always do on the local news, maddeningly dense. She asks if the man is hurt. "He's *dead*," Kennedy says.

In the afternoon Goldstein moves to enter the certified medical records of Fred Batson and Daniel Cherizol into evidence. Hardy objects, saying that, for one thing, their entry would violate Cherizol's privacy, containing as they do such information as the advice he was given not to have sex for six weeks after his discharge from the hospital: defense counsel doesn't want the jury holding *that* against Batson, too. Rettinger says he appreciates Hardy's working so hard — and God knows he is — but there's no issue whatsoever that these records have a place in the trial. Before the jury sees them, both he and Goldstein can go through and request redactions.

The records are entered into evidence, the jurors are brought in, and the People rest.

During the lunch recess Hardy tells me that he will not call Batson to the stand. There's nothing to be gained by it: after all, he was in the area when the crime occurred; his arrest proves that. But the defense will call Mrs. Batson, a prospect that makes Goldstein nervous, since he has no idea what she will say. He was not permitted any "discovery" with her, since she did not supply written materials to Hardy, and Hardy claims that he and Batson's first lawyer took no notes during their interviews with her.

She is the third witness on whose every word the audience will hang (Rettinger even asks Hamlin to disconnect the phone), though some assistant district attorneys here as spectators, talking among themselves just before she takes the stand, speak sarcastically of the approaching "big moment" and the "bullshit story" of the wife.

Denise Jacobs Batson is smartly dressed in a green business suit. Her black hair hangs straight, Cleopatra style, and she wears glasses. After taking the oath and stating her name and residence, she's asked about her employment. The wife of Fred Batson, the dreadlocks-wearing "persistent, violent felon," turns out to be an assistant vice president at Shearson Lehman Brothers.

Until June 1990 she lived with her daughter and her husband, with whom she also ran a lingerie boutique in Brooklyn. Yes, he is currently on Rikers Island, a fact Hardy finally brings before the jurors for its apparent sympathy value, which may now be worth more than the improbable illusion of his voluntary attendance at these proceedings.

On the morning of June 13, 1990, Mrs. Batson says she stayed home from work because she was wearing an eye patch for an injury she'd sustained at Shearson the day before. She asked her husband to take care of something at the boutique. He would need a power drill, and she asked him to get one at a store on East 23rd Street in Manhattan, not far from New York Eye and Ear Hospital, where she had gotten the patch and to which she was planning to return that afternoon for persistent pain. She told him to meet her at the hospital around four o'clock.

She never went there, however, because she got a call that her sister was having an emergency cesarean section at another hospital. She had no chance to call and tell Batson she wouldn't be able to meet him. She saw the news report of her husband's arrest on the television in her sister's hospital room and got hysterical. Since she was in the middle of a high-risk pregnancy herself, her sister's doctor wanted to admit her to the hospital, too. But she decided to go to her mother-in-law's house to contact a cousin and a lawyer.

Goldstein, sensing an easier time than he expected, nicely modulates the tone of his cross-examination between respectful and withering. Was there anything special about the power drill she wanted? She describes one with ordinary features. "So," says the prosecutor, "more or less a standard power drill. And you live in Brooklyn, right?" She admits that there was no one around when she asked her husband to get the drill at that store in Manhattan, and no, he did not complain of any injury before going to New York.

The flimsiness of the story (do Shearson executives really go to the emergency room for follow-up treatment?), coupled with the witness's belligerent demeanor, must by now strike Goldstein as a gift from the judicial gods. Still, cautious and thorough, he goes to the back of the courtroom (the jury is out of the room) to consult with four other A.D.A.'s about what questions to ask. (Should they check the records of the hospital where she says her sister was?) But it's all finished soon after Mrs. Batson retakes the stand. No, as far as she's aware, her husband of two years (they've known each other for six) never bought the power drill. After a quick redirect by Hardy she leaves the courtroom, barely looking at Fred Batson on the way out.

The defense rests. On Wednesday morning there will be a "charge conference" between Rettinger and the attorneys. The juror at the end of the top row can have his exploratory surgery and be back for the closing arguments on Thursday.

Outside the courthouse Goldstein, toting the machine pistol and other evidence in his shoulder bag, seems relieved, almost up, happy it's nearly over, though he will make no prediction on how long the jury will take.

As for Mrs. Batson, Consuelo Fernandez, the prosecutor in the Marla Hanson case and one of the D.A.'s who's been observing Goldstein, tells me she thinks she made a terrible witness — contemptuous and incredible. But wasn't she surprised, I ask, to hear that this previously convicted bank robber was married to an assistant vice president at Shearson? Not really, says Fernandez. She's prosecuted bank tellers with perfect work records who by night were holding up Chinese restaurants.

On Thursday morning the jurors show up with overnight bags. Hardy says he expects his closing argument will take sixty or seventy minutes; Goldstein forecasts sixty to ninety for his. He's never had a summation take more than forty-five, but he's never had a case last four weeks, either. Since the burden of proof never shifts from the People, he gets to go last, with no rebuttal from Hardy, a nice way in which the state makes a convenience of virtue. There are a number of Batson partisans here, including Mrs. Batson and her baby boy (the product of that problem pregnancy), who gurgles and makes noise before being taken out into the hall. The spectators' benches on the D.A.'s side will fill up later on when more young prosecutors, like a trio of backup singers, show up for Goldstein.

After Rettinger reminds the jurors that arguments are not evidence, Hardy begins. A few of them have trouble looking straight at him as he asks them not to be influenced by prejudice and not to hold their own disgust with crime against his client. His voice is full of true, untheatrical emotion — one of the appealing things about Hardy is that he has trouble affecting sarcasm — as he tells the jury what he really meant, weeks ago, when he said Mr. Batson "has not run and has not hidden." He admits that the defendant has been in jail since the afternoon of the robbery, but he has still "chosen" to come here. The nature of this choice remains unclear, more metaphysical than real, but Hardy presses on, saying that there have been times during the past few weeks when he thought he was dreaming: 90 percent of what Mr. Goldstein presented was no more than "cumulative evidence of the fact there was a shootout." When they "cut to the chase" — an unfortunate figure of speech — they will discover that there were only between two and five witnesses in this case who really had anything to do with Fred Batson.

He asks the jurors to use their common sense about the green T-shirt. If a bullet had penetrated it, then that bullet would also have penetrated the black shirt underneath. But that shirt isn't here. In any event, if Batson had been in that wildly shot-up CAT room, there would be blood on the green shirt, and "it ain't there." Hardy is overexcited, shouting too much, and it's a turn-off, but he continues, relentlessly attacking Derrick Harri-

son, attacking Dr. Lebowitz, saying that while we can't speculate on how Batson was cut, we do know he was put down on
the ground, hard, by Steven Moses and the cops. Why were the
keys not found when Batson was frisked? And how convenient
it is that Officer Rivera was alone when he found them in the
patrol car! And "think of yourself trying to get to your back
pocket while you're handcuffed sitting down." (Come to think
of it, how many people carry keys in their back pocket?)

Goldstein objects a number of times that Hardy is distorting
evidence, but Rettinger overrules him: the jury can remember
what the evidence is. So Hardy keeps going, as the bloody tote
bag found with Carlton Julien Jerrome's body lies on the D.A.'s
table. "Carlton Julien Jerrome is dead. Maybe he got what he
deserved," says Hardy, "but we're not here to try him." In
another appeal to "common sense," he suggests that the keys
and the black hat were really in Jerrome's tote bag, and were
later planted as evidence against Batson by cops who didn't
know who the second man in the bank was.

So he has come out and stated his theory of the case: police
frame-up. "There's no evidence that Mr. Batson was in the
bank" — never mind Curtis Jones's identification. What's more,
he says, "this bank had a camera in it." The Citibank security
chief was brought in to "clean up" Curtis Jones's testimony. The
police photos of the crime scene were taken from angles that
wouldn't show the camera. Forget Darlene Smith's testimony;
Curtis Jones was at that off-site ATM every day. He ought to
know whether or not there were cameras.

By now Goldstein is shaking his head. But Hardy continues
his impassioned performance, creating a hush when he brings
up the name of Michael Callender. He and Price and Harrigain
were the initial conspirators; then Carlton Julien Jerrome was
brought in. "If there was a fifth, it was not Mr. Batson," though
we have "the very ironic situation" of having arrested somebody
who happens to be Michael Callender's cousin. At least that's
what Hardy imagines the police saying to themselves in deciding to frame Batson and not pursue Price, who Hardy suspects

was the second robber in the CAT room. The reason Callender
never looked at Batson while on the stand? It's that Callender
knew he was lying.

It is hard to believe that anyone who saw Michael Callender
can think his gaze was averted by anything other than fear, just
as it is hard to believe that jurors — let alone police frame-up
artists — would describe the overwhelming coincidence of Callender's cousin being captured as something merely "ironic."
Why, one wonders, didn't Batson concede that he was, say, the
lookout for the robbers? Curtis Jones's identification was shaky
enough to make his presence in the CAT room plausibly deni-
able, but isn't claiming that he just happened to be running
through a neighborhood whose ATMs were being robbed with
the cooperation of his cousin too much of a stretch? But then
one remembers the reasons to go for broke in defending a
"persistent, violent felon." Going for broke is what Hardy does
rhetorically, too. "Christ died on the cross because someone
swore falsely," he says. Whatever "strange, strange, strange"
coincidence this case involves, there's plenty of reasonable
doubt.

Goldstein, who knows the weight of evidence is overwhelmingly on his side, has one or two doubts on another score. When
Hardy is through, the prosecutor talks to the other A.D.A.'s and
expresses nervousness about the short black woman juror who
was nodding her head at everything defense counsel was saying.

Goldstein begins his own summation just after 12:30 with more
rhetorical flourish than one expected from him, though he remains, beyond anything else, methodical. He starts by going
after Mrs. Batson's alibi and the "extraordinary coincidence"
the jury is being asked to buy, and after he gets rolling, the
prosecutor has his own nodding juror: a white woman with a
pageboy haircut moves her head up and down when the assistant D.A. says the question is not whether Curtis Jones can
remember Fred Batson's face but whether he can ever forget it.
And as for the cameras: did Warren Gervais, that Citibank

employee for twenty-two years, come all the way down here just to commit the felony of perjury? And if Officer Rivera wanted to frame Batson, why not just say he found the keys in the defendant's pocket? "See this for what it is," he says of Hardy's case, as the defense attorney sits at his table looking exhausted.

"What corroborates Michael Callender?" asks Goldstein. "The entire case." Two eyewitnesses say Batson fired at Daniel Cherizol. (Actually, Cherizol never claimed to have seen Batson's face, only that the man in the doorway joined his partner in firing.) Callender also testified that the defendant had a .38. There are two bullets — one recovered from the scene and one from Cherizol's body — that were fired from it. Before he finishes, nearly an hour and a half later, Goldstein allows himself a bit of sarcasm: "All of you know that people from all over the East Coast get their power drills from Twenty-third and Lexington." Finally, he tells the jurors just to keep their eyes on the ball.

The judge's charge, all of it read into the record so those appellate judges will know the jurors were sent to deliberate with a clear sense of the law, goes on for a couple of hours. For all the mayhem and suffering it covers, it begins after a while to sound unbearably tedious. Rettinger does the best he can, alternating the rhythms of his speech into a singsong delivery that makes the recitation seem like a bedtime story, even if the point of his technique is to keep an audience wakeful rather than sleepy. By the time it is over and the jurors are about to go into their small conference room and make a judgment, their silent faces, which one has been regarding for a month, seem particularly Delphic.

Goldstein now "makes a record" of his own, establishing in the transcript that during the trial the Batson family have cursed him when he passed through the corridor outside the courtroom. Rettinger takes note of this and calmly scolds the family for the "Mickey Mouse" behavior.

*　　*　　*

Fred Batson would be convicted on seven of the nine counts. On the most important of them, the attempted murder charge, he was acquitted — the jury apparently feeling uncertain, despite the bullet that fell from the pressure pants, that Cherizol's wounds could be clearly attributed to one gunman or the other. On count six, the first-degree assault charge (that the defendant, "with intent to cause serious physical injury to Daniel Cherizol, caused such injury to Daniel Cherizol, by means of a deadly weapon, to wit, a loaded pistol"), the jury was hung. It was a conscientious verdict, logically consistent, since counts one and six were the two involving the issue of intent and requiring jurors to believe that Cherizol was struck not only by bullets in the hail fired by Carlton Julien Jerrome, but by one from Batson's gun, too.

But the verdict's logical character belies the passions that attended its arrival on Saturday, November 23, at 1:50 P.M. By Friday night Hardy, beset by tension and exhaustion, had broken down and cried; he said he and Batson could not go on any longer, and Rettinger shut down deliberations, sequestering the jury — to their annoyance — for a second night. At one point the jurors sent out a note professing deadlock, but Rettinger soothed them with his "Jewish mother routine," according to Ned Hamlin. The judge's most controversial instruction to them came when they asked a question about the law's definition of "acting in concert" as it applied to counts two and three, the attempted-robbery charges. Rettinger told them that if they believed Carlton Julien Jerrome did what he is said to have done, then Mr. Batson would have to "pick up the tab." Hardy roared an objection that this courtroom was not a restaurant.

Goldstein was pleased with the partial verdict, to which, aside from embracing Hardy, Batson did not react at all. On January 21, 1992, he was sentenced to 15 years to life, which he will spend upstate in Attica or Clinton. Ned Hamlin says that "realistically, he'll probably do at least twenty." One reason the judge may have refrained from imposing the full 25-to-life is that such a sentence would, in Hamlin's words, "more or less close [Batson's] life." With freedom waiting in a future too distant to imagine, he would be more likely to commit violence in prison: what difference would it make? Still, there is additional time he must serve on a previous conviction for robbery, and after all that, he'll be deported to Trinidad. Aside from everything else, he's been in the country illegally.

The jury never heard about an FBI report that has Michael Callender claiming his cousin was given $12,000 from the earlier Citibank robbery of April 1990. Batson had not been a participant in that one, but he saw what the robbers came away with, and as Callender, the cousin who looked up to him, put it, "You don't say no to Fred."

On June 13, 1990, Daniel Cherizol said no.

Death Rally Days

My diary from July 5, 1978, tells me that I spent much of the day, and the night to follow, on a train, the Transalpino, all the way from Rome to London. The couchette in which I was riding up the Mediterranean coast was overloaded. Designed for six people, it would eventually hold eight: myself; Signora Carla Bianco, an anthropologist from the University of Florence whose specialty was Italian-Americans ("Oh, yes, there are many Sardinians in Port Washington"); a retired Englishwoman; and an Italian family — mother, father, uncle, and two little boys — who were on their way to Boulogne for a wedding. The boys (I remember them now) were a happy handful. The diary says: "God, how their father adores them, giving them, especially the little one, big, schmoozy kisses just after he's swatted them for something. I've never seen people pay more attention to their children than in this country. They are never left out or pushed aside. However smothering it must be, and whatever heartbreak it must plant like a time bomb in parents, there is something wonderful about it."

Allowing for the time difference, it must have been during these hours when I was chatting with Signora Bianco and looking out at the Italian coast that two sixteen-year-old boys from

Mira Mesa, California, Michael Baker and John Mayeski, were, in a blend of new and old all-American-boyishness, pulling into a Jack-in-the-Box restaurant in San Diego on their way to go fishing. Before they could finish their fast food, twenty-five-year-old Robert Alton Harris and his brother, Danny, would commandeer their car and force the boys to a spot near a reservoir outside town. Robert had recently gotten out of jail after doing two and a half years for beating a man to death, and the Harris brothers wanted a car for an armed robbery they were about to commit.

To hear the brothers tell it (Danny testified against Robert), the kidnapping wasn't supposed to turn violent, but it did. Robert describes the killings as having been committed in the kind of sleepwalk frequently spoken of by capital offenders. Still, in the event, he managed to tell young Michael Baker (who was on his knees pleading for his life after the Mayeski boy had been shot) to cut it out and "die like a man."

The singular revolting detail that would ensure the crime's being remembered as the Jack-in-the-Box murders was Harris's lack of squeamishness, afterward, in finishing off the boys' hamburgers. The irony of his injunction to Michael Baker about dying like a man would also not be lost on those observing, subsequent to Harris's conviction, his eleven years of appeals, leading, at last, toward an execution date set for 3 A.M. on April 3, 1990.

Robert Alton Harris arrived at San Quentin in 1979, exactly four hundred years after Sir Francis Drake made his landings along the northern California coast. Parts of the prison Harris is in have been standing since 1852. The assertive architecture of San Quentin makes it seem more akin to San Francisco, across the bay, than to Marin County, of which it is actually a part. The town of Larkspur, just southwest of the prison, is a growing community (Robert Alton Harris has lived here longer than many of his neighbors), but in anti-development Marin, new structures tend to be placed apologetically, almost furtively, onto the land. An office building atop a hill near the Larkspur ferry slip seems to have been set there, with its brown, downward-sloping roof, so that as few people as possible will notice it, and so that those who do will see its fealty to the natural contours of the earth. The builders of San Quentin seem to have been less ashamed of what they had to construct.

The jokes and clichés about life in Marin are too true — you really can't order an unhealthful Coke at The Good Earth restaurant — to require much elaboration. But the idea that an execution is scheduled to happen here, an officially proclaimed nuclear-weapons-free zone, so borders on the fantastic that one searches one's mind for an inverted equivalent. A Socialist Youth Congress in rural Mississippi? Nine hours before Harris is to die, the Tiburon Wellness Group will be meeting, with "facilitater [sic] Hetty Herman Minsk," at the Belvedere Community Center. The group "uses Barbara Sher's books *Wishcraft* and *Teamworks* to help meet your goals, dreams and wants."

By Friday morning, March 30, less than one hundred hours before the scheduled execution, the Harris story has become national news. Joan Lunden split-screens Steve Baker, father of one of the murdered boys, and Robert Bryan of the National Coalition to Abolish the Death Penalty. Baker plans to fly up from San Diego to San Francisco (his first trip here) sometime on Monday to witness the execution. If that happens, an unusually complete circle will have been drawn: Baker was one of the San Diego police officers who arrested Harris on July 5, 1978. At that moment he thought he was only helping to catch two bank robbers. He didn't yet know that one of them had killed his son a little while before.

Bryan expresses rote sympathy for the Bakers and Mayeskis, but quickly gets to his own point, which is that countries with capital punishment have the same or higher rates of violent crime as ones without; indeed, we should be mindful that executing Harris may actually *increase* crime in the United States.

Mr. Baker is then asked by Joan Lunden if he thinks the death penalty is a deterrent. "Not when it takes twelve years to carry it out," he says.

Having come to California to cover Harris's execution as part of the "nonwitness media pool" that will spend Monday night inside San Quentin, I look at the list of instructions that arrived with my credentials:

> Do not wear Levi or jean-style blue, black or gray pants.
> Do not run. In a prison, this indicates someone is in trouble.

The West Gate, through which the press must enter by 10 P.M. Monday, is just off Sir Francis Drake Boulevard, a short walk from the slate-colored Larkspur Landing shopping center below my hotel. On my way to check it out, I pass a small wildlife habitat that includes Remillard Pond, the sign for which explains that

> A POND IS A BALANCED HABITAT COMMUNITY. IT'S [sic] INHAB-
> ITANTS DEPEND ON ONE ANOTHER FOR LIFE. REMILLARD POND
> PLANTS INCLUDE: ALGAE, CATTAILS AND WILLOW TREES. THEY
> USE SUN, WATER AND INORGANIC MATTER TO GROW AND MUL-
> TIPLY. ANIMALS FEED ON OTHER ANIMALS AND USE PLANTS FOR
> SHELTER AND FOOD. DEAD PLANTS AND ANIMALS DECOMPOSE,
> FERTILIZING THE POND AND PROMOTING GROWTH OF MORE
> PLANTS AND ANIMALS . . .

If Harris dies on Tuesday morning, the human ecology of the state of California will have shifted, slightly but unquestionably. It is the only thing upon which people on both sides of the capital punishment issue agree. If the death penalty, whether as deterrent or retributive ritual or simple punishment, is once more, finally, carried out (it has been imposed on 275 men besides Harris now in San Quentin), then the state pond, for better or worse, will be a more primitive place, and the chain of predation more circular. Indeed, one gets the feeling that what really hurts many of those carrying "Not in California" signs of protest is the sensation that they will be perceived as being morally out of step with the Western European countries that have embraced abolition and thereby, presumably, achieved a higher degree of civilization. One is struck more by their embarrassment at the prospect of joining the southern "Death Belt" states than by their outrage.

The death penalty has had the overwhelming support of Californians, not only in every sort of poll, but also when the question came before them on the ballot in 1978. Governor George Deukmejian was, as a state legislator, one of the authors of the death penalty statute created to bring the state into compliance with guidelines established by the U.S. Supreme Court when capital punishment was made once more permissible in 1976.

The first Governor Brown of California, Jerry's father, Edmund "Pat" Brown, has recently, at eighty-four, published a morally engaging book on the subject. In *Public Justice, Private Mercy: A Governor's Education on Death Row,* he reviews the various clemency dilemmas he experienced from 1959 to 1966. A vigorous opponent of capital punishment, Brown nevertheless allowed thirty-six people to die in the gas chamber during his two terms in office. (Crowds heckled him when he did commute a sentence, which was often.) Some have been tempted to draw a parallel between Governor Brown on capital punishment and Governor Cuomo on abortion — two men distastefully upholding laws with which their private consciences cannot agree. But the parallel does not run very far: Cuomo has not campaigned to bring the laws into line with his personal convictions, whereas Brown risked, and perhaps eventually lost, his political future by repeatedly asking the state legislature to do away with capital punishment.

At least one poll suggests that Californians would be more inclined to part with the death penalty in exchange for "life without parole." In fact, there *is* a sentence of life without parole in California, and has been since 1978. But what is statutory tends to seem hypothetical when pollsters ask about it, because people simply don't believe that the courts will really keep the cells locked forever. Neither do criminals, according to

Governor Brown: "Every prisoner knows that those laws have built-in escape hatches. Felons convicted under the California law before 1982, for example, automatically have their cases reviewed by the Board of Prison Terms, which can recommend clemency to the governor after twelve years. Those convicted after 1982 have to wait thirty years, but even that is a short enough period to legitimately frighten a large segment of the population." Brown still favors life without parole, but notes that if it is to "save court time and taxpayers' money [when] used as a guarantee in return for a guilty plea," then, ironically, "the state also has to have a death-penalty law on the books — to motivate a murderer to give up his right to a full trial."

On early Friday afternoon, things look peaceful and routine around San Quentin. Some inmates in blue work shirts spend weekdays like this weeding ground between Sir Francis Drake Boulevard and some of the modest cottages of corrections personnel living inside the gates. The main entrance to the prison is through a small road, inaptly named Main Street, off the freeway. After one or two outlets it's really a cul-de-sac ending with a white STATE PROPERTY LINE and the prison gates, near which stand an adobe-style U.S. Post Office, the prison crafts store, and a little house that is the prison law office. Its wooden sign shows a bird flying through bars. The street is sunny and wholesome-looking. You can descend a short flight of steps to a small beach and sit on the rocks, amidst buttercups and larkspur, watching the bay, oblivious of both the prison and the neighborhood on the promontory behind you.

Up there a group of people are keeping a vigil that's gone on for seven weeks; some of them are fasting. The officers at the gate seem relaxed, knowing that their real troubles will begin on Monday. The parking restrictions set to go into effect at 3:30 this afternoon hardly seem necessary yet.

And, as it suddenly happens, they may not be for quite a while longer. By late afternoon the news is out that Judge John

T. Noonan, Jr., of the U.S. Court of Appeals for the Ninth Circuit, an anti-abortion Reagan appointee, has just ruled favorably on a motion by Harris's attorneys for a new hearing to determine whether their client received adequate psychiatric evaluation at the time of his trial in 1979.

Even in the unpredictable judicial realm of impending executions — Pat Brown recalls how his predecessor's clemency secretary got through to the San Quentin warden two minutes after the cyanide pellets dropped into the sulfuric acid beneath a murderer named Burton Abbott — Noonan's decision comes as something of a shock. The considered opinion of most people with an interest in the matter had been that Harris, whose case was reviewed by Judge Noonan once before on other grounds, would die on Tuesday morning. Two days ago a federal judge in San Diego ruled against Harris's claim that he was a victim of fetal alcohol syndrome and organic brain damage. Since his initial conviction in 1979 — the boys he killed would now be approaching their thirties — his case has been appealed four times to the California Supreme Court and another four to the U.S. Supreme Court.

Between now and Tuesday it will be the turn of the state to appeal to Justice Sandra Day O'Connor, who takes emergency matters from the western states, that the court vacate the stay granted by Judge Noonan. This appeal will be filed — faxed, actually — by state Attorney General John Van de Kamp, who is running in the Democratic primary for governor. An opponent of the death penalty, Van de Kamp has taken a beating in recent opinion polls from his competition, Dianne Feinstein, the former San Francisco mayor, who is in the luxuriously electable position of being both pro-choice on abortion and pro–capital punishment. Van de Kamp must therefore backpedal into Governor Brown's old position, that regardless of his personal feelings he will carry out the laws of the state. The weekend will prove to be a somewhat unseemly bonanza for him. Not a news broadcast will go by without this nonbeliever in capital punishment telling the people of California how zealously he is urging the U.S. Supreme Court to allow the state to kill Robert Alton Harris at 3 A.M. on Tuesday. He says that for now Harris will even be denied certain visitors: they've just discovered marijuana in his pillowcase.

Most of the weekend will be lived out in an atmosphere of inscrutable suspense. No one feels confident predicting what Justice O'Connor or the entire Court will do. In the meantime reporters descend anew upon the families of the dead boys. John Mayeski's mother says that she's trying not to lose faith in the legal system. When asked if she has any advice or wish to express, she is succinct: "Speed it up."

Saturday's most pictorial news is the march of anti-death-penalty protesters across the Golden Gate Bridge. The demonstrators carry 121 black mock coffins — on TV they look like a toy train of coal cars — to stand for all those who have been executed since a firing squad did away with Gary Gilmore in 1977. The demonstration was planned long before yesterday's unexpected stay and was probably meant to have the mournfulness with which one awaits foregone conclusions. But anything can happen now; Attorney General Van de Kamp has announced that the Supreme Court has agreed to hear the state's appeal of Judge Noonan's decision. The hope is that it will rule by the end of the working day on Monday — 2 P.M. out here in the West.

Outside the main gate of San Quentin, things are still sunny and peaceful. I go back and forth between the handfuls of pro- and anti-death demonstrators. Each side concisely reiterates its articles of faith — take an eye for an eye; execution costs more than life imprisonment (all the appeals expenses) — statements of instinct more baldly implacable than those clustering around any of the other issues perpetually before the nation. One comes to feel that if ever there was a topic about which nothing more can profitably be said, this is it.

I try to engage Angie Frabasilio, a College of Marin student from San Rafael, in a discussion of whether her belief that the state has no right to take a life forces one, by logical extension, into a completely pacifist position. But when we get to the question of drafting an army, she says, "I was a little young when that issue was around." Wendy Zolla, holding the other end of Angie's banner (WHY DO PEOPLE KILL PEOPLE TO SHOW THAT KILLING PEOPLE IS WRONG?), has been coming here every twelve hours since Thursday. She has previously protested nuclear weapons at the Nevada Test Site and has participated in letter-writing campaigns against capital punishment in Georgia, Louisiana, and Texas. "I include Robert Harris in my prayers every day," she tells me, even though she's here on behalf of everyone on what San Quentin actually calls Condemned Row. "I don't live in fear of people being released from prison. I live in fear of paying taxes and being a part of a murder myself."

The antis are on the side of the street with the prison law office and crafts shop. The proponents are across from them, just down from the little post office. One of them is Bill Fling, a Church of Christ minister from Orangeville, above Sacramento. He gives me a tract he's written and tells me that I will be able to find much pro-capital-punishment material in the New Testament, "which some people think is more lenient" than the Old. "In my personal life, I'm to be willing to turn the other cheek, but civil government is made to protect me, because my cheeks could get pretty raw."

He's with Gay Wamble, a stern, crew-cut man who for twenty-two years was a part of the civil government as a corrections officer of the state prison at Vacaville. (He once directed Pat Brown's tour of the facility.) When the death penalty was overturned in the early 1970s, Vacaville received from San Quentin many prisoners whose sentences had been commuted to life, and Mr. Wamble worked with them "day after day after day after day" in the Maximum Custody Unit, S-Wing: "I know their inwardmost thoughts and their mind about capital punishment . . . They can tell you, 'Oh, I don't pay any attention to that death penalty. It wouldn't change what I want to do. I'd do it anyway.' But I'm here to tell you that that's not his inward feeling . . . I hear them talking to each other about the death penalty. I hear one convict saying, 'Well, when I get out of here I'm going to get that guy because he did such and such to me.' His answer would be, from another convict, 'Hey, man, you better watch that stuff. They snuff people for doing stuff like that.' So that shows you . . . a convict is afraid of the death penalty and it keeps him from committing capital crimes. Now, in their fit of anger, and circumstances, they do it anyway sometimes."

I ask Mr. Wamble, who says he preferred Reagan and Deukmejian on matters of law and discipline, but the Governors Brown when it came to pay raises, about life without parole: "I think it has the tendency to fill the prisons up with people that's going to have to stay there until they die. I don't know of a prison in this country anywhere that isn't overcrowded already."

Across the street is Stephen Souza, an Amnesty International member who broke a six-day fast when the stay was announced. The lack of sustenance has not taken the edge off either his California good looks or sparkly politeness. He tells me he wants a new trial for "Bobby Harris," who is "just the first sacrificial lamb that we want to sacrifice on the altar of inhumanity." (A new trial would, the antis feel, show that Harris's organically damaged brain was not guilty of premeditated murder.) Souza feels that the death penalty violates the Universal Declaration of Human Rights — "the greatest document that's ever been written in the history of mankind" — and would prefer to keep things at life without parole. I ask him if that means he believes certain people really are incorrigible, beyond rehabilitation — a notion that strikes me as an unlikely one for him to hold. I'm surprised by his answer: "I personally think that there are individuals that cannot be rehabilitated, and they should serve the rest of their life in prison."

One has to wonder how much of this hard line isn't just the practical politics of the moment, and how much longer it would be drawn once the gas chamber's door was permanently shut. I notice that one sign on the antis' side of the street — JAIL HIM

AND THROW THE KEYS AWAY, BUT DON'T MURDER HIM —
is tucked out of sight, facing the ocean instead of the street, as
if someone finally couldn't bear to display its expedient tough-
ness. And by Monday a slim vertical placard with the single
word REHABILITATE, in rather small letters, will have appeared.

The Larkspur ferry to San Francisco glides right by San Quentin, and on Sunday afternoon, which is sunny, breezy, and rou-
tinely perfect, the facility offers no unified impression to the
passing traveler. The part of it you first go by looks like a World
War II aircraft plant with big, barracks-style sheds and Quonset
shapes. The yellow stone of the old prison, whose barred green
windows look like giant tongue depressors, seems at a distance
like part of some huge dam or pumping station, until the boat
comes closer and you see how powdery the stone appears, the
industrial impression giving way completely to that of a sand
castle.

Some gulls — whose narrow, purposeful faces remind you of
Gay Wamble's — fly the whole trip across the bay in a straight
line behind the ferry. You wonder what sort of torment or peace
the sight of them brings to the inmates living day after day
under the arcs they describe. It's the same with the lone kayaker
who paddles in front of the ferry: does he provide them with a
diversion or a rebuke?

If the free-flying gulls do insult the prisoners, it is possible
that their revenge will come early Tuesday morning, when, after
killing Harris, the cyanide gas must be vented into the atmosphere. Bob Cleek, a former guard at San Quentin who is now
an attorney, recalls for a columnist in the *Marin Independent
Journal:* "We used to hear stories about all the dead seagulls on
the prison roof following deaths by poison." Sulfuric acid is
dumped into the bay as well. "It'd be interesting to know if the
prison possesses a toxic waste disposal permit," Cleek wonders.
"Imagine Harris's life being spared because of an Environmental Impact Report." And sure enough, Wednesday's *San Fran-*

cisco Chronicle will report that phone calls from death penalty opponents have led the Bay Area Air Quality Control Board to make inquiries to the prison. According to Steven Hill, who manages the board's toxic evaluation section: "If we determine that the gas emission could cause harm, we would not issue a permit to operate [the gas chamber]."

On any weekend but this one, tourists on the ferry are more attentive to Alcatraz, the real bird-associated attraction in the bay. You pass it just before coming into the Port of San Francisco, whose piers house more restaurants than ships. Harry Bridges, the longshoreman leader who convulsed San Francisco with a general strike in 1934, died on Friday. Reminiscences of him, and the old workingman's city, share the weekend papers with Harris, whose picture, taken last Monday, appears on the front page of today's *Examiner*. In it he hugs the baby son of a visitor to San Quentin and smiles benignly.

You note that the big clock over the electric Port of San Francisco sign is an hour slow. No one has yet moved it forward for daylight savings time, which began at 2 A.M. If the clocks in San Quentin have been pushed ahead, is Harris, while weighing the odds, feeling cheated out of an hour of life?

Passengers disembark not far from a statue of Gandhi that was set up in 1988: NONVIOLENCE IS THE GREATEST FORCE AT THE DISPOSAL OF MANKIND. IT IS THE SUPREME LAW. BY IT ALONE CAN MANKIND BE SAVED.

"This is not the end of it. This is round one as far as I'm concerned." It's not one of Harris's lawyers. It's nice Pat Orr, who lives at 58 Main Street, just a few houses down from the prison gates. She's the head of the San Quentin Village Association, and we're chatting, late Monday morning, on the wooden steps leading up from her small flower-filled yard. She's annoyed because this is a county road, not prison property, and even though the demonstrations were planned seven months ago, her group was never consulted. About a month and a half ago she began talking to the county sheriff's office, the Board of Supervisors, and other authorities, but the only consideration members of the San Quentin Village Association have been shown is being told to move their own cars off their own street to keep them from being damaged. Pleas that the demonstrators be moved to the West Gate out on Sir Francis Drake have been ignored; law enforcement, Pat reasons, cares more about traffic than homeowners. But she hasn't given up. She's ready to use the legal process, expensive and protracted though it may be. The dues for her organization are only $10 a year, but "we'll have rummage sales if we have to," she says. Actually, some of the residents are making a little money here. They've rented their yards and garage aprons to the TV people for their trucks, whose grinding motors bother Pat much more than the reporters and technicians themselves.

We're joined by Michelle, another resident, and her small son. According to Pat, people on the block have a variety of opinions on the death penalty — Michelle seems opposed to it and thinks the matter of Harris's supposed fetal alcohol syndrome deserves consideration — but the Village Association has decided that that's not their issue. The media carnival is. Pat says a handful of demonstrators have been here for fifty-seven days, but it's usually the press who form "a substitute crowd." In fact, they've been around so long that when we say goodbye to each other, she says, accidentally, "Nice to media you," and we burst out laughing.

By noon the press is here in force. People are expectant: the Court should say something within the next two hours. Gay Wamble and Bill Fling are tirelessly giving interviews. Steve Souza does the same, smiling his endless-summer smile. One protester alternates between relaxed conversation with the others and quietly kneeling on a pillow while she reads from the Book of Common Prayer. People are in a good mood. It isn't gallows humor, it's the weather. The day and scenery are so spectacularly beautiful that it's hard to be otherwise. For all the suspense and all the handicapping of the outcome, it's difficult to think of the yellow prison with its crenellated battlements as a jail at all. One might as well be out in the sun in front of some other sprawling piece of California architecture, San Simeon or the Mission Inn.

At 12:40 the clergy come up Main Street, most of them Unitarians in long, cheerful stoles. The press rush like antennaed insects to film an impromptu debate between kindly, white-haired Bishop Francis Quinn of Sacramento and the fundamentalist minister Bill Fling, who's still passing out the pro-capital-punishment tract he handed me Saturday. The two of them are a videocameraman's dream. They will occasionally clasp each other's hands in a friendly way as they argue Deuteronomy 19, racial inequality in the application of the death penalty, and the soul of George Deukmejian. "The governor's not a murderer," says Fling. "Oh, I know," responds Bishop Quinn, who later, going back to the Bible, asks Fling if he thinks adulterers should be put to death. The bishop gets some kibitzing support from the circle of anti-death people around him. Meanwhile, a blond TV reporter tries to get it all straight: "If the Supreme Court upholds the stay, that means there's no execution and you start [tonight's demonstrations] earlier." When told by Steve Souza that that's just so, he says, "Gotcha," with some relief.

"Paul is now going to play his flute to calm down the situation. He's such a typical Berkeley Unitarian." This is said affectionately by one of the MASK (March Against State Killing) demonstrators, who is popping some pills — for stress, she says. Paul Sawyer sits down near the post office steps, and when the video people hear his flute and spot his colorful stole, they're on to one of the best photo ops of the day.

Rev. Sawyer leads some singing, a spiritual about how we have to walk down that lonesome road all by ourselves — not a particularly optimistic choice for today, one thinks. He preaches to his converted colleagues about all the other kinds of violence done by the state, from Vietnam to Central America to the black community. A cameraman attaches a tiny microphone to his stole, the better to catch all of this. Sawyer hopes for a world in which "no one, no thing, will be destroyed," and he pays Robert Alton Harris the ultimate northern-California compliment: he compares him to a nonhuman life form. "We would do this as fittingly for the redwood tree being destroyed." He asks the people gathered in a semicircle if they want to say anything, and a long-haired young man who was out here all night says: "I just have thanksgiving for you, man." Rev. Sawyer deflects the compliment back to him. A pediatrician then speaks about her experiences with fetal alcohol syndrome (a subject on which Bishop Quinn also seems to have become recently knowledgeable), and soon it will be the turn of the priest with the "Boycott Salvadoran Coffee" button to have his say.

Five officers from the Department of Corrections have just taken up positions along the state property line, standing calmly with legs apart and hands behind their backs. The cameras scurry in their direction. I exchange a few words with Bishop Quinn, who tells me there are two California bishops named Quinn, but that it's "just a Quinn-cidence." I decide that I like him, which is why I wish he wouldn't do what he does next. "I'm going to go say hello to the guards," he says. He works his way down the row of five, as if the property line were a communion rail, giving each officer a smile and a friendly tap on the chest. They receive this pleasantly enough, but obviously have orders not to unclasp their arms, so the bishop comes away with no handshakes. Perhaps they're just thinking he's a friendly old crock, but the little scene seems depressingly cruel: he's soothing the leashed beasts, trying to keep them calm, because we all know how they can be when aroused. It's also pointless, because tempers and emotions are under control, even as 1:30 approaches. I chat with Meg, another Unitarian minister, from Sunnyvale, who tells me she's got to get back to a meeting of her congregation tonight. "I can't believe it," she says with a disappointed smile, like a mother with a conflict between a school play and the Brownies.

The woman with two placards, one in each hand, keeps marching. Bill Fling and Steve Souza, like the bunny in the

Energizer battery commercials, are still going, indefatigably
talking to all media comers. I walk across the street so that I can
hear the ocean. "It's got to be close to two o'clock," somebody
says. A protester in a chair is wondering what will happen "if
we win." That's what it is coming down to. There's the feel of
an old-fashioned election night now, with people gathered to
hear the returns come in from the other coast. At 1:50 someone
asks Souza what the situation is. "Pretty soon we shall know,"
he says. A woman asks him who some of the people on his list
of speakers are. "Human beings who reside on the planet
Earth," he answers. One newsman is reminded by a colleague
that it was calm and warm like this just before the October
earthquake. "Standing by and ready to go at any time," another
media person tells her troops.

Some motorcycle cops noisily arrive on Main Street and the
photographers go off to snap them as they park. The Reverend
Victor Carpenter of the First Unitarian Church of San Francisco
compares the way cyanide deprives a gas chamber victim of
oxygen to the way the death penalty deprives society of its
moral oxygen. Paul Sawyer takes up his flute again before
joining the rest of the antis in a prayer circle. They sing: "This
Little Life of Mine, I'm Gonna Let It Shine," and Sawyer, in
the most outrageous falsehood anyone will utter today, tells
some elbowing media person: "We're not here for the press,
we're here for life." In fact, in just a little while, after a recitation of the Twenty-third Psalm, Meg will race to the cameras
to tell, angrily, of a parking restriction that was just imposed
on her and of how she was threatened with arrest for walking
up a ramp. She says this kind of restriction and intimidation
may explain the relative lack of protesters here, and she is
applauded.

Portable toilets arrive shortly after a picnic cooler — which
for a moment I think might be a mock coffin — is carried up the
street. By 3:00 there is still no word out of Washington. Reporters listen to their radios: prisoners inside will be under a lock-
down in order to avoid disturbances if the execution goes for-

ward. Policemen have appeared at the top of a hill inside the gates and to the right.

And then, at 3:20, like a grotesque version of a scrubbed space launch, it's suddenly over. Everyone clusters around the preppy blond reporter, whose radio or phone is saying that the Supreme Court, by a vote of 6 to 3, has declined to vacate Judge Noonan's stay. The Harris case will go back to the Ninth Circuit. Even if, from here on, everything goes the state's (and Van de Kamp's) way, there will be no execution for months.

Bishop Quinn is "overjoyed." The antis hug. A smiling Steve Souza goes running up the street, arm in arm, with a woman. Rev. Carpenter makes an emotional speech of gratitude for the "overwhelming joy" he's feeling. Paul Sawyer asks, bewilderingly, for "a great round of sympathy" for Judge Noonan, that Reagan appointee. Applause.

A bustle of departure begins. "Great day, huh?" someone going past me says. "Paul, let's go!" cries a smiling Rev. Carpenter, hurrying his loquacious, flute-carrying colleague along. It is time to unplug cables, store cellular phones, head for the makeshift parking lot down by the freeway. I take a business card from the Reverend William Wood, who, while happy, worries that "we have a long journey ahead of us" ensuring that Robert Alton Harris survives the coming months and courtroom procedures ahead.

I start down Main Street, whose name will soon again, at least for a while, seem unlikely. Out of one of the pretty flower-bordered houses comes the unexpected sound of a saxophone. The tune is neither celebrational nor some mournful piece of prison blues. It's just "Row, Row, Row Your Boat." For the first time today the two victims come to mind. It's impossible not to wish them this day, and the sunburn on one's own face; impossible not to wish that their appetites hadn't delayed, so many years ago, their arrival at the lake, where they might have whistled, not learned, that life is but a dream.

POSTSCRIPT

Fred Batson is now serving his sentence in upstate New York, and on April 21, 1992, Robert Alton Harris died in the gas chamber at San Quentin. After my trip to the West Coast, two years of legal battles were added to the twelve that preceded them. The hours before his execution were such a chaos of stays and reversals (Harris was already strapped into the chair when one stay was granted) that some commentators wondered if the appeals process, as now practiced in capital cases, isn't itself a form of cruel and unusual punishment. One of Harris's most passionate and principled defenders was Michael A. Kroll, executive director of the Death Penalty Information Center. Mr. Kroll wrote me shortly after the appearance of "Death Rally Days" in the conservative *American Spectator* and expressed surprise at its inexplicit viewpoint:

> I guess you are for the death penalty, but that is only a guess and does not come through from the text of your piece. . . . Judging from the individuals you named whom I know (Steve Souza, Rev. Sawyer, Bishop Quinn, Mrs. Orr, for example), I commend you for filling me in on those last days. At the time of your descriptions, I was holed up with the Harris family (brothers, sisters, nephews and nieces) awaiting word as to whether Robert would be gassed or not. It was a strange place to be, given my own emotional involvement. But that's where I was, and it was one of

the most isolated vantage points to have of those last days —
especially after brother Randy and I were barred from visiting on
the suspicion (never more — never any charge) that we had somehow smuggled marijuana to the condemned. . . .

You quite appropriately end your piece with a reverie on the
two boys whom Robert killed twelve years ago. While I find such
thoughts both entirely understandable and appropriate, I also think
there are victims here who virtually never garner the thought of
anyone, and I refer to the family of Harris himself. These are
guiltless people (except for the brother, Danny) who are shunned
by all. . . . Perhaps they are made to be villains for the simple fact
of wanting their brother to live. Whatever, I urge you to cast a
thought in their direction from time to time.

In my response to Mr. Kroll, written in the summer of 1990,
I reflected on the death penalty debate and stated my position
with a directness I had deliberately avoided in the article:

I was struck, and refreshed, by your letter's genuine attempt to
inform and enlarge the recipient. This sort of utterance was, I
thought, in short supply at San Quentin early in April. I think I
said something in my article about how discourse on this subject
seems entirely a matter, on both sides, of pointless repetition.
Perhaps that's true of most public issues, but it's numbingly so for
this one. Even the sincere people (I would count Steve Souza and
Bishop Quinn among them) don't really expect to be listened to
or heard, and so their speech often becomes as robotized as that
of the cause-junkies and zealots. Anyway, your letter was different, and I appreciated it.

Your guess is right: I do favor the death penalty and am
unpersuaded by arguments, including recent ones, on Robert
Harris' behalf. It's not a position I take with any pleasure or from
a rigid consistency. I would not have been inclined to execute, say,
Ted Bundy, who seems to me an obvious sort of genetic catastrophe. Perhaps Harris is an environmental or biological one, but I
cannot, finally, see it that way. Insofar as I do approve of executions, I would not claim to do so on grounds of deterrence. I think
they are always fundamentally retributive, and I accept them as
such.

I believe you are sincere in your grief for the boys; I am
prepared to believe that Harris is, too. I was grateful for your

reminder of the sufferings of his family. I will heed your advice and include them in my thoughts, as well as my prayers.

This exchange of letters began a correspondence on the subject of capital punishment that has continued intermittently to this day. I thank Michael Kroll for his friendly attempts at persuasion and for his permission to quote from his first letter to me.

Politics

Rhode Show

NOVEMBER 1990

"This is by no means a done deal," says Rick Gureghian. "I think these polls can move." He means downward, but five days before the election, the campaign staff of Senator Claiborne Pell hardly seem worried. Their headquarters, here in Providence, Rhode Island, on the fourth floor of the converted Davol rubber-goods factory, are busy but hardly frantic. Gureghian, the press man, is merely making the don't-tempt-the-gods remarks required of front-runners. Such Grecian caution is perhaps in order, since Gureghian, like Pell's campaign manager, Mary Beth Cahill, used to work for Michael Dukakis — "in the good days," he tells me.

Claiborne Pell is almost seventy-two years old and has served Rhode Island in the Senate since 1961. Except for his 1972 race against John Chafee, another of the state's disappearing Brahmins, his campaigns have been walk-throughs. This one was supposed to be different. The Republicans have nominated Claudine Schneider, a popular five-term congresswoman from the western half of the state. Still only forty-three, she is pro-choice, conspicuously pro-environment, and except for a bit of Republican parsimony, dependably liberal. (In 1987 she voted against President Reagan more frequently than any other

Republican member of the House.) The state, while overwhelmingly Democratic, can be generous with ticket splitting (Chafee made it to the other Senate seat in 1976), so early this year Schneider was regarded as the kind of Republican with a good shot at moving up.

But it is proving to be tricky. Pell, who speaks in a soft, aristocratic slur, a millionaire who wears threadbare suits, is an institution, someone seen as simultaneously befuddled and effective. He fathered the Basic Educational Opportunity Grants in 1972, "the cornerstone of federal aid to students," as Congressional Quarterly's *Politics in America* puts it. They were officially rechristened Pell Grants in 1980, and since then have been a continuing advertisement of his name. About 160,000 Rhode Islanders have had them to date.

If Schneider could find a way to do what Mondale couldn't in 1984 — gently suggest that the nice old man is past it — it was thought she might pull it off. During a debate in August she asked Pell to name the last thing he'd done for Rhode Island, and he answered: "I couldn't give you a specific answer. My memory's not as good as it should be." (He later said he thought she was talking about legislation targeted toward individuals, such as a bill to help resolve someone's immigration status.) This could have been her breakthrough, but Iraq invaded Kuwait the next day and Pell, as chairman of the Foreign Relations Committee, had the heaven-sent photo opportunity to lead a congressional delegation to the Middle East. To no one's surprise, he has since found little time to debate Schneider, and she has slipped way behind in the polls. They've hired the best in campaign consultants (she's got David Garth, and he's got Bob Squier), but what was supposed to be a hard-fought, if unideological, contest has turned out to be like many of his past races. Frustrated, Schneider has let slip a crack about the senator's being "out of it," and that hasn't played well. "First they were nice, then they were subtly negative, then they were negative, and now they're nice again," says Gureghian, a heavyset smoker who cast his first vote for McGovern and who, for all his ability to talk to you in press releases (Pell has been "a leader on women's and family issues in the Senate"), would probably relish a bare-knuckles fight with this sparkly woman who looks different in each picture; who was born in the steel town of Clairton, Pennsylvania, but whose conversation has a hint of New Age crystal; and who has gone so far as to endorse those tapes pushed by Tony Robbins, the coiffed Cro-Magnon of mail-order motivation.

As far ahead as Pell seems to be on November 1, it probably *isn't* quite a done deal. No one knows for sure just how disgusted the recent budget fiasco has left people feeling, or whom they'll take it out on. The country could be at war by Tuesday, and Claudine Schneider has energy to burn. So the Pell strategy is, rather like the man, slow and steady. Today they've had him shaking hands at a UPS shift change and going to Blue Cross–Blue Shield at lunchtime. In a little while he'll be getting ready for two evening fund-raisers (one a "high-dollar" affair, the other a "low-dollar" one, according to Gureghian) on the same floor of the Biltmore Hotel in Providence.

At 6 P.M., in a room around the corner from the Bacchante Room (which, if one judges by the size of the shrimp, must be the high-dollar affair), Pell is holding a quick press conference with Senator George Mitchell, the majority leader, and some candidates lower down the state Democratic ticket. In his shy, patrician way Pell makes sure that Kathleen Connell, the secretary of state, comes up to "bask in these wonderful TV cameras," before he introduces Mitchell as someone who would make a "wonderful President of the United States."

Mitchell proceeds to show, instantly, why he would be no such thing. He speaks in the soothing, excessively sane way of a bereavement counselor. He supposedly does harbor presidential ambitions, and it is not beyond possibility that he will become the final pod-candidate for the Democrats, the terminal case of the progressive anemia that has afflicted their presidential offerings since McGovern. He talks up the Pell Grants and says that their creator "has conducted himself with dignity and honor in a manner that has earned him the respect of every member of the Senate, Democrat and Republican." Pell, who looks like a geriatric boy, clenching and clasping his hands, says, "You make me feel very humble." He probably even means it. The secretary of state continues the tribute to his manners, noting the dignity with which he's conducted this race, even though it's been a tough one. The race, in fact, has not been tough, and the implication, that Schneider has been un-dignified, isn't true either, but the Democrats, who love the *noblesse oblige* of aristocrats with a fervor beyond anything Republicans can summon, are reveling in the opportunity to gaze upon Pell as a gentle, stammering FDR.

Mitchell takes a question on the just-past budget crisis. "I'm glad it's over," he says to needlessly hearty laughter. He gets some applause when he says, "It's time the Republicans stopped soaking the middle class," and he follows that up with some sarcasm about the President's "passionate commitment" to the rich, but there is a kind of mad decorum to his thumping of these old party tubs, as if Julie Andrews were attempting to do Sophie Tucker's act.

When it's over, Pell shuffles out of the room behind Mitchell, saying — more patrician modesty — "I'll take one percent." Out in the hall, a kid in a suit, the head of Youth for Pell, says, "That was nice, huh?" to a TV reporter, before engaging some other guys, including Scott Wolf, the young, not-much-of-a-chance candidate for Congress in the first district, in some chatter about what a terrific guy Pell is.

The kid is Patrick Kennedy, Teddy's son, among the youngest of the second Kennedy wave, that *tsunami* of new and future officeholders. Born in 1967, Patrick is already a state rep in the Rhode Island General Assembly, from a little Providence district up by the statehouse. Rhode Island is the small neighboring estate that the Kennedys have leased for a family baby short-changed by political primogeniture, and it is probably safe to say that few state assembly campaigns have been conducted at a higher per capita cost than his first one was back in 1988.

He is actually a nice boy; perhaps the friars of Providence College, where he went to school, put an extra coat of manners on him. He has his mother's pleasant eyes instead of the cold ones of the Kennedy males. He displays a trace of his uncles' nervous nodding, but whether this is a matter of genetic encoding or an acquired characteristic derived from watching videos of the Republic's longest family home movie, it's difficult to say.

He stands outside the Bacchante Room, where the high-dollar fund-raiser has begun, and talks up Senator Pell to me at a length beyond the call of duty, showing an awareness of the statistic Rhode Island politicians use to focus themselves, the way an alcoholic uses the serenity prayer: the state is second in the nation in its percentage of senior citizens. "There's no one who's done more for the elderly than Pell," he asserts. "You know the COLAs? That's Senator Pell." But he'll be good for young people, too. When it comes to possible war in the Persian Gulf (where "a lot of kids from my college in the ROTC program" have gone to serve), Pell is a good bet because "he knows the mistakes from last time," like the Tonkin Gulf Resolution.

As for the race against Schneider, Patrick offers some postmodern polspeak ("She failed to articulate her own campaign, her own message") and the by-now standard tut-tutting about how she "went negative." The Democratic algebra for this particular contest is clear: multiplying a negative by a negative will yield a positive. Or, more simply, make people think she's acting like a bitch, and the aging gentleman will catch an armful of boomeranged ballots. It's "such a hard thing to convince people what's wrong with Senator Pell," says Patrick, and I tell him this race reminds me of the one Robert Kennedy ran against nice old Senator Keating of New York in 1964. That time niceness didn't help, and the snowy-haired Republican went down before the little brother. (My own Catholic town, in a burst of tribal grief, gave Bobby a majority even as it went heavily for Goldwater.) But Claudine is no Bobby Kennedy, and the Democrats are determined to make this a referendum on good manners. Pell is "somebody you can't campaign against in any traditional way," says Patrick, and he's right.

It was during that 1964 campaign, of course, that Bobby Kennedy was charged with carpetbagging, and I ask his nephew whether he still gets such complaints about his own relocation. Not really, and in any case he's decided not to be defensive: "I can't live my life like that." As he greets acquaintances outside the Bacchante Room in this hotel just off a plaza named for JFK, it's hard not to feel sorry for him, starting that life as the print of a negative that's already been dipped too often. But he seems to enjoy it. When I ask him if he'd like Pell's Senate seat for his own, six years from now, he laughs. "I'd have to pull a Joe Biden," he says; he'll be just under thirty, as was Delaware's senator-elect in November 1972. He says he just wants "to stay in politics right now at the local level," to become more focused and efficient. But one notices that he's done the arithmetic.

Rhode Island's chief airport, in Warwick, is named for Theodore Green, who stayed in the Senate to a much riper age than Pell has attained. It has a fancy briefing room with soundproof walls and rows of swivel chairs. But the impending Friday morning arrival of Bob Dole, who'll be campaigning today for Schneider, isn't filling them. A few minutes before things are supposed to start I'm alone in the room with Jody McPhillips of the *Providence Journal*. She talks to me about Schneider's image and about how impressed her editor was by all the bouncing energy Claudine displayed when she announced her candidacy — on Valentine's Day. "She's forty-three years old," McPhillips says she told him. "What the hell's she jumping up and down for?" Just as Robert Frost told John F. Kennedy to be more Irish than Harvard, one wonders if Claudine wouldn't do better by being more Clairton than cutesy. But McPhillips says that one

TV ad showing a sepia picture of her father's tailor shop was done so poorly you could hardly figure out what you were supposed to be looking at.

By the time Schneider and Dole arrive, the number of press has swelled to five or six. "Good morning! Afternoon! What is it?" chirps Claudine, who does at this first glance promise an exhausting perkiness. The suit she has on is blazing red, but it's cut along dress-for-success lines, a strategic change, according to McPhillips, from the kookier outfits toward which she's more naturally inclined. Schneider announces the day's schedule and then Dole takes over for a while, saying this is still a "winnable seat" in a "volatile state." He says he's happy to respond to any questions, "except about the Red Cross." This joking reference to his wife's new job makes one wonder if Schneider won't be replacing her as secretary of labor, a reward for going up against Pell.

If Schneider, for all her energy, looks older than forty-three, Dole seems younger than sixty-seven, and friendlier, too, less like the Prince of Darkness than he does on television. Still, when he walks he glides, and it seems as if he is keeping his real self just out of sight, perhaps behind one of the padded walls. As he goes on with his canned campaign talk, you get the feeling that his detachment proceeds from self-loathing, as if he's wondering why he, unlike you, has nothing better to do.

Schneider stresses her independence and compliments the state's voters on theirs, noting that she ran ahead of Reagan here in 1984. "I have had ten years of sticking to my guns," she says, and Dole promises it will be all right with him if, when she gets to the Senate, they don't always agree. The party needs diversity. He suspects, however, that as Republican leader he'll "be visiting with Claudine from time to time." What President Bush might call the Woman Thing plays well between Schneider and Dole, who brings up Nancy Kassebaum and notes: "I serve with two powerful women, one in the Senate and one at home." Schneider, down in polls of her own sex, contrives to make one comment "as a woman" and to answer a female reporter's question "woman to woman." A softball query to Dole, about how he would feel working with as many as five women in the Senate, a (slim) possibility after this election, is a plant: the questioner is really Schneider's field director.

Dole says he doesn't "run around attacking [his] colleagues in the Senate," and when he's asked what's wrong with Pell, the best he can come up with isn't much better than what Schneider has. You have to "look down the road ten, fifteen, twenty years."

It's been years since New York cab drivers had much to say to their passengers, but Rhode Island ones carry on the tradition of pontifical chatter. "I don't like negative campaigning," says Doug. "It turns me off." (A moment before, when I told him I wasn't sure of the address of the Cranston Senior Services Center, at which I'm next supposed to find Schneider, this same sensitive soul said, "We'll find her. Just look for a tall, ugly broad.") Doug is not politically uninformed, and one gets the feeling that he now knows what, as far as this particular race goes, the Democrats want him to know — that he is supposed to dislike Schneider's negative campaigning.

So is he voting for Pell? Not necessarily, but he's leaning that way. He didn't like Bush's original tax proposal this season, and he inveighs against "millionaires" with the kind of gusto George Mitchell should study. But he can still make a pretty even-handed assessment of the candidates. Schneider, if no beauty, is "a nice person," and he thinks she's done "a lot of good work." He also buys into one of her arguments about Pell: he "could care less about the Foreign Relations Committee." Doug isn't sure Pell's "done much for the state of Rhode Island in the past six years," which is Schneider's point exactly; she'll try to get on the Commerce Committee to correct that. In New York, Alfonse D'Amato is happy to be called the "pothole senator" and leave the statesmanship to Moynihan. Schneider is something of a conceptualist herself, but this committee-assignment argument is one of the few wedges she has available to drive between Pell and the voters, and over the next few days she'll push on it repeatedly.

But Pell fixes potholes, too. "I've never heard of him refusing to help someone," says Doug. "I think he's a decent man, an honest man." Schneider's chief hope when he goes to vote is Doug's concern that Pell "may have outlived his usefulness."

He refers to Bruce Sundlun, the Democratic candidate for governor, as "Bruce," and tells me about campaign advice he's given him between Providence and the airport. Doug has had them all in his cab, and talking with him is a reminder of how funny federalism can be. Rhode Island Senate races are fought in a state that's more like a midsize city, where the candidates spend every campaign tripping over each other, and where the only way to take things is personally.

"There are no strangers here," says the sign inside the Cranston Senior Services Center. "Only friends we haven't met yet." At I I A.M. on Friday folks at the center are waiting to meet Claudine, who will try to meet every one of them. The Magic-Markered schedule of activities (Billiards, Oil Painting, Ceramics, Reminiscing with Christine, Exercise with Ida, Hi-Lo Jack) makes the seniors' days seem as fully empty as the round of factory gates, shopping centers, and fund-raisers now filling Schneider's. She arrives with Dole and is greeted by "Ms. Senior Sweetheart of Cranston, R.I., 1991," who wears a purple dress, gray boots, and a tiara. The queen's proud consort tells me his wife was crowned in a regular pageant, in which her talent was singing, and that she has a year of scheduled appearances, just like Miss America.

"It's very close, so spread the word," says Claudine to a woman whose hand she shakes before bopping into a big room and joining a line of tap dancers. She gets a lot of applause, and I'm reminded of the little heel-bouncing imitation of her that Patrick Kennedy did for me last night outside the Bacchante Room. "I want you to meet Senator Dole, who's come to help campaign for me," she says in the overexplanatory way one uses with the very young. But if this place, its Halloween decorations still up, seems to infantilize the seniors, it also seems to humanize the politicians. Dole is an absolutely different man from the one he was at the press conference an hour ago. He *loves* posing with the old girls, squeezing and teasing them into photos. Fully present now, he seems to experience the whole thing less as the practice of politics than an escape from it. You wonder how he could have failed in New Hampshire two years ago: too many press conferences, probably.

To the tune of "Music, Music, Music," Schneider, who is in fact rather attractive, sits and chats and bops up again, clasping both hands of the ladies a head or two shorter than she is. She and Dole move on to the Adult Day Care section and eventually upstairs, where the minority leader tells some exercisers that he uses his treadmill 25 minutes each day. Claudine, whose expression is never under 100 watts, determinedly connecting with everybody every second, says she's willing to join him on the treadmill of the Senate. I'm having trouble hearing in here, with the windows open and the traffic passing, and I wonder how people with three or four decades on me are managing. But Dole and Schneider are clearly making contact. "I recognize good people and good candidates when I see them," he says, proceeding to turn the Age Thing, for a moment, to Claudine's advantage: she's young and aggressive and will take care of their children and grandchildren, he insists. You wonder why she doesn't take a risk with the issue herself. The *Kansas City Star* reporter who's here following Dole tells me he's seen Pell dozing off in committee meetings. Why not bring that up with these old folks, whose perceptions of aging are likely to be a good deal less sentimental than those of Youth for Pell? Besides, what's she got to lose?

After a stop in the painting and ceramics room, Schneider says she's ready to get the show on the road. Before she can leave she greets a reporter ("I was so thrilled to get the *Warwick*

Beacon endorsement") and responds to my question about one of the very few graspable differences between herself and the incumbent: she voted against Moynihan's Social Security proposal and Pell voted for it, "without doing his homework," she says, because it was "politically expedient." But she doesn't expect it to come up again in the next Congress, so as gunpowder available for blasting open this race, it's pretty wet by now.

And she's off. The Senior Sweetheart's husband tells me he thinks Claudine "deserves a chance." She's "a worker." But he knows a lot of people will vote for Pell, because, like them, the senator's been around a long time.

Pell is coming to Cranston, too, for lunch at the Boston Submarine Sandwich Shop, whose back room the owner, Joe Pashalian, has made into a kind of noontime forum in which local politicians and commentators give speeches and take questions. It's a TV writer's dream of a blue-collar setting, although the group around the table seems to include some small businessmen and a professional or two. Pell arrives with his daughter, who tells me that she's all for his running again: "He's got the stamina of a forty-year-old combined with the wisdom of being his age." One admires her loyalty, but the truth is he looks terribly fragile.

He sits down at the long table near the six-decker ovens and the great spread of Armenian cracker bread. One feels there ought to be musical accompaniment, perhaps "What Do the Simple Folk Do?" "Senator," he's asked, "what will you have?" He takes a plate of tuna salad, just tomatoes, no lettuce, and a glass of water — considerably less hearty fare than people usually come here for.

Someone calls the diners to order by pounding a mallet on the podium. Pell gives a short speech after a standing ovation. He talks about a meeting a couple of days ago with President Bush, and how he helped convey the message to "go slow, go easy" in the Persian Gulf. Risking a reminder of his own advancing years, he concludes his remarks by recalling the story of a senator who dreamt he was making a speech on the Senate floor and then awoke to find that he was.

Anna Minicucci, who introduced herself to me as Joe Pashalian's "unpaid publicist" and who is more than a little reminiscent of Rhea Perlman, asks him a question about "human potential." Pell is interested in ESP and extraterrestrials, and is lucky that Schneider is known to like astrology, or else there might be a real Flake Factor to overcome. He responds with talk about the exceptional physical and mental feats people can sometimes perform, like reading and retaining a whole page of print in a flash. "I remember John Kennedy had that skill," he says by way of shrewdly chosen example. "I think these areas should be explored."

He gets a laugh by calling the White House chief of staff Mr. Say-No-No, and thoughtful attention when he calls for a longer school year. "Some of you may have heard of the Pell Grants," he says, a little like LBJ going into a nursing home and saying, "Perhaps you've heard of Medicare." But he is not all ADA-sponsored boilerplate. There's a kind of intellectual *droit du seigneur* about him, a measure of independence that is also, one supposes, a privilege of age. "I'm sort of sympathetic to it" is his surprising answer about a proposal to make English the official language, though he's glad he's not had to make a decision on it. He's supported bilingual education in the past, but fears that if a child has it for too many years it becomes a crutch. And he was against forgiving Egypt its foreign-aid debt as a reward for its support in the Gulf crisis: there are many recipient countries supportive of the United States, so how do you choose one and not another? On the Foreign Relations Committee he'd prefer working once more with the "reasonable" Senator Lugar as ranking minority member. Jesse Helms "is just" — he pauses, closes his eyes, shakes his hand near his head while searching for words — "very difficult to deal with." That's the highest pitch of nastiness he'll reach in the campaign.

He reminds the group that in his own case "memory may be a

little less, but judgment's a lot better." One guy, in a friendly way, gets up from the table and excuses himself by saying: "I've got to go to work. I've got to pay my taxes." Joe, not far from one of his ovens, thanks Pell for being his own man. "We know you don't take money," he says, and besides, "we only give dough."

Arlene Violet, a former Sister of Mercy, served as Rhode Island's attorney general in the mid-1980s. As a lawyer she'd gotten the nickname "Attila the Nun," but a perception of incompetence in office queered her reelection. Now back in private practice, she is currently filling in for Vincent ("Buddy") Cianci, who has put aside his radio talk show to run as an independent for mayor of Providence. (Cianci was mayor from 1975 until 1984, when he pleaded no contest to a felony charge of assaulting the man he thought was his wife's lover with a fireplace log. Seventeen individuals associated with his administration went to jail for corruption. But the billboards in town tell you, "He never stopped caring about Providence," and Buddy is now given an almost even shot at regaining his old job.)

Schneider does Violet's radio show from 4 to 5 P.M. Arlene is sympathetic to her, and uses her buzzsaw accent to fend off hostile callers: "*Aaaar* you *se*-rious?" she demands of one guy.

The candidate does what pitching she can, along already familiar lines: the gently xenophobic (in a changed world, aging Rhode Islanders could use somebody on a "health-related" committee, not Foreign Relations); the feminist (her "good women's intuition" tells her it's close — and, by the way, asks Arlene, "How many women *aaar* there in the Senate?"); the independent (not every Republican "is cast in the image and likeness of the President"); and the anti-incumbent (she's for a twelve-year limit on House terms, and wishes that her "altruistic [*sic*] belief" in the willingness of voters to get rid of the entrenched when need arises was more frequently borne out by elections).

One caller takes her to task for claiming on *Face the Nation* that she voted to override the President's veto of the civil rights bill when in fact the House never voted at all. She just "misspoke," she explains; she was *prepared* to vote that way if the matter went beyond the Senate. Schneider does seem to have a tendency, beyond the ordinary one of politicians, to claim more credit than she's entitled to for certain initiatives. Clippings containing stories to that effect have even crept into her own campaign press kit. But it's clear that a number of the hostile calls coming in are Pell-campaign plants: they're too sound-bitten to be otherwise. "Is this what we're to expect from Claudine Schneider in the Senate?" asks one of them, like the last line of an attack ad, in the course of a complaint about her supposedly "going negative." After a couple like these, Claudine and Arlene have a laugh about it. They even seem to recognize one of the voices. "It's fixed," says a sympathetic caller. "We know that," Schneider says gratefully. One wonders if it isn't a bit of karmic comeuppance for her field director's having pretended to be a reporter at the press conference with Dole.

In the last several years radio talk shows have become crass town meetings — democracy as bitch session — and the Rhode Island version inevitably has the state's everybody-knows-everybody intimacy stirred into it. Before the hour has gone by, Anna, from the sub shop in Cranston a few hours ago, is on the line to refute any notion of Pell's frailty: "I tell you, Arlene, he looks well."

Schneider tells Anna that it's "ludicrous" for her to assume she's running for the Senate only because President Bush wanted her to. "Nobody tells me what to do," she says, pointing out with some validity that Republican leaders urged her to take Pell on in 1984 only to have her tell them she wasn't ready. Now, presumably, she is. But she admits that her decision to run this year was based partly on the assumption that Pell was planning to retire. Then the Democrats, afraid of how strong she might be against anyone else, urged Pell to run one more time. Schneider didn't realize, as she bounced through her announcement on Valentine's Day, that she had just overplayed her hand.

* * *

Friday night brings a couple of hundred Democratic faithful, who have ridden behind the party mule from Deal to Frontier to Great Society and through the mostly desert country of the past twenty years, to a big hall in Pawtucket. This is a tired town, with an unusual number of funeral homes, hoping for some new life in the form of an off-track betting parlor, if the voters approve the relevant referendum on Tuesday.

In front of the state flag, which, when draped against its pole, looks like the Vatican's, Mayor Brian J. Sarault introduces Pell, who thanks him by telling the truth: "You make a much better speech than I do." Unimpressed by any need to show dynamism, Pell rambles on about the nature of compliments: "I often thought it would be fun to announce your own death, sit in the back of the church, and see who comes." He refers to the Republicans as our ad *ver* saries, and advises the crowd against complacency with the example of "poor Mr. Bellotti," who lost the primary in Massachusetts to John Silber despite all the polls that said he wouldn't.

The lieutenant governor who follows Pell, Roger Begin, receives loud applause when he takes note of how the senator never refers to his opponent by name: "That's part of the gentleman of Senator Pell." As the election nears, his *noblesse oblige* is turning from a mere selling point into a holy legend. The way tonight's speakers go on about the Pell Grants, one would almost think they were golden guineas extracted from the velvet bag of the senator's personal fortune. It's clear by now that the Democrats think it's ill willed of Schneider to be campaigning at all.

"Sign Up! Fun! Food! Phones! *For Senator Pell,*" says the poster near a table with various campaign materials. (Campaign buttons, it seems, are almost extinct, having been replaced by those plastic stickers you peel off wax paper.) The faithful sit at banquet tables and are called up for their food by table number, like guests at an understaffed wedding. Attractive, white-haired Mrs. Pell mingles easily among them before she and the senator leave to "a nice round of Pawtucket applause" ordered up by the mayor, who has meanwhile introduced some state senators and school committee members.

It's not all that different from the Cranston senior center — one can imagine Claudine bopping in and getting the hokey-pokey going — and one suspects that a good many of the people seated at the tables are pensioned city and state workers now living in Pawtucket's John F. Kennedy Housing for the Elderly. These ferociously vulnerable senior citizens, eager to vote out any inattentive politician, vastly outnumber the sprinkling of adolescents here. In Pawtucket, where the bus back to Providence leaves from an abandoned Peerless department store across from the historic Slater Mill, one realizes that the immediate political future has everything to do with the slightly more distant past.

On Saturday afternoon I decide to catch Schneider at a scheduled campaign stop at the Ann & Hope discount department store in Cumberland, in the northeast corner of the state. The chain, particularly its Warwick branch, is a sort of lucky spot for her, and she's supposed to arrive at three — after appearing at the Almacs supermarket in Bristol; the First Congregational Church bazaar/lunch, also in Bristol; an Episcopal church in Woonsocket; and a high school football game in North Smithfield.

The Cumberland Ann & Hope is less a discount store than a literal factory outlet: the chain uses the name of the old textile mill in which the Cumberland branch is located. But unlike Pell's headquarters in the old Davol plant, this is no piece of boutique architectural restoration. The store was simply thrown into the vast old structure, with pipes and ducts and electrical tape above your head wherever you walk. A little conveyor belt, adding to the industrial effect, takes your shopping cart from the first floor to the basement while you use a flight of stairs. The current decorations — huge red-white-and-blue signs shaped like candidates' rosettes, proclaiming "Unbeatable Values" — seem just the right backdrop for the challenger's appearance.

But by 3:30 there's no sign of her, and I call the headquarters in Warwick. She's been delayed in East Providence, I'm told. But I thought she was coming from North Smithfield. The aide on the other end of the phone doesn't know about that. She says the schedule is shaky because it was drawn up in such a rush: they didn't know when Claudine would be allowed to escape Washington and the budget crisis. She says, twice, that the schedule "travels with" the candidate in her car; the phrase sounds like a metaphysical feat, effect backflipping over cause. But if I'd like, I can probably catch her at the St. Joseph's Veterans Association supper, up in Woonsocket, sometime between 6:30 and 7:00.

Woonsocket has a large French-Canadian population; today's local paper carries an ad for the state legislative campaign of Rene Menard, chaired by Roger Valois. Now, a little before six o'clock on a Saturday evening, a few St. Joseph's veterans are outside their cinderblock hall, drinking beer and frying the steaks for tonight's supper. They tell me they don't know anything about Claudine Schneider showing up, though she was here twice in the past week or so, for two different benefits. They let me hang around as dinner gets prepared and then under way, and I assume the schedule has once more traveled with the candidate, into another dimension.

But eventually a car pulls up carrying Mrs. Nenette Cmarada, "Claudine's Mom," as her name tag says, along with Andrew Oser, a friend from Washington who's helping in the campaign. Mom has already been in Warwick, Lincoln, and East Providence today, though here in Woonsocket she's in her most effective venue: a Belgian native, she's made lots of phone calls in French to the locals. A lively woman who's a great deal more youthful than Claiborne Pell, she tells me that this stuff about negative campaigning is nonsense. Claudine is "clean-living . . . a clean person." She wouldn't do that, and besides, "she and Mr. Pell were friends all the past ten years she's been in Washington." Washington has been her daughter's big problem. Being stuck there has put her under "a lot of pressure and stress. It's been a very difficult time for her, very frustrating."

Daughter arrives, in a dark dress and a long string of pearls, and plunges into the roomful of tables, greeting the diners with her usual pitch. "It's a very close race," she says, putting her hands on the backs of their chairs. "Don't cut my Social Security," one of them tells her, to the whole table's laughter. "If you cut my Security, forget it." "Not me!" says Claudine.

She's schmoozing as fast as she can. She was supposed to have left here before she even arrived. It's 7:20 now, and she goes from table to table under the blue, green, and pink ceiling lights as the tape plays "Sixteen Candles." One guy tells her he's a "Democrat, straight through."

"I thought those days were behind us," says Schneider, who here in Rhode Island likes to stress the supposedly declining significance of parties.

"I'm a hard man to kill," he responds.

She gets serious. "I'm sorry he wants to vote for the party . . ."

"I'm only pullin' your leg."

It's time to see massive turnovers in the Congress, she says. We all need shaking up. "We're going to be competing with *Eastern* Europe soon," says this daughter of a Czech tailor.

I ask her about something she said to Arlene Violet yesterday, about not wanting to be in politics forever. I tell her I believe she means it, that it's more than just a convenient thing to say when trying to retire a longtime senator. And if that's the case, where does she see herself fifteen years from now, whatever happens Tuesday? "I really don't have a clue," she says, before telling me about the crisis of her adult life: a diagnosis of Hodgkin's disease when she was twenty-five. "That made me stop, look, listen, and think" — and wonder, she says in her New Agey way, about how she might leave the "planet" a better place. Recalling that time, she says: "I had prayed that I would live." She beat the disease, thereby sustaining the relevance of her old feeling that she would have several careers, "maybe four or five" during her lifetime. What they are she doesn't know, but after politics she'll have "earned an easier lifestyle." Meanwhile, "Mr. Pell should feel the same way. He's given thirty good years, and I would think he would welcome some retirement."

She'd probably welcome some sleep. But before the night is over there's still a fund-raiser in Slatersville, and then a Portuguese event in Pawtucket, and then another in Bristol.

The polls say she'll probably get her wish of a new career sooner than she'd like. But as she gets ready to hit the road to Slatersville, her friend Andrew Oser asks me, matter-of-factly, if I'll be coming to their victory party Tuesday night.

One measure of the clout of the elderly in this state is that you can take that common mode of old people's transportation, the bus, from Woonsocket to Providence, a forty-minute ride, for $1.25. Back in the state capital, I end the day by having a nightcap with my caustic old Shakespeare professor from Brown, Elmer Blistein, now retired, and his wife, Sophie. I ask him how it feels to be approaching the age at which he's almost ready to run for office in Rhode Island. If Claiborne Pell, Bruce Sundlun, and Fred Lippitt win on Tuesday, the senior senator, the governor, and the mayor of Providence will all be over seventy years old.

The next morning Claudine Schneider is in her royal-blue Sunday best — a full-skirted dress and a wide-brimmed hat — racing into the Pond Street Memorial Baptist Church on Providence's black south side. It's 11:20 as she arrives for a service she thought started at 11:15, but worse luck — Pastor Virgil Wood actually begins at 11:00, and as she stands in the foyer listening to the P.A., she hears him making announcements from the altar. Senator Pell, he tells the congregation, was at a rally in the church parking lot yesterday, and he called the reverend at home last night to thank him for the use of the church's property. Pastor Wood asks the faithful to remember the Pell Grants and "to show the brother we appreciate what he did." Before marching in, Schneider tosses me a look that combines mock horror and *oy vay*. But she gamely enters and sits down a few pews from the front. When Pastor Wood asks visitors to stand up and identify themselves, she goes right ahead and says her name, adding in a friendly way that she wishes he hadn't taken sides. Both the congregation and the minister, who must have given up on her coming, seem genuinely tickled, and he responds with lighthearted graciousness: "I can only tell you that some people listen to the pastor, and some people don't." The maroon-robed choir launches into "So Glad You're Here," and she claps along. It's agreed that she'll speak to the congregation at the fellowship after the service, downstairs.

That's a long time to wait to make one more speech, but she seems genuinely to enjoy the service, tapping her blue pumps to songs like "Take Me Higher" and "Pass Me Not." Pastor Wood's sermon doesn't just raise the roof; it threatens to pulverize the cinderblock walls. Schneider, who ordinarily makes up in pep whatever she lacks in eloquence, must be feeling like George Mitchell.

But downstairs at fellowship, after a very polite audience gathers in front of the coffee urn and punch bowl, she has the best fifteen minutes I see her display all week. She says that people in this congregation know what it is to be stereotyped, and she hates being stereotyped as a "cold-hearted Republican," not when her party has brought forth such heroes as Abraham Lincoln and . . . She struggles for a second name and is saved by the thought of that progressive environmentalist, Theodore Roosevelt. She talks about her fight against cancer and her "mission on this earth," proclaiming that she knows her "purpose," and praising the "unified power" people can have. She connects solidly with the most attentive audience I will hear her address. But it is also one of the most politically sophisticated, politicians being no strangers to the Pond Street Memorial Baptist Church. I suspect that on Tuesday they will have no trouble voting against this woman they seem to like so much.

The *Providence Sunday Journal* carries an endorsement of Schneider ("Claiborne Pell's significant accomplishments are now largely behind him") and a big curious ad announcing that she has also been endorsed "By Members of Our Nation's Most Distinguished Bar Association" — that is, the cast of *Cheers*. (It's because they "share her vision for the future.") The only real campaign news of the day comes in the form of an afternoon debate among the three candidates for mayor of Providence, during which Buddy Cianci displays his brutal charm against Fred Lippitt, the septuagenarian east-side WASP reformer, and Andrew Annaldo, the sleepy endomorph unaccountably nominated by the Democrats.

Annaldo is actually one of the stars of an evening rally put on by a Democratic ladies' auxiliary, at Lombardi's restaurant, a big place way out on Charles Street in North Providence, past a thinly beaded string of neighborhood bars. Lombardi's turns out to be loud, happy, and packed ("I hope you're not taking the count for the fire department," one guy delightedly says to me when he spots my pad), and the crowd seems to be younger than the one that gathered Friday night in Pawtucket. But those are the ones standing. Sitting down at the banquet tables are the old people, sipping red wine, prepared to vote, and probably dreaming of Boca Raton. For all the noise in this room, one has to wonder why anybody would go into politics up here in Rhode Island: it seems an obsolescent industry, its market dying off as inexorably as newspaper readership.

Annaldo arrives to the sounds of "Mack the Knife" and an absolutely mystifying show of enthusiasm: "An-*drew!* An-*drew!*" There's enough of a crush to make you worry that Senator Pell will be squeezed and broken when he tries to move from the entrance to the microphone. As he makes his way in, I ask Mrs. Pell if, after thirty years, she ever gets tired of this stuff. "It's always different," she assures me. I ask her what's different this time. "Possible defeat," she says in a surprisingly spontaneous way.

Her husband makes his speech, drawing attention to the "absolutely nip-and-tuck" mayoral race, another usage whose quaintness the crowd no doubt likes. It seems so *him,* just as the other day he declared not that the United States couldn't be the world's policeman but rather that it couldn't be its *gendarme.* As a woman in one of his commercials says, "He's just Senator Pell," something that you'd think would be defunct by now but you're pleased to discover is still, on rare occasion, to be found, like a campaign button.

Monday, November 5, 1990: Thirty years ago today John F. Kennedy, on his way home to Hyannis to vote, addressed an election eve rally in what was then called Exchange Place, in front of the Providence City Hall. The rally was large and memorable enough to make Exchange Place seem, several years later, the right spot to be renamed Kennedy Plaza. Now, at a tiny noontime rally for the Democratic ticket, the speakers keep invoking what happened "thirty years ago today" as a motivation for victory "in thirty hours," as Scott Wolf, the not-much-of-a-chance congressional candidate, puts it.

The Democrats will no doubt have a good day tomorrow, but this attempt at a street rally is an almost morbid exercise in nostalgia. The big blue Teamsters truck parked on the south side of the plaza might contain a gross of respirators. At least, after days of balmy weather, it finally feels like fall, nippy even; Mrs. Pell stands near the platform in a long woolen coat. The outgoing mayor of Providence introduces Jack Reed, another congressional candidate, as honest and "smot," and Reed tells the voters to make it simple for themselves: "Democrat, Democrat, Democrat."

Teddy Kennedy, the main attraction, his complexion alarmingly red, arrives on the platform to cheers, bringing Pell up with him and upstaging the candidate for governor, who's just begun to speak but gives up the notion, saying he "can't think of a greater privilege" than to start talking when the two senators are arriving. He quickly gets off and lets young Patrick Kennedy get on with the introduction of Pell, whose best line is a promise "not to be here thirty years from now."

The elder Kennedy comes on after an introduction by his son and proceeds to mispronounce the name of the gubernatorial candidate who was so privileged to be interrupted by his arrival. But he goes on to give such a hammy, forceful presentation — a lunch-bucket speech at the top of his lungs, as body-slamming a performance as Pastor Wood's this time yesterday — that he almost makes you think this is a real event, almost makes you forget that his outdoor audience isn't any larger than what Pastor Wood had inside the snug Pond Street Baptist Church. Before going full tilt he mentions his mother, Rose, one hundred years old up there on the Cape, claiming he chatted with her just this morning about Claiborne Pell. It's a charming bit of blarney that doesn't bear much looking into, perhaps no more than does this senator's reference to his commitment to "minimum standards of decency."

Beyond the massive urban reconstruction going on near the state capitol stands the University of Rhode Island's College of Continuing Education, an unpretentiously inspiring place full of "adult learners." Schneider was supposed to arrive at six, at the student center, where people are cramming in a bit of homework or eating a vending-machine sandwich before going upstairs to a night class. "If she don't show up before seven, she ain't gonna meet anybody," says one woman to another out in the hall.

A minute later she's there, looking fresh in her red suit, which is draped with an extremely oversized scarf (the telltale kooky touch). She goes from table to table ("It's very close"), handing out Xeroxes of her *Providence Journal* endorsement, striking up and artfully concluding one brief conversation after another. "Hiya, Miss Schneider," says one young woman, as if she's greeting the most popular teacher at the high school. Her mother is working the tables too ("Are you her mother? You're so short!"), until she seems too tired and goes off to the side. Her daughter seems not to be tired at all — is planning, in fact, to get up at five and go greet workers at the Electric Boat factory gate.

But in the early darkness of autumn a sadness comes over the scene, over this talented woman's miscalculated enterprise, which is heading down the drain. "If she could touch everyone in the state . . . ," one of her aides says to me, meaning shake every hand. In this duchy it's not so much a fantasy as a near-plausible might-have-been, if not for the budget mess. Only about three quarters of the way through this stop does she learn that the rules do permit her to get up on the student center's stage and make a speech, and by then it seems too late. The aide doesn't think it's such a hot idea anyway, but I find myself wanting to tell her to go and do it: get up there and go positive and negative simultaneously, like a magnet. Tell them you're one of them, a kid from Clairton who's ambitious, and that there's nothing wrong with that, and if they're here on a Pell Grant, terrific, but they should remember that that money isn't his; it's their parents', and theirs, and it's been taxed out of them like anything else. Think of what Teddy Kennedy could do with this crowd, much less Pastor Wood.

But time is running out. I head back home in the dark, pretty sure she has no chance, that the conventional wisdom is this time wise. It's true that the mammoth construction I'm passing involves changing the course, literally, of two rivers that run through Providence. But while it would be a nice metaphor, I don't think it's going to apply.

Despite the rain forecast, Election Day turns out to be bright and chilly, with high winds that keep white clouds scudding above the bank towers of Providence. Schneider has spent the day driving around the state, meeting and greeting, with a stop in Narragansett to cast her own vote. At 9:00, when polls close and television coverage begins, one suspects that Rhode Islanders will be paying more attention to the election up in Massachusetts, that angry argument they've been hearing through the ceiling, than to the series of civil contests down here.

The Republicans are at the Marriott, where the band plays the sort of selections one would hear at a Republican wedding ("C'est Magnifique," "Isn't It Romantic?") and where in the course of the evening some good Republican fur coats swim into the crowd. But these Republicans are not what Dan Quayle would call happy campers. Across from a fat little girl with braces, who's offering people entering the ballroom one last campaign sticker, a woman in a black dress stands mutely, as she will for the next couple of hours, like a hired mourner. Just before 9:00 people are waiting for *Matlock* to leave the TV screen and for WJAR to come on with the returns. They chat with a complete lack of suspense. Outside the ballroom, Arlene Violet (a Republican, believe it or not) asks a guy if he's "workin' haaad."

Exit polls have, of course, made election nights a matter not of counting but of handing over "the envelope, please." It's a fast-forwarded awards show, and by about 9:02, except for the mayoral race, predictably crazy, it's all over. The Democrats have steamrollered the state, and Schneider is expected to get no more than 38 percent of the vote. The incumbent Republican governor, who raised taxes, gets 26 percent against an opponent he beat twice before. "We thought he had more family than that," says one reporter. The only Republican to survive it will be Congressman Ron Machtley, but even his opponent, not-much-of-a-chance Scott Wolf, will get enough votes to give him a good scare.

The woman at the podium introduces the man who was the Republican state chairman during Watergate — we'll get through this, too, is the message. He praises the candidates as "courageous" for having, it seems, the foolhardiness to run at all. One by one they come to the microphone with their concession speeches. The band's selections now range from the chirpy and obvious ("Put On a Happy Face") to the subtly sadistic ("But Not for Me"). Stephen R. Deutsch, who ran for lieutenant governor with a promise to abolish the office, finishes conceding to his opponent across town by reminding "Roger that the only reason we let him win this race is that he promised to buy dinner."

"Get ready for Claudine," I hear one TV technician tell another. A few minutes later she's on her way in, to the theme from *Rocky,* what they played the day she announced. Andrew Oser, her Washington friend who Saturday night invited me to their victory party, looks stricken. Claudine, however, seems to be liberated. She's wearing her hair down, in that too-youthful way she prefers. And she's bouncing.

But then you realize that this is a last heroic effort, and you like her better when you realize that she's not going to take it like a man. The tears come halfway through the speech, and they're painful to see from this woman to whom perkiness is breath. But it's okay: that sense of having been spared eighteen years ago, the kooky sense of destiny wrapped up in the lingo of Tony Robbins and Washington press releases, kicks in. "Claudine Schneider will always be Claudine Schneider," she says. "I will always have an agenda." You realize that this woman — bright, energetic, and sometimes a little tacky — probably does have a future, even if she won't be starting it tonight.

It's also a relief to see that she's just a little bit angry. A few minutes later, on a taxi driver's car radio, I hear her being short with a reporter, and tomorrow morning's paper will quote her as saying what's only true: "People decided to cast their vote as a thank you for the past, as opposed to an investment in the future." Pell's fatherly response to her telephoned congratulations — "I know it's hard" — probably didn't help her mood.

I arrive at the top floor of the Biltmore, full of bellowing, yammering, hog-heavened Democrats, just as Pell is finishing his victory statement. It's what it would have been even without the crowd — largely inaudible.

As it gets toward midnight Buddy Cianci and reformer Fred Lippitt are simultaneously claiming victory in the mayoral election. The uncanny assurance that Cianci displays about how the absentee ballots will turn out is, one suspects, probably reliable. Meanwhile, the Democratic parties going on throughout the Biltmore, the social centerpiece of Rhode Island as it was thirty years ago, are just hitting their stride. There are four of them in progress right here on the twelfth floor, and by the early hours of the morning the stairwells are draped with firehoses, and some glass lies gaily smashed. At about 2:30 A.M. a security officer tells me it's so bad he's thought about calling in the Providence police. But he would prefer not to, since Rhode Island's governor-elect, whose victory is being celebrated, is a part owner of the hotel.

Travels with My Veep

Between Dan Quayle and four members of the working press sit nine men with guns. *Air Force Two* is heading toward Memphis, Tennessee, for a day of charity, politics, and golf. As soon as the plane was "wheels up" from Andrews Air Force Base, at 9:04 A.M. on this warm June morning, one of the nine Secret Service men reached for a wall phone in the main cabin to report that the vice president was aloft. The schedule for this day trip runs to fourteen pages, though its bulk is more reflective of precision than frenzy:

> 6:50 P.M. THE VICE PRESIDENT arrives Tournament Room and remains standing.
> Mr. Jim Barksdale makes brief remarks and introduces THE VICE PRESIDENT.
> 6:55 P.M. THE VICE PRESIDENT proceeds to Stand Up Microphone and begins Brief Remarks.
> 7:00 P.M. THE VICE PRESIDENT concludes Brief Remarks and proceeds to motorcade for boarding.

The all-capitalized title is perhaps a warning not to expect much breach of majesty. Quayle remains unseen while boarding (a quick transfer from his helicopter) and throughout the flight.

The press corps accompanying him today is small but dis-

proportionately high-powered. The CNN White House correspondent, Charles Bierbauer, is along, and so is the *Washington
Post*'s David Broder, who is alternating coverage of Quayle
with Bob Woodward for a jointly written series. A White House
advisor is described in one morning paper as urging the vice
president to watch out for these two "rabid skunks." Broder,
however, could hardly be more gentlemanly — not one Quayle
joke will escape his lips today.

The absence of Quayle's chief of staff, Bill Kristol, and his
press secretary, Dave Beckwith, whose daughter had a nasty
accident yesterday, leaves a group of junior staffers in charge.
Don Sundquist, the Republican congressman whose district
we'll be in, seems like an acting chief of staff. Back in the VIP
lounge at Andrews, he explained that he's "been trying to get
[Quayle] to come down since January." Then the congressman's
thoughts turned to redistricting, how Annunzio of Illinois will
probably lose his seat, while "Rosty" survives. It's an obsession
beyond fund-raising, of course; if you passed by Sundquist just
before boarding, you could hear him explaining to someone: "If
I keep Dickson . . . "

Breakfast on *Air Force Two*, far above the airlines' average,
consists of French toast and Canadian bacon served with glass
salt-and-pepper shakers and cloth napkins. The press are billed
for it along with the coach fare they pay, but each Secret Service
member pays $5.10 in cash, the collection of which is a regula-
tory comedy, Peter paying Paul at thirty thousand feet. When
the agents are through eating, they sit back and read novels, or
Runner's World, and their instructions for the day: NO LONG
GUNS will be used on this trip, perhaps because the MEMPHIS
POLICE WILL PROVIDE HIGH GROUND OBSERVATION. It appears that the afternoon will be trickiest: "VP Participation in
the Golf Event has been publicized and large galleries are expected."

Photos of Dan alone, Dan with George, and Dan with Marilyn hang at the front of the main cabin and in the space beyond,
in and out of which staff members come and go, greeting the

press ("Glad y'all are with us"), answering questions, bustling about with film canisters and a shopping bag full of presents. When the plane touches down at 10:00 Memphis time, there is still no sign of Quayle, but his golf clubs, protected by blue cozies with the vice presidential seal, move down the aisle and deplane from the rear. One agent remarks on how hot it's going to be outside, and asks another if he's wearing his "vest." "I never leave home without it" is the response, made during a week when Ronald Reagan is phone-lobbying for the Brady bill.

Under a hot sun, Dan Quayle descends into the city of the two Kings — Martin Luther and Elvis. If he were a base broadener, he might, instead of golfing and speaking at a synagogue, spend some of the day at Graceland, or at the Lorraine Motel, which next week becomes the National Civil Rights Museum. But he has no special gusto for odd venues and lions' dens. After three years of being battered by the press and stagnant in the polls, he seems to seek the familiar, to have his wounds licked by friendly elephants. He is smaller than you expect, and curiously sexless for somebody so handsome. Though wrinkled around the eyes, he sustains the appearance of extreme youthfulness through a carriage that borders on the apologetic. Before getting into a Cadillac Fleetwood, he shakes hands with local officials and some party faithful, as well as the fire chief of Leningrad (*sic*), who's in town for a conference.

The motorcade moves along the Martin Luther King Expressway, which has been cleared of traffic, making its way toward Danny Thomas Boulevard and on to the immense St. Jude Children's Research Hospital, founded by the entertainer in 1962 and since then expanded to formidable proportions. The vice president will spend fifteen minutes touring the facilities; this afternoon's golf tournament, an annual fund-raiser for the hospital, will claim him for several hours.

He is scheduled to chat with some patients in the medicine room after coming through a doorway near a plaque bearing a poem about a boy who died of leukemia. The children who have been assembled for his visit this morning evince a cheer and calm that belie their distressed physical appearance. Bloated or thinned from cancer, and bald from chemotherapy, some of them would be of indeterminate sex and age did the hospital not hand out a list with their names, ages, and illnesses. Their mothers sit close by, among them Eric Rushing's, an attractive blonde who holds her five-year-old son, his head distorted by a brain tumor, on her lap; every so often she gives him a quick, happy kiss.

Some young nurses near a wall decline one mother's humorous urging that they come closer to the center of things. "This is where we stand every time," one of them says. "This is my spot." The seated mother jokes about the "patient-nurse interaction" that's missing. Owing its life to celebrity, this hospital named for the patron saint of hopeless causes is accustomed to and canny about it. The President was here late in 1989, and Mrs. Bush just weeks ago. When asked if any Democrats ever stop by, a hospital spokeswoman says, "That's a good question, actually."

Actually, here comes a likely one now. Phil Donahue, married to Danny Thomas's daughter, Marlo, has just entered the room with his brother-in-law, Tony Thomas, and the vice president, who says a few words before making a progress past the children and mothers. Eric Rushing, whose condition can't help but remind one of the terrifying *Life* magazine photos of the terminally ill Lee Atwater, gives Quayle a "shot" with a toy hypodermic and then tenderly applies a Band-Aid to the vice presidential hand. As he goes around the room, Quayle is gentle and stiff, appealingly so, with the children, quite good in a set of circumstances that, for all their choreography, are straining the emotions of some of the press in the room. He talks to a boy (a look at the handout shows he's really twenty-three) from Angola, Indiana: Craig Dunlap is a bone-cancer patient whose right leg has been amputated above the knee. Quayle tells him about the times he's been in Angola for its Fourth of July parade. When introduced to Steven Knoll ("sarcoma — stable disease") from Stuttgart, Arkansas, he recognizes the town as a rice-producing center and jokes that he'll tell George Bush, who's meeting soon with Prime Minister Kaifu, to urge the Japanese leader to raise import quotas for rice. He carries this one off with an impressive charm; it lightens the atmosphere and seems to please even the media, who largely ignored Quayle's recent trade trip to Japan.

A "press availability" will follow in the boardroom upstairs. On the way to it, Phil Donahue, who shows some surprising low-key charm of his own, attracts autograph seekers, and we hear one woman, a patient's mother perhaps, someone with too much stake in this place to be starstruck in any but a purposeful way, say to him, simply: "Keep up the good work of your father-in-law."

Upstairs the press have little to ask, and Quayle has little to say. He tells the story of Eric and the Band-Aid, holding up his hand for the cameras. He mentions his wife's work against breast cancer, drawing a distinction between priorities in that field (early detection) and what's vital for patients at St. Jude's (aggressive treatment). Appearing reasonably briefed about the hospital, he plugs the golf tournament that's being held for it this afternoon, and then he moves over to shake some hands, thereby permitting a closer view of his face (more sunburnt-Irish than WASP-pink) and three plaques on the boardroom wall, which offer proof that the energetic directors of St. Jude's do indeed know how to get along with Democrats: flanking one that commemorates a research fellowship endowed in honor of John Sununu are two others bearing the names of George Mitchell and Richard Gephardt.

"Let's hustle!" says the advance man, the scold in charge of press van number two. (Norma Greenaway, my new friend from Southam News of Canada, tells me I should experience Kennebunkport in the summer: that's where they *really* treat you badly.) The motorcade makes its long, trafficless way across town, passing down prosperous streets like Walnut Grove, a few of whose suburban gentry are curious enough to come out on the lawns of their ranch houses, and finally onto the grounds of the Racquet Club. "Yeah," says a reporter, "this looks like Danny's kind of place, doesn't it?"

The promise of Quayle has sold three hundred tickets to the Shelby County Republicans' $100-a-plate luncheon. The all-white crowd is abuzz with good-natured excitement at numbered tables topped with two red roses and glasses of iced tea. The press set up in back, and in a corner just behind them the officer in dress whites carrying what appears to be the standby nuclear "football" takes up an inconspicuous position.

"Do you think Dan Quayle needs a patron saint of hopeless causes?" Norma asks me just before he enters. If the country were composed of nothing but Shelby County Republicans, you'd have to give her a no. The ovation is warm and standing. Still, it's generated not by any imminent ecstasy, any prospect of going limp in a bath of charisma, but rather by the call of duty, a rare opportunity for audience participation; those applauding are ready to *help* this poor boy against all those bastards at the back of the room.

The invocation by Dr. Maxie Dunnam, senior minister of the Christ United Methodist Church, seems to prove that God has moved on from copiloting and super-salesmanship into something like middle management: "Forgive us," asks Dr. Dunnam, "when we don't make You a factor in our political equations." Congressman Sundquist's introduction of Quayle refers to the way he's "weathered a barrage of criticism and too often an unfair press," and challenges the perpetrators of his image to disseminate the "sensitive, caring, and thoughtful" Quayle that was on display in the medicine room of St. Jude's: "I hope it's captured on film, and that it will be shown on national TV tonight." That, of course, is the only way the event will have any political reality, and when on Friday night some seconds of it do show up on CNN, Sundquist may feel he's accomplished his mission. For the present, however, he seems to succeed only in encouraging Quayle to drain the humanity from those few minutes back at the hospital. After the vice president has taken the podium to another standing ovation, made an Elvis joke and an obligatory reference to Tennessee's Andrew Jackson ("the media gave *him* a hard time"), he once more brings out the story of Eric and the Band-Aid, one of those "moments that you will never forget." This time the moment isn't so much retold as retailed, complete with a little Reaganesque lump in the throat. The crowd sighs appreciatively. I guess you had to not be there.

This is all warm-up to a preelection pep talk, and throughout this preamble Quayle adopts a somewhat maddening little-boy persona; it's as if he longs for the protectiveness and reassurance the crowd is happy to give him. They will *get him through this,* the way you nod encouragement to the kid in the pageant as he tries to recall his lines. The sheer cooperativeness of the crowd is, finally, less indicative of political affinity than low expectations. They laugh more lustily, applaud more heartily, and sigh more feelingly than even an inherently gung-ho occasion like this requires.

The main part of the speech involves, naturally enough, throwing red meat to the already convinced, and as such it's not bad: Quayle has been extraordinarily successful raising funds for the party all across the country. His rhetorical style has some oddities — rather as Jimmy Carter used to pause in peculiar places, the vice president sometimes alternates shouts and murmurs with little correlation to his text — but he makes his points with sound-bitten economy. Despite what the Democrats say, George Bush *does* have a domestic agenda: "what they mean is that this President doesn't have *their* domestic agenda. We know what their agenda is: higher taxes, more spending, socialized medicine, more governmental regulation. Well, that's *their* agenda. Let me tell you what *our* agenda is: growth, low taxes, strong national defense, *true* equality of opportunity, *real* reform in education — and that means giving the parents the right to choose where their kids go to school!"

Republicans are also the party of "public safety," apparently the new term for law and order. "I can't wait for this campaign to begin!" Quayle says, a prospect so dreary that even these good Republicans of Shelby County can't bring themselves to applaud it. But they clap mightily when he's through, even though the luncheon's guest of honor isn't staying for lunch. There's no time for that. The motorcade is pulling out toward the next event, the principal one of the day. As the advance man (a more pleasant one this time) informs the occupants of press van number two: "We're gonna go right to the first tee."

On our way to the Tournament Players Club for the Federal Express St. Jude Classic Celebrity Pro-Am, there are speculative jokes about the show-and-tell Band-Aid, about whether it was a replacement and whether he'll still have it on tonight. Bierbauer wiggles his hand to indicate "so-so" when asked by somebody if he thought the now legendary hypodermic shot was really such a good photo op. No matter: it's the image of the day, and you can already picture the generic Democrat who will be rounded up to respond to Quayle's luncheon message on the six o'clock news: "Well, Brad/Heather, that's unfortunately typical of the Republicans' approach to social problems. Just put a Band-Aid over them."

At 1:45 there's a crowd behind the first tee, as the touring pros, along with the local establishment figures and philanthropists who get to golf with them, are introduced. Tony Thomas and Phil Donahue ("Danny's son-in-law") emerge from the clubhouse, and the latter again shows a non-hammy charm by saying only "He's so much thinner in person" into the microphone. The crowd enjoys this imitation of itself, but its display of good feeling doesn't extend to those who've come to cover Quayle. "Down in front, media! We had to pay, they didn't!" is the cry you hear before kneeling down to grass-stain your pants. After Quayle comes out to another standing ovation, it's clear that these spectators have more than visibility and value on their minds. They know why the press is here — to hurt Dan — and from behind the ropes they try to practice the same sort of protective dandling the luncheon audience did. "He looks *fine*. Leave his checkered pants alone," says somebody to a reporter who's asked the most innocent question imaginable — why

Quayle isn't wearing the checkered golf pants that Craig, one of the patients in the hospital this morning, had inquired about. "That's only inside my own congressional district," Quayle banters back to the questioner. "I would never wear them outside Indiana." "Who's the better golfer? You or your boss?" DQ: "There are some questions I will not answer. That is one of them." He spots Broder, now in shirtsleeves, and says, "David, you look like you belong out here." He's no Jack Kennedy at this sort of exchange, but he's no Nixon either. In fact, the only thing undercutting the ease he demonstrates is a genuine eagerness to start golfing. He's already made his remarks boosting St. Jude's and paid tribute to Danny Thomas in the same verbless phrases Bush would use ("Danny Thomas: talented"), and he'd like to be heading toward the fairway now.

He'll be golfing with Ben Crenshaw, who gets as big a hand as Quayle before teeing off. Finally, it's the vice president's turn. The emcee notes that Quayle is the only amateur with the courage to go off the pro tee, and the veep responds, "We'll find out if it's courage or stupidity in one minute," a line no one would touch with a nine iron. When the minute comes, it proves to have been neither courage nor stupidity, just earned confidence. The tee shot he makes is a display of grace and strength, even better than Crenshaw's, and the smile he flashes is the expression of a man who, probably for the first time today, has gotten to be himself.

He's at it for fourteen holes, four hours in the hot sun, until it's time for the last public event of the day, a speech at Memphis's Baron Hirsch Synagogue. In the manner of the President coming in to address a joint session of Congress, Quayle receives two standing ovations before uttering a word. Rabbi Rafael G. Grossman (who from a distance bears an amusing resemblance to John Sununu) talks of how the congregants have come to love Quayle, and, despite any lingering tendencies to vote Democratic, it's clear that those assembled in this huge and beautiful building regard him as their man — at least on one issue — even more possessively than the Shelby County Republicans.

Audience protectiveness is once again the order of the day. (Before the press departs, one member of the congregation will enjoy the chance to buttonhole Charles Bierbauer about the fourth estate's sins against Quayle.) One wonders for a moment if the crowd's eagerness to be of help won't in fact be needed when Quayle, describing his recent (and, in truth, undercovered) travels, refers rather oddly to the "opportunity" he had to represent President Bush at Rajiv Gandhi's funeral. But he is soon hitting a good stride, even with those needless alternations in volume, comparing the children of St. Jude's to Israel herself (they're both fighters) and recounting his visit to Auschwitz with his wife and two of their children. He decries bigotry and hate crimes ("In this new world order there is no room for persecution") and brings on joyful applause by mentioning America's assistance in the recent rescue of Ethiopian Jews. His single specific Middle East proposal is the repeal of U.N. Resolution 3379, the one equating Zionism and racism. He finishes to a third standing ovation, bringing the day's total to six.

Rabbi Grossman, a longtime activist on behalf of Jewish emigration from the Soviet Union, has obviously kept his congregation at a high level of political awareness, and in thanking the vice president, he seems to be trying to dispel any suspicions of expediency: "What you said is what you are . . . I know as a personal fact that you meant every word of it." As the rabbi explains what the Torah is and presents him with a Bible, Quayle stands beside him like a student on prize day.

Part of the inscription in the Bible reads: "Your leadership has ennobled our nation and the human race." This may be laying it on thick, but by now the mutual-admiration stakes have piled up uncontrollably. A moment before, Rabbi Grossman observed unblushingly that what Quayle said "took great courage." Actually, despite the occasionally courageous speechmaking Quayle undertakes (forthright opposition to aid to the Soviets), this particular talk is what one of the older boys on the bus says they used to call a "giant pander," even less nuanced than something Hubert Humphrey might have uttered under similar circumstances.

When talking, like Lloyd Bentsen, about politicians Quayle fails to resemble, perhaps most relevant of all is that he is no Spiro Agnew, a man who after a year in office went in the media-made public mind from being a buffoon to a junkyard dog, at considerable (if short-lived) political profit. But as Quayle leaves to standing ovation number seven and heads toward the airport, you have to wonder if, by coming to love him, the congregation has given him only what he came to it *for.*

No one on *Air Force Two* bothers you with instructions about life jackets and oxygen masks. They don't even tell passengers to take their seats until after the plane has begun taxiing toward the runway. There's a cocktail-party feeling in the aisle as we get ready to head back to Washington: agents, staff, and press examine Graceland souvenirs (from side trips made during the golfing) and pass along the good news that Dave Beckwith's daughter has successfully come through surgery on her arm. The day's other medical news is less pressing, though not irrelevant to the vice presidency: the exhumation of Zachary Taylor has yielded no evidence of arsenic poisoning, and Millard Fillmore, who'd been mentioned as a possible conspirator, is in the clear.

After quite a good dinner ($6.25 for Secret Service), the four traveling press are invited to make their way to Quayle's workspace at the front of the plane. This will be their first really close-up meeting with him, and after filing past *his* souvenirs (a Gorbachev portrait from the Leningrad fire chief) and leftover briefing materials (Danny Thomas's autobiography), they reach the vice president's noisy sanctum. Quayle says hello and offers sticks of sugarless gum all around — an appealing if not exactly awe-inspiring introduction.

He is not relaxed, and you can hardly blame him. It will soon be midnight; the jet noise is formidable; his golf game was not, in the end, so hot; and the reporters sitting down with him have just covered his tabletop with their portable tape recorders. Despite the gum chewing, the intimacy of the setting, and the lack of cameras, this encounter is hardly informal; while not on the fourteen-page schedule, it has figured in the day's planning as definitely as the visit to the medicine room or the synagogue. Congressman Sundquist sits at Quayle's right elbow, and both are fully aware of what sort of people they've just let in.

A number of the questions are pointedly unpleasant. How often does he golf? (Only three or four times a month, and this is the first PGA event he's had a chance to participate in as vice president.) What happened to the Band-Aid? (It came off around the fourth hole.) How much can he really get out of a ten-minute tour of a hospital? (Don't forget all he learns from the briefings beforehand.) The responses are courteous, wary, and generally nimble. One finds a lot more life behind the eyes than when he's being thrust in front of friendly audiences. He acts his age and has, at last, a normal physical presence; you notice that his hands are even prematurely wrinkled.

With some pardonable weak spots, he is perfectly well informed. You sense he's faking knowledge of the Quebec situation, when Norma Greenaway brings it up, but when asked about his own trips to Israel, he precisely recalls their dates, their purposes, and the people who accompanied him. Pressed for his reaction to "the Rockefeller report," he says, "Which one? Health care or children?" and is ready with responses for both (increasing parental tax deductions might be better than tax credits). When the "conversation" turns to the recent space station vote in the House, he displays a relish for the victory he helped put together, even though he had to do some of his arm twisting on the phone from Eastern Europe: "The space station survived with a considerable margin . . . if they take another run at us later on this year or next year, we'll be prepared."

He tells Charles Bierbauer that he always likes to get out of

Washington, but when the lights of the city come into view beneath the left side of the aircraft, he breaks into a smile and looks toward them like a tourist who's been alerted to the presence of the Grand Canyon. This little ordeal, which he'll politely deem "a pleasure as always," is just about over, and the announcement that the press will have to return to their seats for landing is probably the best thing that's happened since his shot on the first tee. As you leave this lifelike, competent man, you know for sure what you'd already guessed: the idea that the Republic should shiver with anxiety at the prospect of his taking over has been ridiculously oversold. That the country could do better than Dan Quayle is not news; that Dan Quayle himself can do better — as he's just done — still is.

Yet it doesn't fill one with new admiration for him. If anything, the display of ability generates a different sort of disappointment, annoyance over the way he permits himself to remain, in public, a controlled substance, a sweet, miniature creature in a Republican petting zoo. This may be what, to some extent, the White House wants and the office demands. But it is so contrary to Quayle's own long-term political interests that one has to wonder if there isn't a psychological motivation as well. After what he's been through in the last three years, would he rather tend to his own wounds than inflict some on others? If he has little chance of being elected President, is it because at some point he became an object of pity to himself? Perhaps it became just too much to do, at least in public, what number two is always supposed to do — try harder.

A week later Dan Quayle will be back home in Indiana, the mother of vice presidents, for a July 4 visit to his hometown of Huntington. Waiting to board the plane that will carry the whole Quayle family there, you wonder if the day will provide him with any unexpected chances to emerge from the plastic chrysalis in which he is wrapped.

The only other reporter aboard this morning is Bob Woodward, whose presence apparently frees David Broder for a holiday barbecue. Red-bearded Dave Beckwith, the press secretary, is along too, saying he's pleased with the *American Spectator*'s July article on the weird disparity between Quayle's press as a senator and what he's suffered since — though he thinks coverage has improved of late. (Quayle himself seems disinclined to take up the subject. When I ask him later if he's satisfied with the press he's getting, he jokes: "It's never good enough.")

There are no golf clubs for the stewards to take off the plane today, but there are seven cartons of personal effects, including the nominating petitions from Quayle's 1986 Senate race, which have been brought along to join the Quayle memorabilia now being exhibited in the Huntington City-Township Public Library by the Dan Quayle Commemorative Foundation, Inc. The exhibit has been "held over," according to the sign outside, and after a brief motorcade from the Fort Wayne airport into Huntington, past cornfields, muffler shops, and frame houses, it's our first stop.

"Oh, no, the Follies!" says Mrs. Quayle, spotting a program from an old Kappa Kappa Kappa sorority show — not far from the vice president's law school diploma, out of which the family dog took a bite. "Tucker, look!" says Ben Quayle to his older brother when he comes upon something of special interest in the display cases containing such items as their parents' wedding announcement and Dad's old sweatshirt. Photos from the 1980 Senate campaign show a Quayle so peach-fuzzy and tousled that he'd be more believable wearing a paisley shirt and singing a Donovan song than — it's even harder to believe now — doing what he was doing back then: aggressively killing off Birch Bayh.

The Quayles enjoy this curated attic enough to throw off the schedule a bit. (As they linger inside the exhibit room, the librarian runs to get copies of *The Brethren* and *The Final Days* for Woodward to autograph; all copies of *The Commanders,* she tells him, are out.) Quayle at last emerges to a press availability across the street, near Wilson Realty, where a sign welcomes him home and thanks him for saving the Patriot missile. A local reporter calls him "Dan" and asks how it felt to see his old Little League shirt. "We were having a little debate," replies the vice president, "on what year I played for the Kiwanis team." There's really no way he could "open up" an encounter like this one, but back out in the sunlight, here at the corner of West Market and Poplar, he has once more undergone that reverse photosynthesis, taken on that deathly affable look, that face that someone's described as looking as if it hasn't been lived in. His verbal gaffes have gotten more than enough airplay, but you almost wish he'd let loose with a real open-mike blooper on the order of Ronald Reagan ("We begin bombing in five minutes") or radio's Uncle Don ("That ought to hold the little bastards for a while"): call Albert Gore an s.o.b., or George Mitchell a fool, anything to get some mud on the Little League uniform the national press still has him in, and which he keeps pressing and putting on himself.

Before today, it's been eighteen years since Huntington had a Fourth of July parade, but Dan Quayle's return is such a regional draw that nearby New Haven has canceled its own festivities. The parade's staging area is the parking lot of Huntington North High School, where '55 Fords take their places as antique cars and politically incorrect kids dressed as Indians mount their horses. It's a pleasantly corny spectacle, and one local reporter orients an out-of-towner with a list of surprising hometown attributes: "All three networks! And indoor plumbing!"

The press ride standing up in a pickup truck just ahead of the Quayles, in a position to keep cameras trained on them every step of the way. The family marches five abreast, glowing with good looks and health, and of course way too wholesome ever to pass muster with the arbiters of glamour. "We appreciate you!" someone calls out from the curb, and as the crowds thicken along the route leading to the center of town, the applause and cries of encouragement reach a critical mass of heartiness. "Hey, Danny Quayle!" "*Go* for it!" "There's our man!" Signs appear: WE ❤ THE QUAYLES and, rather curiously,

BUSH WON'T FAIL QUAYLE — the vice presidential name separated in a way that leaves one unsure whether it's meant as a
direct object of the three other words.

Long ago Jacqueline Kennedy was heard to say that if you
bungle raising your children, whatever else you do won't matter
very much. Years from now, whether it's the White House or
Huntington that lies beyond the storm of ridicule they're still
walking through, one suspects that Dan and Marilyn Quayle
will find reason to be satisfied with the way they've brought up
their daughter and two sons. The children walking with them are
impressively modest: they won't wave to the crowds, not out of
sullenness but from a clearly instilled sense that all this is not
because of *them* — even though Tucker, a sort of returning New
Kid on the Block, is in possession of some sign-carrying female
fans of his own. (His big star trip today consists, on the way
home, of going back to the galley of *Air Force Two* for an extra
piece of pie.) There's an attractive easiness between these parents and their kids: chatter, laughter, physical nudges and hugs,
none of it canned, and all of it, one has to remind oneself, more
important than having the esteem of Arthur Schlesinger, Jr.

Or, of course, Dan Rather: CBS GO HOME. AMERICANS BE-
WARE OF THE NATIONAL NEWS MEDIA says a placard held by
one grim-faced Huntington elder. Indeed, the parade is, in a
way, a double celebration for those returning from combat in
foreign territory. As one big sign on a housefront declares:
WELCOME HOME V.P. DAN QUAYLE & FAMILY. WELCOME
HOME TROOPS. The day's main event, after the parade, will be
the unveiling of a plaque at the courthouse where, on August
19, 1988, Dan Quayle began his campaign and the citizens of
Huntington memorably jeered the media that had been eviscer-
ating its native son. "There's the famous courthouse," Dave
Beckwith tells Woodward as we come in sight of it, near the
railroad crossing and Finney's Corner Tavern. "We'll throw a
few things to make you feel at home," says another aide.

"A few weeks ago," Quayle tells the crowd below the steps,
"my staff came to me and said, 'We have a special Fourth of

July prepared for you and your family . . . You're gonna be with people who are smart, who have common sense, and the same values that you do.' I knew at that moment I was gettin' the heck out of Washington, D.C.!" The Huntingtonians love it, and they listen applaudingly as their man protests "historical revisionism" (the kind that would knock those paleface Indians off their horses); extols other local heroes like the early astronaut Gus Grissom (even though the air base named for him is on the hit list for closing); and talks up a new exemplar of the American dream, Supreme Court nominee Clarence Thomas, a name this all-white crowd already seems to recognize as one the uncommonsensical people of Washington will be out to destroy. After the speech is over, and the brass band has played, and the plaque has seen the bright light of day, the vice president walks across the street to pay an unexpected visit to the offices of the *Huntington Herald-Press* (est. 1848), where, almost twenty years ago, J. Danforth Quayle worked, for a short time, as a member of the press.

On the way home it's clear that the trip has done him good, though whether it's the kind of good he really needs — more stroking by the faithful — is open to question. What's indisputable is how much more relaxed with the press he is on this plane ride than on the one home from Memphis — even though half of today's press consists of Bob Woodward, a man who can banish presidents and raise CIA chiefs from the dead. He and Woodward seem to like each other, and Quayle is confident and joshing in his presence, entertaining him with an ambiguous, off-the-record review of *The Commanders,* which he's just finished.

Once again Quayle displays a confident command of information on everything from Saddam Hussein's remaining warmaking capability to Clarence Thomas's prospects: he suspects the nomination will turn on abortion and feels sure that Thomas's spoken admiration of Lewis Lehrman's *American Spectator* article on natural law does not constitute definitive opposition to *Roe v. Wade*. He disputes the charge in a recent *New Republic* piece that NASA has him "on a leash," and says that from his point of view the "Livermore plan" to get to Mars on the cheap with inflatable modules is "absolutely" still alive and worthy of consideration. (Why not ask George Bush if he could go out and give a speech on its behalf?)

His half-hour performance is better than some of the ones his boss puts on, either behind a White House podium or on *Air Force One*. And yet it remains so at odds with his public image that you can't help but think of the *Saturday Night Live* sketch in which Ronald Reagan leaves a goofball press encounter for a closed-door meeting with advisors, at which he turns into a Metternichean wizard. The disparity in Quayle's case is hardly so vast or comical, but it remains wide, not only because of the media's investment in the caricature they have drawn, but also from the vice president's apparent unwillingness to defy the enjoined docility of his office, to cut back on friendly fund-raising and disprove the image, dramatically, in more unlikely, ruleless arenas. The real story, still waiting to come out, is that Dan Quayle is no Dan Quayle.

POSTSCRIPT

You can't please all of the people all of the time. My liberal friends in New York needled me over how *nice* I had been to Dan Quayle, whereas one *American Spectator* reader, Alfred B. Wright of Buffalo, New York, declared to the magazine that "Mallon's derision of the vice president is buried in subtlety like a knife in the back," and criticized the editors for paying me to write "this interminable, empty, and redeemingless disquisition."

It wasn't nearly so long — and in some ways not nearly so nice — as the series of articles that Bob Woodward and David Broder finally presented in January 1992 and published in a book a couple of months later. While not uniformly so, the series was sufficiently flattering to ensure its being much discussed. The *Washington Post*'s characterization of Dan Quayle as an astute politician and administration insider seemed less the work of "two rabid skunks" than a version of the editor's old dream headline, MAN BITES DOG. The newsworthiness of such a slant surely did not escape the foresight of the limelight-loving Bob Woodward, but the series did contain plenty to substantiate its measured praise. The season of "family values" and misspelled potatoes lay ahead.

Up in Rhode Island the administration of Governor Sundlun was, from the start, tumultuous. He had to close down the

state-chartered system of banks and credit unions after embez-
zlement brought it to the brink of ruin. Mayor Brian Sarault
was, in February 1992, sentenced to five and a half years in
prison for extortion, which made the contiguous cities of Pawtucket and Providence able to claim the distinction of having
both elected felons (one past, one future) to preside over them.
Young Patrick Kennedy wasn't charged with or convicted of
anything, but he did spend some uncomfortable time testifying
at his cousin's rape trial a year after Senator Pell's reelection.

Claudine Schneider continues to maintain a home in Rhode
Island, but despite some speculation that she will run for governor, she has so far confined her cleanup efforts to the larger
ecology, working in Washington for the Wilderness Fund and
another environmental group called Renew America.

The Old
World Order

The Golden Pearl

At 7:06 A.M. local time on December 7, 1941, the Opana mobile radar station on Oahu picked up an enormous blip. The activity was duly reported, but higher-ups told the radarmen not to worry: it could only be the big squadron of B-17s due in from California to reinforce the base. Forty-nine minutes later the first wave of Japanese Zeroes began destroying the Pacific fleet. The B-17s, arriving later, would land amidst American anti-aircraft fire.

Fifty years later to the week, the skies over Oahu are once more crowded with aircraft. Plane after plane carrying members of the Pearl Harbor Survivors Association is landing in Honolulu for the attack's golden anniversary, the red tail markings this time signifying not the Japanese air force but TWA. On Wednesday, December 4, all 433 passenger seats on Flight 1 from St. Louis are filled, and a coach traveler can look forward over dozens of septuagenarian heads — gray or bald, and capped with PHSA headgear — sticking above the seat backs. The men and their wives wear badges and pins identifying former outfits and home-state PHSA chapters, and across the aisles they ask each other questions like: "Are you going to the dinner at Schofield Saturday night?"

These men, the barracks mates of James Jones's Robert E. Lee Prewitt, are here because they were spared eternity, and they are willing to sit hour after hour, time zone after time zone, to get back to the spot where their war began.

The pilot announces that the plane today weighed 734,000 pounds at takeoff, but now, descending toward Honolulu, is hundreds of thousands less, having burned off the fuel required to carry it here. The statistics, like the instructional safety film that preceded them hours ago, carry the mind to the focal point of this anniversary, the sunken USS *Arizona,* which, at the bottom of the harbor, beneath its memorial, still holds what remains of three times as many men as are on this crowded plane, and which every day, even now, continues to leak two or three of the million gallons of fuel that were pumped into her shortly before the attack.

"Survivor" is a term embraced today by Americans claiming triumph over a host of humiliations ranging from incest to smoke in the workplace. The eager self-love with which the word is spoken into talk-show microphones is embarrassing, but it cannot entirely dilute the word's power, and during early December, as it appeared stenciled and stitched on hundreds of aging chests and heads, the term surely still had meaning. Separated from death by just yards and seconds and fate, these men could scarcely think of themselves as anything else. One theme of discussion at the commemorations would be whether or not the war, fifty years later, is truly over. The President would say yes, but some of those arriving on Flight 1 might beg to differ. Individual psychologies keep their own timetables, like the oil drops still rising from the *Arizona,* and the Allied bomb, buried near Lehnitz, Germany, that on the evening of December 4, according to Friday's *Honolulu Advertiser,* suddenly exploded, injuring two people and leaving a twenty-foot-deep crater.

There was a danger that December 7, 1991, would be remembered for overkill of a different sort than that unleashed in 1941: the Pacific Command reportedly issued more press credentials to journalists covering the Pearl Harbor anniversary than were given out during the Gulf War. Even so, on Thursday morning, December 5, by which time the commemorations were under way, one could still experience some of the naval station's normal routine. A sign at the Supply Center offered advice to all personnel — "Here or Away — Make It a Safe Day" — and there were no doubt hundreds of sailors doing the same things sailors were getting ready to do on that long-ago morning when no one was paying any special attention to safety. Nowadays a lot of navy men can be seen jogging around the base, making one realize that if an aerial attack were to happen in 1991, many fit enlistees would be strafed to death in their Nikes instead of killed below deck while sleeping off Saturday night. Above present-day Pearl Harbor one does see occasional dark clouds being pushed so fast by the trade winds that they might be mistaken for smoke, but the only things that drop from the skies are rainbows — great, thick, durable ones that follow sun showers.

At ten this morning, outside the *Arizona* Memorial Visitor Center, the 111th Army Band (Hawaii National Guard) is playing at a ceremony that includes the laying of wreaths against masts symbolizing the nine state-named battleships damaged or sunk in the attack. Some junketing governors are here to see the flowers placed, with the assistance of a park ranger, by a survivor from each of the ships. Taps is sounded, and followed by a rendition of "God Bless America" as one has never heard it — slow, mournful, and *a cappella*. It's one of several astute theatrical calculations that will be made this week, displays whose effectiveness is guaranteed by the emotions lying just below the skin of those who have come back. In this case immediate relief comes when the song is sung a second time, to quick, peppy musical accompaniment by a children's choir.

The simple monument to the sunken USS *Utah,* which lies off the far side of Ford Island, is sometimes called, according to *Life* magazine, the Forgotten Memorial. There are no tourist shuttles to it, as there are to the *Arizona;* visitors have to ride the regular ferry for naval personnel out to Ford and then cross the island to the site of the wreck. Ford was decommissioned as a naval air station in the spring of 1962, just weeks before the dedication of the *Arizona* memorial. The jet age had rendered its short runways obsolete, and now only small private planes practice touch-and-go landings there. On the side of the island closest to what was once Battleship Row, one finds a mix of new construction and older buildings, including a dispensary to which the wounded were carried all day on December 7, 1941. But farther inland, on the short trip to the northwest side, one feels that the island hasn't changed at all in the last fifty years. Its small frame houses look much as they would have then. According to Thurston Clarke, in his excellent book *Pearl Harbor Ghosts: A Journey to Hawaii Then and Now,* on the afternoon of December 7, 1941, "Two hundred *Arizona* dead were lined up on the lawns of officers' bungalows. Their blood soaked the ground and blackened the grass. Survivors gathered dismembered arms and legs from roofs and trees."* On this Thursday afternoon fifty years later, when a small ceremony is planned at the *Utah* memorial, the only unusual item on one of the bungalows' lawns is a sign proclaiming it "Ford Island Yard of the Month."

The Utah was one of the first ships hit. She took two torpedoes to starboard and fell over on port, sinking after only eleven minutes. Fifty-five of her men went down with her. Her death, if untimely, was not the robbery of youth suffered by most of those who died inside her. The *Utah* was an old ship. Her World War I service was well behind her, and she had not had battleship status since 1932. In fact, in the months before the attack she was serving as a target ship for American planes that practiced bombing runs by dropping bags of flour onto her timber-covered deck. (According to Walter Lord's *Day of Infamy,* says one of the memorial speakers today, an excited Japanese pilot

*I am indebted to Clarke's book and to Stanley Weintraub's *Long Day's Journey into War: December 7, 1941* for some of the historical background and detail in this essay.

mistook the timbers for small planes, delighting in the possibility that, despite espionage reports to the contrary, an American carrier might be at Pearl Harbor after all.)

The Forgotten Memorial, dedicated twenty years ago, is little more than a plaque, a flagpole, and an L-shaped dock from which to observe the half-submerged hulk. Today the site gleams with a newly tarred walkway and a coat of fresh paint. The shipwreck itself, at least what's visible, is so badly rusted and rotted that it probably won't last much longer. Some green shoots grow up through it, and the occasional bird lands on one of its crumbling edges.

The speakers at this afternoon's ceremony sit on the dock, and the honored guests gather under a canopy. The wind whips pleasantly as the short talks begin, led by a master of ceremonies who is actually air force: General Matthews is here because his father served on the *Utah* in the First World War, before moving to his ship's namesake state, perhaps even for sentimental reasons. Senator Jake Garn, whose own father was a World War I pilot, takes his turn at the lectern to recall his mother crying with fear, when news of Pearl Harbor came, that her husband would be called back into service. The younger Garn, a naval aviator in the 1950s, used to land seaplanes here, and twenty years ago, as mayor of Salt Lake City, he came to the memorial's dedication. Governor Norman Bangerter comes next, using his time to register an objection to the Forgotten Memorial tag. He has written to tell the editor of *Life* that the memorial is merely quiet, in the eloquent manner of, say, the Gettysburg Address.

And then it is the survivors' turn. On December 7, 1941, the PHSA's Utah state chairman was actually aboard the USS *Medusa,* a repair ship anchored about a mile away from the *Utah.* "What are those army guys doing on a Sunday morning?" he asked himself as the bombs started dropping, a reaction he says was "pretty typical": it could only be some sort of drill, thought everyone. Don Larsen, who *was* on the *Utah,* follows him to the microphone in his aloha shirt, looking like any happy, healthy retiree on his Hawaiian vacation, but within moments of starting the story of how he escaped his ship, he is sobbing. "What we had left wasn't worth a dime." Before the governor's proclamation is read, General Matthews soothes the rawness by summing things up in military-speak: "What a stressful, difficult, challenging experience was had by all who were present."

When a new flag has been raised over the memorial and the program is over, I ask Milton Matson, who'd been sitting under the canopy, about his own stressful morning fifty years ago. Looking through his trifocals, he tells me: "One thing that stands out in my memory is, after the ship started rolling over, I was talking to one of the shipmates there, and he says, 'Well, there's one thing about it. I won't have to wash those damned dishes this morning.' " Matson slid down the side of the ship, holding on to a ten-inch hawser. "I got my butt scratched a little bit with barnacles." Eventually he was transferred to the USS *Detroit,* where he "continued to do [his] twenty." He makes it sound as if that morning at Pearl Harbor was just part of his hitch, but he acknowledges that this is probably his fifth trip back.

The navy's tour boat has been especially busy the past few months; they've gotten it out as early as four in the morning to take groups around the harbor and to the *Arizona* memorial. Some of the participants in the *Utah* ceremonies, including Milton Matson and Don Larsen, who looks exhausted, are on it later in the afternoon. The guide points out sights the men never saw during their service here, such as Aloha Stadium, as well as more eternal features of the Oahu landscape, like the Dole pineapple fields. As on December 7, 1941, there are no aircraft carriers here, and aside from some submarines that make this their port, the harbor is filled mostly with destroyers and frigates. The battleship is a naval anachronism, and the mooring blocks of what was once Battleship Row are like pedestals without statues, bearing only the names of the ships tied to them fifty years ago. The guide also directs attention to the three paths taken by the Japanese bombers, one of which runs right between the upper floors of two postwar skyscrapers.

Approaching the *Utah* from the water, one sees the side of her that wasn't visible during the Ford Island ceremony. That "side" is neither port nor starboard; it is her deck, forever capsized toward the water's surface. From this vantage the sight is more moving than it was from land. One notices the gun turrets sticking uselessly up through the water and the splintered, rotting teakwood on which the sailors walked through each peaceful day. From Ford Island the hulk seems like an accident; from the water it looks like an atrocity. The sight of his old ship brings tired Don Larsen back to life, and he politely corrects a couple of the guide's mistakes.

The *Arizona* memorial is judged by Thurston Clarke, not unfairly, to be lacking in "the necessary morbidity, the power to move even the most ignorant to tears." Anchored on two sides, it nowhere touches the sunken ship over which it floats, and for all its gracefulness is an odd-looking structure, a carved soapcake. A pattern meant to depict the Tree of Life has been cut into it, but the resulting shapes seem, at least from a distance, peculiarly like Japanese ideograms. Alfred Preis, the Austrian refugee who designed it, visited his most famous construction yesterday, recalling that his first proposal, "a sunken sarcophagus" into which viewers would be lowered for a look at the wreck through thick glass, was considered *too* morbid. What was built instead seems, in the strict sense, heavenly, more celestial than nautical. It has the clean lines of a modern painting, whereas the living-dead hulk of the *Utah* is something Géricault might have put on canvas. The *Arizona* survivors have been apotheosized; the men of the *Utah* are still scrambling for shore.

None of this can deny the effect that Preis's quiet creation has on many visitors. (This afternoon, before stepping off the tour boat to enter it, one older man takes the trouble to comb his hair.) In the shrine room, beneath a tablet bearing the names of all the men still below, one finds small floral tributes sent from the VFW posts of towns all across the country. Looking down and off the side, one can spot small fish swimming toward the rusty gun turrets lying just beneath the water. Aerial photographs of the whole arrangement are eerily spectacular; the white memorial, floating perpendicularly atop the still-visible sunken ship, seems like the armature of a giant crucifix.

On early Thursday evening the memorial's deck is strewn with television cables for live feeds to the mainland, and at 5:30 circular floor lights, like the ones on the edge of a modern subway platform, come startlingly to life, as if switched on by those below. If one looks out over the side from which the huge number-three gun turret can be seen breaking through the water, the tiny oil slick made by each day's escaping fuel is visible. The spectrum of shiny colors it makes under the setting sun is pretty, almost gay, though nothing to match the actual rainbow that has just dropped over the enormous ship nearby, the USS *Missouri,* which sailed into the harbor this morning, and upon which, forty-five months after the sinking of the *Arizona,* the Japanese empire surrendered to the United States of America.

The corner of Lewers Street and Kalakaua Avenue is a good place to watch the survivors' big parade on Friday morning. Whenever one of the sudden showers falls, you can duck into the McDonald's (offering the McTeri-Burger Deluxe, as in teriyaki), and reemerge to hear a small cheering section of older women break into one more round of "Let's Remember Pearl Harbor."

The heartier men walk behind banners identifying their old ship or their PHSA chapter, and the frailer ones come by on trucks. A contingent of former marines actually marches, in time, looking smart; a more casual participant in another parade unit manages to keep up as he videotapes the videotaping crowds along the sidewalks.

During a lull, when some space opens up between units, one woman on the corner moves over to let a girl walking a bicycle cross the street. The girl says, "Excuse me," but she was in a hurry, and the woman, upon noticing her Oriental features (the girl was almost certainly an American citizen), can't stop herself from laughing and saying to the man next to her, "Still pushy." The girl will never know she's been made a surrogate Japanese for one of the many nervous little ethnic jokes the week produces. Nonetheless, for all the old wartime scores and all the new economic resentments, there is plenty this morning to indicate the assimilationist accomplishments of present-day Hawaii. When Senator Inouye, maimed during his World War II service in Europe, rides by, one can hear a Caucasian spectator, presumably a resident, saying to his wife: "Hey, the home team!"

The PHSA is taking care to assure its perpetuation, through an offshoot called the SDPHS, the Sons and Daughters of Pearl Harbor Survivors. They, too, are in the parade, in identifying red and white attire. There is probably nothing wrong with their history-minded presence — after all, even the D.A.R. is here (two prissy old gals in a convertible) — but one has to wonder if this isn't something other than historical consciousness, if it isn't a peculiar species of codependency. In 1990s America, if you haven't yourself survived something, it's *de rigueur* to be related to somebody who has.

One offshoot of the desire to keep the memory of Pearl Harbor ever fresh is the continuing historical attention, principally from amateurs, to the question: did FDR know? That is, did he allow the catastrophe to take place because he saw it as the certain way to get America into the war? The askers of this question are not generally so flaky as the Kennedy conspiracy theorists, but the motivating tendencies are the same. The "investigators" of each "conspiracy" claim to be engaged in useful historical revisionism, but what they are doing might better be characterized as historical *pre*visionism. For the Pearl Harbor contingent it is always 7:54 A.M. on that Sunday morning, a minute before the Japanese planes come through the clouds, and for the JFK gumshoes the Hertz sign in Dealey Plaza says 12:29, not 12:30. General Short and Admiral Kimmel are still preparing for their Sunday morning round of golf, and Jack and

Jackie are still waving. The theorists claim as their intention the laying to rest of each disaster, something that cannot occur until the "real" truth is finally established; but their actual purpose is more like the opposite. The information is not so much hidden as hiding, which somehow makes the thrilling, sickening event forever *about* to take place. The buff can keep scanning the skies or peering over at the grassy knoll happy in the knowledge that this awful, sublime moment doesn't yet have to be over.

Thurston Clarke argues that the Hawaiian islands' explosive development in recent years makes it "easy to overlook how their beauty unhinged the purpose of their defenders." Paradise made war unimaginable, and even now a paradise that's been leased and subdivided retains charm enough to let its population, temporary and resident, ignore even such benign reminders of unpleasantness as the survivors' parade. Waikiki's beach lies only a block or two behind Kalakaua Avenue, and as the parade goes by, there are plenty of swimmers and sunbathers — among them three older Japanese ladies holding hands, dunking themselves and laughing — content to let it pass unnoticed. The Sawada Art & Golf shop is open for business in a nearby mall, and in the pink world of the Royal Hawaiian Hotel, looking much as it first did in 1927, the bar is ready with mai tais for survivor and sybarite alike.

It is, just as incongruously as fifty years ago, Christmastime, and on Friday night there is to be another march, the Public Workers' Santa Parade, featuring floats that are really city trucks from agencies like the Board of Water Supply. President and Mrs. Bush will be checked in at the Hilton Hawaiian Village, but the more important long-range news for the hotel appeared in Wayne Harada's "Show Biz" column in the December 5 *Advertiser:* "Don Ho ends his affiliation with the Hilton Hawaiian Village when he closes tomorrow evening at the Dome. He'll reopen Dec. 22 — and launch a new era — at the Hula Hut on Beach Walk."

As the old men in the parade go by, atop their trucks and behind their banners, dozen after dozen of them, one realizes that as much as anything else they are still-living monuments to the good life. A lot of them had been poor enlistees trying to escape the Depression. Their postwar upward mobility took them by surprise — and eventually on retirement trips like this one. The poignancy they finally make one feel is something larger and more generalized than that which came from the disaster they endured. If they weren't survivors, if they hadn't lost buddies, if they had never seen war, never done anything more remarkable in their lives than go to the prom, they would still be unsettling, as evidence of what life does to all those who were once boys: it makes them old and then it makes them die.

"Reflections of Pearl Harbor" is the title of the Friday afternoon program outside the Visitor Center. Under a broiling sun attendants pass cups of water to the older members of the sparse crowd. None of the scheduled speakers is a survivor of the attack, since this event, as James Ridenour, director of the National Park Service, explains, is designed to show how there were more "victims of Pearl Harbor" than the people there that morning. If "survivor" is American talk-show diction, "victim" belongs to the academic lexicon. Its utterance leaves one suspiciously anticipating a sensitivity lesson, the kind of upsidedown breast-beating that will make the attack have been America's fault.

The first speaker actually does something like the opposite. Alfred Preis, the *Arizona* memorial's designer, talks with the patriotic love of the refugee (in his case from Nazi-occupied Austria), thanking the United States for "having given me life." In a pained, wheezing voice he speaks of the curious foreshadowing experiences that gave him his aesthetic sense: at five years old he was taken by his mother to the emperor's funeral and overwhelmed by the beauty, the feathers, the music, the "display of power." A strange dream of entering a cave also shaped the imagination of this man who would one day memorialize a thousand trapped men.

Then Edward I. Ichiyama, once Pacific area manager for the Social Security Administration, talks of the "very tragic constitutional failure" of the internment of 120,000 Japanese-Americans, including his American-citizen wife, whose brother was in the U.S. Army. Ichiyama himself became part of "the most decorated unit in American military history," the 442nd Regimental Combat Team, whose Japanese-Americans performed such feats as rescuing a Texas army unit from Germans who had them surrounded in the Vosges mountains. Ichiyama and all five of his brothers and brothers-in-law received Purple Hearts, and no one would think of denying him the title the printed program gives him: "Distinguished American." But the speech he gives is a litany of victims — the radiation sufferers of 1945, the blond German youth he saw lying dead. All of their agony is certain, but one feels uncomfortable with the implied idea that it is impermissible to think of carnage suffered without also thinking of carnage dealt, as if the globe might fall apart unless equally strong vectors of right and wrong were seen emanating from all its points at every moment.

Still, Ichiyama's speech seems intellectually bracing compared to the one James Michener gives next. The novelist's remarks are not without charm, including as they do the story of his Pennsylvania aunts' delight in accepting his Japanese postwar bride, however appalled they were to find out she was a Democrat. But Michener is peculiarly fulsome in his praise of the Japanese. He asks if the audience realizes even now how complete the Japanese victory at Pearl Harbor was (a debatable point, in fact), before praising the "heroism" of this formidable opponent, a curious attribute to highlight for an audience here to commemorate a surprise attack. He says that the Japanese surrender was "complete and honorable," noting that during the occupation not one American was killed by guerrilla action on the Japanese mainland. "Onetime enemies had become trusted friends." "Devoted" and "miraculous" and "amazing" are the other adjectives he applies to the cooperation of the two countries. Mr. Michener, according to Mr. Ridenour, is a "citizen of the world," a world apparently without ironies or third acts.

In the hours before the actual anniversary dawned, a visitor to the harbor could see the *Missouri* strung with white lights, like a suspension bridge, and hear some distant strains of music. An orchestra practicing for the morning? Or maybe a few musicians who decided to stay and jam after tonight's "Battle of Music"? (The "Battle" was a re-creation of the December 6, 1941, contest in which the *Arizona*'s band placed second, earning it the right to sleep late — which would mean forever — below deck.)

The parking lot behind the Consolidated Media Center is filled with satellite dishes for the morning's coverage. If satellites had existed fifty years ago, no one would be here now, but any reporters wishing to ride up to the National Memorial Cemetery of the Pacific (Punchbowl) will have to be on the bus by 3 A.M., with their instructions that, of the more than 36,490 graves there, only those of Ernie Pyle and Colonel Ellison Onizuka (the *Challenger* astronaut) may be photographed. Traveling up the extinct volcano — the cemetery is in the crater — one looks back down at the lights of Honolulu and thinks of all the seamen who, at this moment fifty years ago, were on Hotel Street, paying a girl to make love, for the last time, as four time zones farther west Prime Minister Tojo was calm enough to keep sleeping.

The grave markers at Punchbowl are flush with the ground, in neat rows just like the suburban houses the World War II GIs returned to buy and live in. In the dark the markers look like footprints, and the occasional floral arrangements stick up like hands. Big flags brush the sides of the bus as it climbs and comes in sight of other buses, and more buses, and more still — all of them chartered to bring the survivors and their families up the mountain. Aging men and women step out of them on uncooperative knees and look around in the chilly darkness. A marine bugler quietly rehearses taps as the stars shine on in the night sky.

At 6:15 the band is playing the jaunty march from *Bridge Over the River Kwai,* and people in the crowd inevitably begin whistling, conscious or not of its being fifty years ago to the minute that Admiral Yamamoto's planes were completing their carrier takeoffs for the 230-mile flight to Oahu. The pilots could home in on KGMB, which between songs gave them the weather report: "Partly cloudy, with clouds mostly over the mountains. Visibility good. Wind north, ten knots."

The presidential motorcade makes its timed arrival at sunrise, blue and white signal lights flashing like sparklers, up along the esplanade, past the flags, past the crowds from the charter buses. After some mournful music, George Bush's speech seems strangely throwaway. Neither the microphone nor the rhetoric is turned up high. There is a paragraph apologizing for the internment of Japanese-Americans; a quick tribute to those who fought "the cause of Korean and Vietnamese freedom"; mention of a Hawaiian boy who died in Desert Storm. Even with allowance made for the setting, the President's delivery is so completely unemphatic as to feel unseemly, at odds with the substance of his text. There is no applause until it is over, and an hour will pass before one realizes that George Bush's problem is not an absence of emotions but a surfeit. Up at Punchbowl he is husbanding them for what lies ahead, down in the harbor.

Back at Pearl, as 7:55 A.M. approaches, a weird feeling, not just silent but nervous, an awed and superstitious mood, takes hold. The "moment of silence" would probably be happening without its being on the schedule. It is broken by a roar of planes, whose location and direction are acoustically uncertain until one sees the four of them — and then, in "Missing Man" formation, only three — streaking westward above the harbor and over the *Arizona* memorial, where the President is waiting to make a speech and cast a wreath into the water. The ceremonies there are for invited guests only, and so the press watch them, with a crowd of World War II veterans, over a big Panasonic TV on the Kilo 8 pier.

From there one can look out upon the memorial or at the *Missouri,* the intentional symmetry being the only nose-thumbing sanctioned by the week's organizers. Earlier plans for gestures of reconciliation were scrapped after loud, quotable complaints from the Pearl Harbor Survivors Association. Right now Bush would probably like to be standing with Prime Minister Kiichi Miyazawa, shaking hands, but a few months ago the PHSA national president, Gerald Glaubitz, said of the Japanese, "They weren't invited fifty years ago, and we're not going to invite them now." The organization's historian, Raymond Emory, made an analogy: "If somebody had raped and murdered our mother fifty years ago, we wouldn't be inviting them over for lunch." The PHSA's clout is such that Emory, not Miyazawa, is sitting between George and Barbara Bush this morning on the *Arizona.*

The Japanese parliament was not able to agree on a particularly apologetic resolution, and it fell to Foreign Minister Watanabe to express "deep remorse," a gesture whose incompleteness was satirized in the *Advertiser*'s editorial cartoon on Thursday. In his *Arizona* speech Bush moves away from the issue entirely, emphasizing instead the perils of isolationism, a bland enough theme, one would have thought, except for the primary challenge he is facing from Patrick Buchanan and the new America Firsters. He also contributes, much to the liking of the PHSA, to the continuing alchemy of Pearl Harbor from debacle into triumph, speaking of the Heroes of the Harbor (capitalized in the official White House transcript), men who "did not panic" but "raced to their stations. Some strapped pistols over pajamas — fought, and died . . . For the defenders of Pearl, heroism came as naturally as breath. They reacted by instinctively rushing to their posts." In making historical lists, anyone now attempting to place Pearl Harbor with the marine-barracks bombing in Beirut will be met by some angry stares.

The President's remarks memorably illustrate the way sincerity can redeem boilerplate. There is nothing exceptional about this speech other than the way in which it moves its speaker. Bush cannot, without choking up, get through his second-to-last paragraph, in which he describes how the harbor's water, "in what now seems another lifetime . . . wrapped its arms around the finest sons any nation could ever have; and it carried them to another, better world." The catch in his throat moves people on Kilo 8 to tears. The report of saluting rifles reaches them through the Panasonic TV before, a second later, it arrives on the breeze.

Few veterans in the crowd on Kilo 8 remember hearing news of Pearl Harbor while "walking across the green at school," namely Andover, as Bush recalls doing after he and the First Lady are ferried over from the *Arizona* memorial; and the President's remark that the Japanese expression of "deep remorse" is "much appreciated" by the United States is greeted with silence. Even so, one gets the feeling that what Gerald Glaubitz said about Bush at Punchbowl a couple of hours ago is true: "He's one of us." It's more than his experience as a naval aviator, which has made him the perfect President for this occasion. It's generational. George Bush still looks much younger than he is, but his recently fibrillating heart has no doubt given him a new feeling of actuarial solidarity with this group. His best moment in this last speech comes when he gets suddenly personal, philosophical, the way one might with friends of a lifetime some summer night on a front porch. The public rhetoric turns confidential: "I wondered: what will my reaction be when I go back to Pearl Harbor? What will their reaction be — the other old vets — especially those who survived that terrible day right here? Well, let me tell you how I feel. I have no rancor in my heart towards Germany or Japan — none at all. I hope you have none in yours." It's said in the vulnerable way friends have of talking about all the hands that have been dealt, and the feelings it stirs are released in applause generated by his next proud and declamatory paragraph: "World War II is over. It is history. We won. We crushed totalitarianism; and when that was done, we helped our enemies give birth to democracies. We reached out, both in Europe and in Asia, and made our enemies our friends. We healed their wounds and in the process, we lifted ourselves up."

It remains for Bush to conjure the dead once more, this time to imagine words they might be speaking: "Don't you think they're saying: 'Fifty years have passed. Our country is the undisputed leader of the free world. We are at peace.' Don't you think each one is saying: 'I did not die in vain.' "

Just prior to the anniversary Frank Deford wrote in *Newsweek:* "We make a to-do about remembering it each year. But we don't. Not really. What we actually do is: We Remember That We Remember Pearl Harbor." There is something to this. Sentimentality could, after all, be defined as the squaring of sentiment. Nonetheless, there is something to be said for trying to remember feelings once felt. If the debate over a Japanese apology has been confused, it has not been unintelligent, and it has for now saved one theater of the war from the specious moral equivalence the "healing" waters of time will inevitably bring. All history's destiny is toward pageant: the German Protestant princes and the Holy Roman Empire are equally colorful, each no more right or wrong than the other, and the Civil War is eventually a chess set. But there is no point in hastening a process that, aside from its inevitability, is destructive of the truth. If the book on Pearl Harbor remains a bit rancorously open, that's not so bad as a wrongheaded rush to Bitburg.

Two hours after the President's last speech, John Duffy's *Time for Remembrance* is premiered by the Honolulu Symphony Orchestra in the parking lot near the Visitor Center. The composer is quoted as saying that he "must have read about 1,000 poems" before coming up with words for the first movement. What he hit upon were lines from Rupert Brooke:

> *Blow out, you bugles, over the rich Dead!*
> *There's none of these so lonely and poor of old*
> *But, dying, has made us rarer gifts than gold.*

It seems a peculiar choice. Brooke was, of course, an Englishman, and his poem is from the early days of the First World War, but Duffy's selection is not the only use of Great War verse during the commemorations. At the *Utah* ceremonies on Thursday, Governor Bangerter quoted from "In Flanders Fields." This small pattern — a complement to the Great War origins of Alfred Preis's aesthetic sense — reminds one that the popular literature of the Second World War, particularly from America, came in the form of bulky disorganized prose — *The Naked and the Dead, From Here to Eternity, The Young Lions* — copious, accessible works for the Everymen who fought the war through, but insufficiently heroic for high-minded anniversaries.

Jones's novel is the literary legacy of Pearl Harbor. The power of the book and of the movie made from it have literally made history, of an inaccurate kind. Thurston Clarke recounts a conversation he had with Herb Garcia, the base's museum curator of the Schofield barracks, which are about six miles inland on Oahu from the naval base at Pearl:

> [Garcia] concedes a dud naval shell from Pearl Harbor fell into a barrel of flour in the kitchen, that a Japanese pilot may have squeezed off rounds while heading for Wheeler, and that empty casings may have fallen into Schofield's quadrangle and been mistaken for live ammunition. "Remember, the soldiers who witnessed this were not trained observers," he said, "just excitable Depression-era kids. Then rumors got bigger in the telling and were reinforced by erroneous scenes from the *From Here to Eternity* movie. Now, ninety percent of the veterans who return say, 'Yeah, I was bombed, I was strafed.' If I argue, they say, 'Look, buddy, I was here and you weren't.' "

I found this perception at work late on Saturday morning when Specialist E4 Matt English drove me from the Consolidated Media Center to my next commemorative stop. English, a pleasant, red-headed twenty-year-old with a shaky sense of direction, told me that, since leaving Michigan to join the army, he's spent almost his whole two and a half years at Schofield. He had talked this week to one seventy-four-year-old Schofield veteran who'd been back for the forty-fifth anniversary and was now back for the fiftieth, and who described how he was doing his laundry when the attack started. English himself lives in C Quad, in an infantry barracks he insists has bullet holes in it from December 7, 1941.

English says that life at Schofield has improved since Prewitt's day, but there's still enough tedium and hardship to make pardonable some contrivance of legend around the place. English and his fiancée, who's also in the army, are getting married on January 4, and the apartment they'll be living in will run them $850 a month. He may reenlist but is not at all certain he's going to be career. To ride down Center Drive on the naval base, through the Military Family Housing Area, is to view the eternal aspects of service life: the cheap green-brown houses with the tricycles out front that, come Monday, when all the cameras have left the base, will again be just someplace halfway around the world.

Compared to much of the naval station, nearby Hickam Air Force Base has a plusher feel, more like that of a well-tended college campus with dozens of creamy beige and brown buildings and houses. What happened here fifty years ago is usually told second or third in the story of December 7, 1941. Hickam held a modest ceremony at the base flagpole late on Saturday morning to honor its dead, and an hour later the base seemed back to normal. One could walk around it hearing nothing out of the ordinary but the departing roar of *Air Force One*. The portable bleachers that had been set up by the flagpole were already being folded.

But Robert ("Johnny") Johnson was still there, counting the names of the dead, twenty-nine of them from the 22nd Materiel Squadron, on the new marker. He had arrived at Hickam in September 1940 to work as a parachute rigger, and can remember being in the hospital with a broken ankle the following summer. After his release in October 1941, he continued to limp for a while, "but that day I don't remember limping." That day was December 7, the day of what he refers to as the "blitz" — the indisputable bombing of the main barracks at Hickam. He had just gotten back from brushing his teeth when it started. "I couldn't figure out what was going on, and I went down below to go get a rifle, but the door was locked up. We had just come off of maneuvers five o'clock Friday night, and everything was turned in." (At Hickam and Wheeler, the focus had been almost exclusively on precautions against sabotage, not aerial attack, which meant locking up ammunition, digging trenches, and keeping planes close together on their runways.)

The Japanese planes, says Johnson, would fly down behind the hangars. Then "they'd turn around and they'd strafe on the way back." Sharing a memory frequently spoken by survivors, he says he "could see those guys sitting, the two of them in each plane, just sitting there, their heads. I could see them as they went by." It was the last strike that hit the barracks. "I got blown up in the air and I sort of came down on my neck and shoulder, and it felt like the shoes had gone off of my feet . . . I was asking the Fellow Up Above to help me get by or get through, and after that I always said, 'Well, if they never got me that day, they're never going to get me.' " Johnson would spend part of a long war — he was discharged in the summer of 1945 — in the Gilbert Islands.

On the morning of December 7, after he got to his feet, he sought shelter against a little tailor shop on the base and then made his way to a baseball dugout, where he managed to pick up a rifle. But "what's a rifle going to do against aircraft, you know?" When the attack was over, the men were told to go down into officers' quarters to be ready for more. "The story was that the island was surrounded . . . We had thought we were going to be attacked that night." At about nine, "there was a plane that came over . . . with the light blinking, and it seemed like all heck broke loose." To this day he's not sure whether the friendly aircraft was shot down. The lobby of the barracks, which have become the U.S. Air Force Headquarters in the Pacific, contains a photo of Pearl Harbor taken on the night of December 7, 1941, as searchlights scanned the skies. Stanley Weintraub's *Long Day's Journey into War* recounts how antiaircraft gunners were by the next morning still so nervous that they began firing at an especially bright object in the sky before realizing they'd taken aim at the planet Venus.

Displayed along with the nighttime photo is the machine-gun-shredded flag that flew atop the barracks that day. It was this that Johnson wanted to see after counting the names of the 22nd Materiel Squadron. Walking toward the converted barracks, whose modernization has deliberately stopped short of filling in the scores of bullet holes that pock the exterior walls, Johnson points to one section and says, "I came out the window over there."

He first returned here in 1971 for the PHSA's national convention, and he's returned to the islands a number of times since. What he's liked least about this current trip is the jam-packed overdevelopment of Waikiki and the talk he hears of how it was the navy that really won the war. He acknowledges "lots of good memories, and a lot of bad memories." Among the latter is one from the mess hall, which he says could seat nine hundred airmen at once: "A kid from my hometown was there. He was a cook, but he wasn't on duty that day. He was making him[self] a lunch to go hiking, and of course he got blown to bits. That was his birthday, twenty-three years old that day. Lawrence Carlson was his name." He enunciates it precisely, making sure I've got it right.

The men leaving Honolulu in plane after plane on Monday, December 9, have mostly retired from whatever work they took up in 1945. But once again they are going home. Their eastward flight path is taking them closer to the wreck of the *Oklahoma* than they have been anytime this weekend, for the *Oklahoma* lies 540 miles northeast of where she first sank, after taking nine torpedoes on the morning of December 7, 1941. Like most of the ships that went down in the attack, she was eventually raised. The others were returned to service, but she was too far gone for that, and so in 1947 she was towed east toward a scrap yard. As if in protest against such a fate, she sank a second time, before arriving at her destination, and she's never been raised since.

While she was still on the bottom of Pearl Harbor, some of the sailors trapped inside made marks on the bulkhead showing that they lived on until at least Christmas Eve.

"Don't you think," asked President Bush about the fallen, that "each one is saying: 'I did not die in vain.' " Eventually, perhaps, the spirits of the *Oklahoma* knew or felt that, but not in those seventeen days, as they breathed the last of the pocketed air over and over. They may literally not have known what hit them, much less its historical meaning. Peace and satisfaction must have been a long time coming, just as they were to many of these survivors, still alive, flying homeward. When the President shouted, with real feeling, "We crushed totalitarianism," a part of him knew he was telling only a half-truth, or more exactly, two thirds of one. The occasion permitted no reference to what another President called the "hard and bitter peace," the era that began with an expedient handshake over the Elbe.

Nonetheless, some of the men flying home in this steel tube, away from all those sunken ones, must be taking satisfaction in the news, heard on hotel televisions as they undressed after last night's dinner at the Sheraton, that the Soviet Union, born when most of them were, has for all intents and purposes ceased to exist. Any sort of boasting about this, during the past two years, as its inevitability grew clear, has been almost forbidden by some national feeling of what is proper. A lot of men in this generation, no doubt because of the war, never had much taste for demonstrativeness in any case. I can remember, years ago, hearing the man who had once been Sergeant Arthur Mallon of the U.S. Army tell me how it was on V-J Day that he returned to New York after service in England as a medic. What did he do? I wanted to know, assuming he had rushed to Times Square to kiss the same nurse in Alfred Eisenstaedt's famous photograph. No, he just got a haircut before returning to his mother's house and going to bed. Even so, if he were still here, I suspect he would join in marveling at the world's growing resemblance to the envisioned one for which he was asked to fight.

The People Next Door

It's 11:05 A.M. on September 25, and here at 321 East 45th Street we're under our benign annual house arrest. In fifteen minutes President Bush will arrive at the United Nations, which is one hundred or so yards away. About a dozen people are in the apartment-house lobby waiting for him to get safely up First Avenue and into the General Assembly Building so they can get permission, from one of the policemen stationed on the block, to leave their own building. On one of Ronald Reagan's visits, we even had the Highway Patrol in the lobby.

When the President isn't making his yearly visit, this stretch of East 45th Street is still one of the safest blocks in the city. The U.S. Mission to the United Nations is on the corner, and a New York City policeman occupies a kiosk outside it twenty-four hours a day. When the co-op board of 321 held its annual meeting two summers ago and considered spending money for another doorman's shift — the last one now ends at midnight — one woman argued that she hardly saw the need: the man with the Uzi near the back of the mission made her feel very safe.

It is highly unusual for the residential-property owners of Manhattan Island to argue against additional security for themselves. But this East River neighborhood is different: if the U.N. has failed in its aim to make the world safe, it can at least be credited with having done that for Turtle Bay. A block up from the U.S. Mission is the Turkish Center, which makes for another cop in another kiosk, presumably to discourage Armenians or Greeks bearing plastique. (The car-bomb barriers around the U.S. Mission are disguised as appealing oval-shaped planters.) But no one worries much about terrorism here; the residents are quite happy to risk the odd international outrage in exchange for all the extra deterrence to street crime. I live on the first floor of 321, without bars on the windows, either.

As I sit at my desk on weekday afternoons, multilingual children's chatter drifts across the street from the International Pre-Schools. I get lunch from the U.N. Plaza Delicatessen, have clothes mended at the U.N. Cleaners, and get my hair cut at the U.N. Hair Cutters. The automatic teller at the nearest bank displays its functions in French. The neighborhood is a gentle mix of brick apartment buildings, old townhouses (a recent For Sale sign offered one ideal for a family "or small mission"), and the sort of tall green-glassed international-style structures that the U.N. brought in its postwar wake. The sloped General Assembly Building and the thirty-nine-story Secretariat tower have stood for almost forty years on the site of some old slaughterhouses, a fact that some internationalists probably took to be hopefully metaphorical.

It gets quiet here early. Workers at the United Nations are not known for burning the midnight oil; indeed, I often catch a bus up First Avenue at about 8 P.M., hardly a late hour for people to be knocking off a day of world-salvational labor, and I am usually the only person at one of the stops closest to "the Organization." (It occurs to me that the racehorse Secretariat may have gotten his name because he always finished early.) While waiting for my bus, I ponder the quiet, enjoy the sea breezes (the East River is actually a body of salt water), and regard the glassy nighttime façades of the buildings that seem both monumental and ephemeral, like empty pavilions at a deserted world's fair.

When I moved here four years ago, I hoped to be able to run in the good-sized park north of the General Assembly Building, but the U.N. permits only strolling there. The slower pace enforces a more lingering look at the sculptures donated by various member states. From Finland there is an uninspiring configuration of rotted-out piping, and from the Soviet Union a heroically pumped-up bronze man performing the surprisingly biblical beating of a sword into a plowshare. In 1975 the East Germans presented *The Rising Man,* who appears more cringing and tormented than anything else. Most popular of all with tourists, who are always photographing themselves beside it, is a 1988 gift from Luxembourg by Carl Fredrik Reutersward: a great big handgun that's twisted into an ineffectual knot atop its pedestal. Its sixties pop art look seems more progressive than nostalgic here, because the rest of the U.N. is eternally cloaked in the atmosphere of the fifties, from its architectural style to the blond woods of its elevators and desks to its great splashy nonrepresentational paintings and tapestries.

WELCOME TO THE UNITED NATIONS! IT'S YOUR WORLD! says the sign for a wall of smiling Kodacolored faces of many lands and races. The U.N.'s tour begins with an explanation of the Organization's origins and the information that "the land of the U.N.," even though it was purchased with John D. Rockefeller Jr.'s money, "is not part of the USA." The Host Country is always a touchy subject, and while the tour starts by adhering to a bland moral equivalence — going past a photo of Reagan and Gorbachev shaking hands, and a kind of ballistic product map ("Nuclear Threat: Ominous Ratio of Warheads to People") — one quickly gets a sense of Who's Really to Blame. There are no fewer than six cases of artifacts (broken crockery, etc.) from Hiroshima and Nagasaki, as well as, from the latter, a radiated statue of Saint Agnes and her lamb. The front is undamaged because, less than two thousand feet from ground zero, it fell face forward at the moment of the blast; the back is charred and mottled. Before moving on from this unsettling display, the guide draws attention to the garden beyond the window. It contains the Peace Bell, a gift to the U.N. in 1954 — from Japan.

The "partial international character of the territory," explains another guide, is illustrated by occasional vexing situations like the American denial of a visa to Yasir Arafat, who wished to address the General Assembly. Whatever American legal rights might have been in this matter, she says, it was really not in keeping with the spirit of the U.N.-U.S. arrangement. When asked if there have been problems like this with anyone else, she comes up with one example, that of Kurt Waldheim, whose picture is still available on postcards in the U.N. bookshop.

The day I begin attending U.N. press briefings as an accredited correspondent is July 31, when word comes that Lieutenant Colonel William Higgins, the American hostage who was serving with U.N. forces in Lebanon, has been killed in retaliation for the Israelis' kidnapping of Sheik Obeid. More than fifty reporters listen to a spokesman for Javier Pérez de Cuéllar, the secretary-general, say that his boss "strongly hopes" Higgins is alive. But hope is followed by contingency mourning: "If the report can, however, be confirmed, the secretary-general can only express his outrage and revulsion."

Just back from Geneva, the SG, as he's usually called, will be having lunch with the Yugoslavian ambassador and will be getting an award as "personality of the year" from some group or other — a piece of news that makes two reporters near me look at each other and laugh. The briefing is a kind of hour-by-hour rundown of the SG's activities along with reports of twitching by the Organization's many acronymic tentacles: there's been an UNTAG report from Windhoek and a discussion of UNIFIL by the Security Council.

One quickly realizes that assignment to the U.N. is the media equivalent of being sent to the glue factory. None of the several dozen reporters is recognizable, except for Jeanne Moos of CNN, who seems to be doing temporary duty here instead of her usual featurettes on subjects like folding umbrellas and a New York woman's collection of pet rats. After the briefing I count thirty-four typewriters — manual Underwoods — in the press room. Only one is being used, by an Indian-looking gentleman. A woman covering the Security Council, which met this morning on the subject of hostage-taking, is on the telephone explaining to someone why she'll be unavailable to do something: "I'm sorry. This is the first thing that's happened in months." The U.N.'s slow season, when the General Assembly is not in session, generally lasts eight months, from January through August.

Still, the press room contains, in midsummer, rack after gunmetal-gray rack of press releases from the U.N.'s Department of Public Information and various individual missions. Correspondents walk along the racks each day and pick up sheet after sheet, automatically, like secretaries sleepwalking past an immense collating copy machine. "New Permanent Representative of Afghanistan Presents Credentials" — add it to your pile. The most important daily document is the *Journal of the United Nations* (*Journal des Nations Unies*), which announces meetings held and meetings scheduled, and which contains, in its equivalent of baseball box scores, a section titled "Signatures, Ratifications, Etc." There is good news on August 18: the "Convention on Prohibitions or Restrictions on the Use of Certain Conventional Weapons which may be Deemed to be Excessively Injurious or to Have Indiscriminate Effects (and Protocols), concluded at Geneva on 10 October 1980" has now been ratified by Liechtenstein.

As Jennifer Metzger points out in a paper for a recent conference, "Media and the U.N.": "Whereas most major newspapers, magazines and broadcast outlets once maintained full-time staff correspondents at the world body, today only the *New York Times* does so." But the press facilities themselves, like the rest of the U.N., retain their lost-in-the-fifties look. The press releases all have a mimeographed appearance: the words on them are snowy and pulverized.

The language of the U.N.'s Department of Public Information is a kind of sweetened Newspeak, a diction so abstract it soothes grammar to sleep. The United Nations Decade of Disabled Persons began in 1983, and correspondents are reminded that "the main goals of the World Programme of Action are prevention, rehabilitation and equalization of the opportunities for disabled persons." Does the World Programme really seek to prevent opportunities for the handicapped? Actually, meaning hardly matters if utterance is viewed as a noble end in itself. In her 1973 study of the U.N., *Defeat of an Ideal,* the writer Shirley Hazzard, who worked there for years, said that " 'productivity' is more often than not assessed in wordage," and that much U.N. documentation is "useless in two or three languages."

Perhaps all bureaucracies seek the stasis of perpetual motion, keep themselves going in order to keep going, but it is the United Nations that sets global standards for circularity. A press release issued on August 3, concerning the meetings in Geneva of the Working Group on Indigenous Populations, notes the following: "During the session, which will last until 4 August, the Group is expected to review developments pertaining to the promotion and protection of human rights and fundamental freedoms of indigenous populations and to give special attention to the evolution of standards concerning those rights." Carts precede horses in an endless parade of deferral. The SG's office on his receipt of the latest Central American peace proposal: "While awaiting reception of an official version of the document, the advanced text which he has seen is being studied in a preliminary fashion."

In terms of reflecting the Organization itself, the rhetoric of the Department of Public Information must be judged wholly appropriate, for it is the department's duty to relay, with zombie-like impartiality, both the meaningless — the king of Morocco has told the Conference on Disarmament of the "great responsibility to prevent the annihilation of humankind" — and the mendacious: "Cuba has no political prisoners," said the Cuban representative to the Committee on the Elimination of Racial Discrimination. "Prisoners were sentenced under the penal code and not for their political opinions. There were, however, counter-revolutionary prisoners who were involved in various subversive activities against the State."

On September 12 the secretary-general issued an advance version of his annual report, noting in the course of his *tour d'horizon* that "natural disasters are too frequently a cause of human loss, economic and social hardship." It was sometime later that month, during the week of Hurricane Hugo, that I began throwing away some of the United Nations documents that, after two months of frequenting the press room, were beginning to overrun my apartment.

"Where's Apartheid?" asks a man behind the information desk of his colleague.

"Trusteeship," answers the colleague, telling me where I'll find the 630th meeting of the Special Committee Against Apartheid.

The Trusteeship Council chamber is one of the U.N.'s many vast auditoria and conference rooms, and today, August 8, the gallery is nearly empty. Only a few reporters seem present, though some tourists wander in and out. I follow the tinny whisper of the translated proceedings through headphones attached below the armrests of the chairs. The acting chairman, Jai Pratap Rana of Nepal, who looks like a central-Asian Sam Nunn, listens as Ann-Marie Lizin, the secretary of state for Europe 1992 and a former member of the European Parliament, says that the "frontline" states in southern Africa have known only war and oppression and that "the search for genuine peace in the region" can be fulfilled only through the elimination of apartheid. She says that for three years colloquia have been held in Brussels on this topic, though "nothing has really changed." What is needed is "a refocusing of attention." Indeed, "what we need to do is attack the problem at its root." That it is impossible to keep attention focused on any topic if you meet to discuss it 630 times is not an insight that would be speakable here.

The chairman acknowledges Miss Lizin's speech with senatorial courtesies ("I thank her excellency . . . for her important statement"). The journalist who follows her, Miranda Ebenezer, a member of the African Women's Organization of Azania and of the Media Workers Association, then addresses Mr. Jai Pratap Rana as "Comrade Chairperson," before approvingly quoting Kwame Nkrumah and discussing the establishment of the African National Congress in 1912. She declares that "the settler regime" has "no rights"; that there "is no room for the imperialist, the colonizer, the capitalist"; and that in the struggle against apartheid, "African women have courageously taken the bull by the horns."

The woman next to me has closed her eyes. Some people on the delegates' floor not far from the place marked for Djibouti are talking loudly. The chairman thanks Miss Ebenezer "for her informative and important statement."

Three days later the Security Council meets at the request of Panama to discuss alleged U.S. violations of the canal treaty. The gallery is perhaps one-sixth full; the green metal chair backs are chipped, and the first couple of earphones I try are broken. Pérez de Cuéllar, who has the appearance of a well-meaning high school teacher too shy to confess his yearnings for retirement, sits next to the council's temporary president, Hocine Djoudi, from Algeria.

"Your country and mine have continued to enjoy cordial, productive relations," the deputy U.S. representative, Herbert Okun, says to the Algerian, before responding to the declaration by Jorge Ritter, Noriega's foreign minister ("The United States is running out of excuses, and the Panamanian people is running out of patience").

Mr. Okun is a calm droner, no Moynihan or Kirkpatrick. He points out that it is General Noriega who has violated the treaties, on nine hundred occasions, and that this meeting has been called to distract attention from the efforts of the Organization of American States to get him to surrender power.

Like the Panamanian people, I am soon running out of patience, and it occurs to me that one reason Pérez de Cuéllar reminds me of my old science teachers is that attending meetings at the U.N. has turned me back into something I haven't been since high school: a clock watcher. I retreat from the gallery to the press room, where a TV monitor shows the videotape the Panamanians have provided as evidence of U.S. violations. It contains shots of a helicopter, a police car, a couple of small boats, and a tank — all of them meaninglessly spliced together. The monitor now scans the representatives watching the video in the chamber. Two Chinese are laughing to each other. Even Pérez de Cuéllar and the Algerian can be seen smiling. But Jorge Ritter insists that these are "real" pictures, not done in a movie studio; furthermore, "there's a great deal more of this film." Jeanne Moos of CNN, sitting in front of the monitor with someone who asks her what she thinks the helicopter on the screen is supposed to signify, responds: "This must be the 'menacing maneuvers.' " In his only Moynihanian moment, Herbert Okun says that you can see worse on the streets of New York every day.

The Committee on the Exercise of the Inalienable Rights of the Palestinian People holds its 164th meeting in the chamber of the Economic and Social Council on August 15, which means that it is 466 meetings behind the Apartheid committee in grappling with its assigned enormities. A guide in the gallery tells tourists that the exposed beams and workings of this room (à la Beaubourg) were deliberately left as they are so that the room's unfinished look would serve "as a symbol" of all the work that the Economic and Social Council still has to do. The tours come in and out as the meeting assembles itself, but even though it's an "open" one, not a single member of the public has come to sit and watch it. It reminds me of a bad poetry reading at a college: perhaps they're delaying the start in the hope that people will show up. I look down from the gallery and see the goateed permanent observer of Palestine, Zuhdi Labib Terzi, whom I recognize from the neighborhood and from *Nightline*. The Cuban representative sits next to the one from Afghanistan. (Do they chat about the Soviets the way housewives talk about boorish husbands?)

The delay has actually been caused by the late arrival of Ronald Spiers, a U.S. diplomat for many years and now a U.N. undersecretary. He finally shows up, with a small entourage and a manila folder. Between the usual courtesies and his inexplicable reference to recent positive developments in the Middle East, he says his experience tells him that "externally derived" solutions for Palestine won't work, although things can be helped "by a fair wind from the international community."

That wind really begins to blow when the committee praises the work of the U.N.'s North American Regional NGO Symposium on the Question of Palestine, which was held in June. NGOs are "non-governmental organizations" that affiliate themselves with the U.N. in order to achieve solutions to such pressing problems as this one. Among the North American NGOs participating in that symposium were the National Lawyers' Guild, the American-Arab Anti-Discrimination Committee, American Jewish Alternatives to Zionism, and the Committee for Academic Freedom in the Israeli Occupied Territories. Yasir Arafat sent his regards. He was "delighted" they were meeting, as well he might have been, since the symposium's Resolution 2 was a rather witty series of calls for the United States to reduce its aid to Israel: first, by "an amount equal to the sum expended by Israel in maintaining its belligerent occupation of the West Bank and Gaza, including East Jerusalem"; second, "by an amount equal to the sum expended by Israel for settlement maintenance and expansion in the occupied territory" — and so on.

With this committee, as with the Special Committee on Decolonization, one quickly sees that the purpose is not the exchange and mediation of opinion, but its creation and manipulation — spreading the message, getting North Americans and Western Europeans to see it the U.N.'s way. It is announced that a Latin American and Caribbean Regional Seminar and NGO Symposium is going to be held in Buenos Aires, and an Asian version will take place in Malaysia later this year. Terzi thanks the government of Malaysia.

The next item on the agenda? Applications from new NGOs to participate in the committee's work. "More and more organizations," says the chairwoman, are applying to participate in symposia sponsored by the committee. "All these NGOs have been screened . . . and the bureau recommends them for approval." There's another symposium in Vienna in August. She's also accepted an invitation to represent the committee at the Non-Aligned Summit in Belgrade in September. And she's "accepted in principle" an invitation for a representative of the committee to go to the Presidium of the Soviet Committee of Solidarity with African and Asian Countries in 1990.

Actually, the real purpose of these meetings is not so much the manipulation of opinion as the assurance of other meetings, just as the real purpose of U.N. reports is that they be written. Ambassador Terzi praises one on the violation of human rights in the occupied territories, saying that it is "worthy of becoming a document" within the committee's larger report.

The United Nations is so involved with death — that is, of the intellectual and moral variety — that with the word "séance," which the U.N. uses as its synonym for "meeting," French seems less like the language of diplomacy than of bluntness. If the U.N. had a school song, it wouldn't be "Kumbaya" or "It's a Small World After All"; it would be "We're Here Because We're Here Because We're Here." On August 24, in order to review the 1979 Vienna Programme of Action, the 97th meeting of the Intergovernmental Committee on Science and Technology for Development took place in conference room 4, which is in fact a vast hall. The participants were scattered like distantly planted shrubs to listen to the Hungarian representative say that "what is essential is for the Intergovernmental Committee never to tire of examining the influence of science and technology on development"; that "programs of a comprehensive nature" must be developed; that these programs must be "monitored" and "coordinated"; and that, in conclusion, "the various programs must be interrelated." We must, in short, "do something; not leave it in the merely theoretical realm," even though "there is no such thing as instant success and easy solutions."

Mr. Alistair Harrison of the United Kingdom had the day before put a little Thatcherite oomph into the proceedings, declaring, as the subsequent U.N. press release put it, that "the Committee had been founded on the myth that problems could be solved simply by declaring a programme of action and preceding it with the name of a well-known city. The vacuousness of such an approach was all too evident ten years later." His statement should have been nothing more than agreeably self-evident, but for the United Nations it bordered on the electrifying. Rhetorical norms were soon restored, however, and three weeks later, at a conference of NGOs on the relationship between environment and development, held in this same room, Robert Savio, the director-general of Inter-Press Service Third World News Agency, would speak to a large audience on the difference between information and communication. Information is a vertical structure; communication is not. He would also consider whether environment "is an event or a process."

After weeks of listening to it, one realizes that such talk isn't meaningless or amusing, but evil. The denial of reality it involves is so total that it has led to a kind of final irony for the United Nations: that it has become a world unto itself, a small clean space colony of frozen bodies sent up to escape a dying planet. Unable to remake the real world, the inhabitants of the U.N. have seceded into a toy one.

Here in Turtle Bay, a corner of Dag Hammarskjold Plaza on East 47th Street has for months now been occupied by Chinese students and rechristened Tiananmen Square. In their very polite way, they ask residents of the neighborhood who are running errands along First Avenue to sign their petitions. (Their two portable toilets are gently labeled S--T and P-E.) Along with the petitions there have been videos of the massacres, as well as signs saying HANG LI PENG! and — a borrowing from the left — PEOPLE UNITED WILL NEVER BE DEFEATED.

On seven successive Saturdays this summer there were services to honor the dead students of Peking. At a Buddhist ceremony late in July, New York politicians like Representative Bill Green and Ronald Lauder bellied up to a small altar hung with black crepe and set out with flowers and fruit. Passing out black armbands and incense sticks, the demonstrators were organized, neat, and smiling — enough to make one think that if American students had behaved this way twenty years ago, their parents would have stopped the Vietnam War out of gratitude for their children's manners. A Japanese tourist bus passed as a Buddhist monk in a saffron robe got ready for the ceremony, which included chanting and the beating of a small hand drum. A man not wishing to be photographed, wearing a white plastic bag over his head (with a smile-button face printed upside down on the back), was led by a woman to the altar to pay his respects. Speeches followed the ceremony, one of them urging Americans to stop doing business with China until the executions stop. With the kind of realism one almost never hears uttered across the street, one speaker reminded potential boycotters that "in the long run you will have the support of one billion Chinese consumers."

"Tiananmen Square" has had a distinctly anti-U.N. flavor: U.N. WHAT CAN YOU DO FOR THE WORLD? SHAME ON U.N., read one sign. There is no mention of the Chinese situation in the secretary-general's annual report, and it is not at all certain it will get on any important U.N. agenda. That it has managed to come up at a meeting of the Subcommittee on Human Rights in Geneva — a fact recently pointed out by U.S. Ambassador

Thomas Pickering in a generally encouraged assessment of the U.N. — is hardly inspiring.

The United Nations concerns itself with only a handful of available evils, chief among them apartheid. A press release of August 9 shows Iceland seeking a clean bill of health from the Racial Discrimination Committee by stating it has no diplomatic relations with South Africa. When the Special Committee Against Apartheid deplores a planned trip to South Africa by some British cricketers, this makes the "Friday Highlights" sheet from the Department of Public Information. The General Assembly is largely made up of dictatorships, but what one cannot do in the U.N. is speak in relative terms. Only a pariah like Israel does that. Without relative thinking there can be no debate, and finally no morality, just a succession of madly absolute statements, but what the United Nations will not admit is the existence of our vicious world of pots and kettles. Indonesia talks of the South African "reign of terror" in Namibia, but it would be impertinent to mention Indonesia's own domestic slaughters of the 1960s. What happens is that the genuine evil of apartheid ends up being tamed by its own enshrinement. Czechoslovakia worries to the Decolonization Committee that "information on the options available to the peoples of small territories [is] not being provided nor [are] all administering Powers promoting the economic development of their territories in preparation for independence." One wonders: would he like those same materials more widely distributed in, say, Czechoslovakia, in case it is ever decolonized by the Soviet Union and given a chance for economic development? But it would be rude to ask.

The General Assembly's huge hall is ringed with vertical beams resembling the pipes of an immense organ. The last meeting of the 43rd session takes place on Monday, September 18, and is a bit of a parliamentary fiction. Insofar as anything at the U.N. is real, the General Assembly had its last real meeting in July, after convening on fewer than a dozen days since the previous December. But now, one day before the 44th session opens, the 43rd must close itself out by agreeing to carry certain items from the previous agenda (like Israeli aggression against Iraq) over to the next one. Still, this meeting provides an opportunity for the U.N. to proclaim its own relevance, something it does with surprising confidence and frequency these days. The outgoing General Assembly president, an Argentine, stoutly declares that "this, more than any other time, is the time for the United Nations." In "the post–Cold War world" of today, the U.N. has "demonstrated its efficiency." (The 1988 Nobel Peace Prize to the U.N. Peacekeeping Forces is the Organization's chief point of pride.) Pérez de Cuéllar, in his annual report, took similar note of the "conciliatory atmosphere around the world" as a nourishing one for the U.N. The superpower thaw is thought to be good for business. (That the INF treaty he extols on page 14 was the result of American willingness to play bilateral nuclear chess is another point that could never be acknowledged.) A prisoner of the U.N.'s inflated language, the SG even oversells the idea of trying not to oversell the U.N., saying there must continue to be a "rigorous analysis" of its limitations and "constant review" of its peacekeeping methods.

The U.N.'s supposed new usefulness is a theme now being echoed by the United States. At an editors' breakfast sponsored by the United Nations Association (with the Department of Public Information's cooperation) on the day the 44th General Assembly opens, Ambassador Pickering says that name-calling at the U.N. has "diminished markedly," maybe 1,000 percent in recent years, and that reductions of the bloated Secretariat staff are under way: the goal is to cut it by 15 percent. A man who looks bland and paunchy sitting down but formidable when on his feet, Pickering, who was U.S. ambassador to Israel and to El Salvador, is also, rhetorically, no Kirkpatrick or Moynihan. But their eras, when the U.S. *was* briefly willing to speak in relative terms, are in the past. The administration of George

Bush, a former U.N. ambassador himself, has decided to play nice. It "strongly welcomes" the U.N. observers for upcoming elections in Nicaragua, for example.

The U.N. is clearly happy with the change of heart, because more than anyone else it is still the United States that — to paraphrase Ronald Reagan — is paying for the microphone. The administration has asked for full funding of U.S. assessments this year, and is also asking Congress to appropriate our "arrearages," the money held back by the Reagan administration in more contentious times. Another reason the U.N. is glad of the rapprochement is temperamental: as Shirley Hazzard has said, the Organization demands "a bedside manner from the world." It simply hates being criticized, even by the oafish United States. One notices how François Giuliani, the SG's spokesman, and other Secretariat people will respond to simple questions as affronts, as if any inquisitiveness necessarily betokens bad faith.

Thérèse Paquet-Sevigny, the under-secretary-general for public information, follows Ambassador Pickering at the editors' breakfast. An energetic Canadian who wears a black pleated skirt and smokes little cigars, she seems yet one more throwback to the 1950s, an appealing one. She says the U.N. places "such great value on U.S. opinion" not only because of the size of the American financial contribution, but because of U.S. values, too. During the past several weeks, this is the only time I have heard American values praised in the United Nations, and it comes as something of a shock. But Miss Paquet-Sevigny's business is public relations. Her office watches a lot of polling, and she is pleased to report that the U.N. has rebounded from a 1985 low point, when 54 percent of Americans thought it was doing a poor job, to the mere 29 percent who think that's the case now. Unfortunately, most Americans just don't know either way, and "an enormous effort" is required to explain the U.N.'s role to them.

If the U.N. does require a bedside manner, the United Nations Association, which was headed for a number of years by

Elliot Richardson, is its most solicitous hand-holder. UNA-USA, which according to one pamphlet seeks to make the U.N. "even more effective," is represented at this morning's breakfast by John Tessitore, a slightly pudgy, gold-wire-rimmed fellow resembling an assistant professor who won't get tenure. He says he's "not here to sell" the U.N., "wonderful product" though it is. Rather, the UNA wishes to use "candor" and admit the Organization's weaknesses along with its strengths.

As it turns out, a number of the speakers laid on for the editors throughout the day display the same testy defensiveness as the SG's spokesman. In the panel "Human Rights and the U.N.," Bertie Ramcharan, a principal officer of the Secretariat, speaks of the six components of the "human rights infrastructure" and the five "building blocks" for dealing with human rights violations, though he seems less than eager when asked to quantify instances where U.N. intervention has really made a difference to someone's human rights. Felice Gaer, executive director of the International League for Human Rights, tells what she thinks is the sadly amusing story of one media organization based in Paris that sent its *wine critic* to cover a Geneva meeting at which the Afghans would be directly questioned about human rights violations. Afterward, no story ever ran. When asked why, the reporter explained that nothing happened after the questioning — no vote, no action, nothing. Of course, it was the wine critic and not Miss Gaer who got the point, but this is the sort of story that makes UNA people shake their heads with the self-satisfaction of the uselessly well intentioned.

Jean-Claude Faby, deputy director, U.N. Environment Program, New York Liaison Office, is actually impressive in his own *tour d'horizon* of global concerns, but he too has the U.N. disease, noting with pleasure that Shevardnadze now devotes five pages of some speech, instead of five lines, to environmental matters. Similarly sympathetic is James P. Grant, the head of UNICEF, who has the craggy good looks and gravelly voice of the actor Hal Holbrook. In talking about his group's dependence on voluntary contributions and fund-raising, he notes that, while still much less than those from the United States, Soviet contributions are now twelve times what they were not long ago. Unfortunately, he adds, they come in rubles, which are supposed to be used to buy Soviet supplies, and in these days of perestroika, a lot of Soviet suppliers won't accept rubles. So UNICEF is trying to get the Soviets to make their contributions in convertible currency. As Mr. Grant is introduced, we learn that forty thousand children die every twenty-four hours from hunger and disease — "a Hiroshima every three days." Mr. Grant is the luncheon speaker, and we learn this while we're drinking wine, eating portions of chicken twice as big as anyone needs, and awaiting a heavy dessert.

The UNA-sponsored day moves slowly along as clouds roll over the East River and the landscape of northwest Queens, whose church spires, smokestacks, and water towers have scarcely ever looked more inviting. The second-to-last speaker, on the subject "Global Hotspots," is Giandomenico Picco, the SG's special assistant, who talks about the U.N.-sponsored Iran-Iraq cease-fire and sees a "renaissance of the U.N." now that unilateralism's failure is recognized. "Multilateralism" is the good word at the U.N., but one suspects that the Iran-Iraq cease-fire was really a triumph of bilateralism — the mutual exhaustion, after eight years and one million deaths, of Iran and Iraq. Mr. Picco says that once you take a side in a dispute you are introducing power, not peace. What he does not mention is what one always learned about the U.N. in elementary school, that what was supposed to distinguish it from the paralyzed League of Nations was precisely its ability to introduce power — its own — into disputes.* The official U.N. tour does not stop at the plaque in the lobby put up "in grateful remembrance of the Armed Force of Member States who died in Korea in the Service of the United Nations 1950–1953."

---

*It should be noted that Mr. Picco did useful work in helping secure the release of American hostages from the Middle East in 1991. Whether the U.N.'s general cravenness in dealing with terrorist states didn't perhaps contribute to the *taking* of many hostages over the years remains a subject worth considering.

Finally Hedi Annabi, the special assistant to the special representative of the secretary-general, Humanitarian Affairs South-East Asia, discusses, somewhat bewilderingly, how the Cambodian peace conference that collapsed in Paris last August was, in fact, a partial success. Keith Burris of the *Hartford Courant,* sitting next to me, whispers an explanation of what the parties accomplished: "They've agreed on rebuilding the country after they have the next civil war."

The 44th General Assembly has elected Joseph Nanven Garba of Nigeria to be its president. Looking down from the topmost gallery on this opening day, one can see the nameplates for countries one's never even heard of. (Myanmar turns out to be the new name for Burma.) The delegates sit behind shiny, lime-colored tabletops as an Austrian is elected president of the Sixth, or Legal, Committee, even though the U.N.'s recent experience with Austria has been more on the criminal side of things. Costa Rica's three seats are occupied by women in bright clothes: two are in yellow tops and another is in black and white swirls. One watches things like this because the proceedings themselves are impossible, though not difficult, to follow. George Orwell came to realize that his public school was "a world where it was *not possible* for [him] to be good," and by now I have realized that the United Nations is a world in which it is not possible to pay attention. The vice presidents of the General Assembly are being elected, and Yemen has "gracefully yielded" its candidature to Iraq. The representative of Bahrain praises Yemen by saying, "A friend in need is a friend indeed," noting that the prophet Mohammed said Yemen is the land of wisdom.

There are 155 items on the General Assembly's agenda this fall, ranging from the eternal (Palestine, apartheid) to the obscure ("Question of the Comorian island of Mayotte") to the purely rhetorical ("Declaration of the Assembly of Heads of State and Government of the Organization of African Unity on the aerial and naval military attack against the Socialist People's

Libyan Arab Jamahiriya by the present [*sic*] United States Administration in April 1986").

But before these items can be discussed, there are the weeks of speeches by heads of state and foreign ministers. Historic utterances (by the new Polish foreign minister, for example) capture more attention here than they might in another venue. But in the world of one-nation, one-vote, the U.N. is seen putting ministers from Fiji, Cape Verde, and Luxembourg under the same spotlight for the same number of minutes. On September 29, Dr. Virgilio Barco Vargas, president of Colombia, receives a standing ovation, mostly for having managed to finish his speech without being assassinated by the Medellín drug cartel.

In a northwest corner of the General Assembly Building the Meditation Room is open to visitors. It seems a place designed more to frighten than soothe, a small stone-floored trapezoid, by my measure fifteen paces by seven at its widest points. An abstract fresco is at the narrow end, and in the back are eleven small benches with straw seats. It is dark in here. A small single bulb in the center of the ceiling bathes a block of naked stone — like a denuded altar — in weak light. Sitting down in back, one has the feeling of being in a ransacked chapel, a place with no clear sign of what to pray to, a place so determinedly universal as to be unreal, like the United Nations itself, which, in its attempt to create one world, ultimately reminds one of those apparently bogus experiments in "cold fusion" — room-temperature panaceas produced on the cheap and, finally, against the laws of nature. We live, after all, in an age marked less by recombination than by an ever greater provincialism. From Quebec to Eritrea, the world, as it becomes ever smaller, wishes to be ever more local. Indeed, one of the Léger murals in the General Assembly hall looks like an amoeba quivering in the struggle to divide. The totemless Meditation Room is the Stonehenge of an era whose hopes never came to pass because it couldn't get people to hope them. After two months at the

United Nations I have seen the past — and it still doesn't work. More than anything, the Meditation Room is a relief from the endlessly verbose Organization itself, providing as it does a chance to sit and follow the instructions on a sign near its entrance, a sign announcing that you have arrived, at last, at a place where "only thoughts should speak."

POSTSCRIPT

The juxtaposition of these two pieces may not be as odd as it seems. If one accepts the bombing of Pearl Harbor as being, in Thurston Clarke's words, "a day that more than any other determined the shape of the next fifty years," it becomes a bookend whose mate is probably the lowering of the hammer and sickle from the Kremlin's flagpole on Christmas Day, 1991. "The People Next Door" was written during the summer of 1989 and as such is already a museum piece, a record of the old bilateral world in the last few minutes of its fifth act. Before it was off the newsstands, the Berlin Wall had come down and the Ceausescus lay riddled with bullets.

The United Nations, inevitably reactive, changed too, and the hopes that it can do some good in a more truthful, less terrified, world are predictably high. "There is an embarrassment of possibilities before him at the moment," said the UNA's head, Edward C. Luck, of the new secretary-general, Boutros Boutros-Ghali, who took office the day after the Soviet Union officially closed shop. In an un-Orwellian world, the United Nations I wrote about, a sort of underwater place, frightening in its unreality, can no longer function as it did. Perhaps it will become useful, though it is much more likely to continue to reflect the world — at the moment, the Pax Americana — than to shape it.

I still live in Turtle Bay, a neighborhood that was a virtual armed camp during the first days of the Persian Gulf War in early 1991. One reason for all the police was that the U.N., having passed a resolution empowering the Allies to use force against Iraq, had ceased to be merely the backdrop for demonstrations and become instead the target of some of them. I can think of no more hopeful sign for it.

Amusements

They Chute Horses

American musical memory knows there was a time when an Oklahoman had to travel up to Kansas City if he wanted to walk to privies in the rain and never wet his feet. By January 1990 things had progressed to the point where he could spend a week at the rodeo without venturing outdoors between his hotel room and an arena with fewer odors than any privy ever had: a "skywalk" connects the downtown Doubletree Hotel to the Tulsa Convention Center, in which the Twentieth International Finals Rodeo was being held atop three thousand cubic yards of trucked-in dirt, whose lower sandy layer succeeded in absorbing the smells.

But if IFR 20 was deodorized, it was not entirely deracinated, as almost any ride in one of the Doubletree's elevators could remind one. One afternoon, as the car came to a gentle stop, a cowboy and his girlfriend let out a steadying *whoa* and laughed about how their insides were flopping, and on Saturday night, on his way to compete in the penultimate calf-roping round, Ken Bailey, number 46, could be heard to exclaim, when the car stopped a floor above the lobby, "One stop's enough for me!" In another two hours Ken would be jumping off his speeding horse, Slick, to rope a calf in 8.7 seconds and tie for second-fastest time of the night.

Fans of the IFR, whose cowboys ride a circuit of over three hundred competitions sanctioned by the International Professional Rodeo Association (IPRA), will tell you it's more real, if less old and rich, than the National Finals held by the Professional Rodeo Cowboys Association each year in Las Vegas. The PRCA evolved over decades and awards a lot of five-figure prizes, but since it moved from Oklahoma City to Las Vegas four years ago, it's been overwhelmed by the Strip. "They start the sessions at seven so everybody can get out early enough to get to the shows and casinos," says Dayna Cravens, who does publicity for the IPRA and whose father, J. O. Cravens, a former bull rider, is its president.

In its twentieth year, the IFR seemed to be literally a step behind its competitor. As the finals were beginning in Tulsa, the city's papers were full of rumors that this would be the last time before the event moved itself and its twenty-five thousand ticket sales to — Oklahoma City. J. O. Cravens complained of a lack of political and business support, but wouldn't say yes or no about moving as the rodeo opened on Thursday, January 18. So over the next several days, along with the fortunes of hometown favorites like barrel racer Connie Cooper and saddle-bronc rider Justin Rowe, Tulsans were following this other drama, wondering if the city would have its confidence, just mending after the oil glut of the 1980s, given a small new shake. Jay Cronley, a columnist in the *Tribune,* said that Tulsa had every hosting advantage over Oklahoma City except the "leadership" needed to keep the IFR from leaving: "You want to live in a small town . . . ? Stick around."

At night around the Convention Center it was easy to get the feeling one already was living in a small town. The downtown blocks, some of them malled over and gentrified a decade or so ago, were now deserted with a kind of neutron-bombed thoroughness. Patrons of the Doubletree exchanged restaurant discoveries in a fundamental way: if you came upon any restaurant open at night, that was news good enough to pass on, never mind the quality of the food. Tulsa is a city of suburbs, and the IFR seemed properly unsure how long it could expect patrons to find their way to a downtown arena that might best be described, in the words of a friend, as centrally isolated.

But if on opening night Tulsa's hold on the IFR seems tenuous, there is no doubting the larger loyalties of the crowd. When Miss Rodeo USA 1989, Lisa Watson of Elmore City, Oklahoma, rides out upon a white horse, carrying the American flag, thousands of cowboy hats go over thousands of hearts. "The Battle Hymn of the Republic" seems a generous choice of an opening song for a rodeo association including so many cowboys from the Confederate states, but it is quickly followed by "This Is My Country," as Lisa is ridden 'round by a circle of flag-carrying attendants in a spectacle that should be grotesque but is instead eerily beautiful: the other women canter, their flags flying in near darkness around Lisa, who is bathed in a white spotlight and gorgeous in the manner of that string of southern Miss Americas from the 1950s.

It is hard to imagine a sports crowd displaying more genuine involvement in an event's patriotic preliminaries. One fears for one's ears, not to mention the horses' ability to stand their ground, during Miss Candi Todd's worst-ever *a cappella* rendition of "The Star-Spangled Banner," but the heart soars again when someone has the nostalgic wit to play — as they will on each of the following three nights — a vintage recording of "God Bless America." Careful equine choreography gives Lisa, left in solitary splendor toward the close, an opportunity to gallop all the way across the arena and disappear through the gate just as Kate Smith hits her final "home."

With lights back up, and hats back on, the flags of states and sponsors begin whirling by, each of their carriers galloping a single furious circuit, seeming to lack nothing but gray tunics and cavalry bugles. The banner of the cowboy chapter of the Fellowship of Christian Athletes takes precedence, followed by the flags of Canada (which sends one contestant) and twenty-seven states. The announcers try to kindle pockets of alphabetical enthusiasm by shouting out state nicknames that might be vaguely recalled from grade school, and the almost impolite hush that greets the flag of New York is probably attributable more to remoteness than hostility. The banner of the Acme Boot Company, sponsor of the Miss Rodeo USA pageant — another contest to be decided this week — brings to their feet the seventeen local queens vying to be Lisa Watson's successor. Miss Johnson Ford Rodeo has come from Sturgis, South Dakota, and Miss WZPR Rodeo, jointly sponsored by Jay's Auto Wrecking Service, is here from Edinboro, Pennsylvania.

The crowd is not entirely local either. Forty-seven percent of it, the paper says, comes from at least forty miles away. On Friday and Saturday nights the stands will seem a little more suburban, but on this weekday opening the hats and jeans seem more like work clothes than going-out drag. Their wearers look over the parading 1988 world champions, give one more salute to Lisa, and are ready for action on what Jerry Todd (Candi's husband) has proclaimed, from the announcer's booth, "the roughest playing field in America."

Rodeo is probably the most compulsively announced sport in the world. The spectator is never out from under an amplified waterfall of statistics (Captain Crunch, a bull, is "unridden" in his last twenty-one outings), jokes, and sentiment. At each session after the first, the announcers do an endless recitation of the previous one's times and scores and places, though all of this information is easily available in the patron's newspaper or program. IFR 20 requires two announcers, Jerry Todd for the timed events and Danny Newland, a former saddle-bronc rider, for the "rough stock" competitions like bareback and bull riding. Rodeo announcers are typically the subject of newspaper profiles, program feature articles, and a level of fan awareness unexperienced by the off-television commentators of any other sport. Danny Newland's battle with Hodgkin's disease and his off-season career as a high school teacher of agriculture are written up as prominently as any stories about the competitors themselves. *Rain or Shine,* Cyra McFadden's fine family memoir, tells the story of her father, Cy Taillon, the "Dean of Rodeo Announcers": "It's still difficult to pay for a drink, in a Western bar, if your last name is or once was Taillon." Cy's own life's journey from "rakehell" to respectability ran parallel to the evolution of his sport. Before Taillon began working in the 1930s,

> rodeo was used to announcers who treated the sport as a Wild West show, part vaudeville, part circus. Cy dignified it, with his ten-dollar words, his impeccably tailored, expensive suits and his insistence that the cowboys were professional athletes. When he intoned 'Ladies and gentlemen,' women became ladies and men became gentlemen; the silver-tongued devil in the announcer's box, as often as not a rickety structure over the chutes and open to the rain, spoke with unmistakable authority.

For all Danny Newland's rodeo lore and info — young southerners tend to get interested in bull riding, Canadians in saddle broncs — his voice is a little nasal, like a TV pitchman's. Jerry Todd, from behind the see-through plastic bunting, seems more in Taillon's line of baritoned professional dignity. He may bring out the same one-liners nearly every night ("UPS couldn't have wrapped him up any better!"; "Triple A, eat your heart out!"), but he consistently directs his listeners' attention to the theme of cowboy effort. Contestants are said to be "working" for the crowd, not performing, and when Mike Pharr from Georgia lands out of the money after missing a calf-roping throw, the fans are reminded to pay him off anyway: "The only thing he'll take with him tonight is what you give him, so be generous with the applause." (Cyra McFadden says that this instruction to the crowd originated with Cy Taillon.) Todd imagines the gloom among two teammates who miss entirely and get a no-time — "I wouldn't want to be in that room tonight" — and when the crowd is distracted by a decidedly uncharacteristic fistfight in the stands, it is reminded to watch the chutes and not "the idiots in the stands," an injunction that brings on applause.

How, one wonders, does a rider trying to stay, for eight

seconds, on an angry, bucking horse, trying to earn a purse and keep his spinal cord whole, manage to concentrate amidst the poorly timed burst of band music for him and the announcer's voice, which as the horse charges out of the chute may still be pitching straight lines to the clown or be in mid-anecdote about some other cowboy? In fact, the riders claim not to notice any of it. As I was told before round five by Steve Danylo, western region bareback-riding winner, "You're so into yourself and what you're gonna do."

What they're going to do is wait for any clatter in the chute to die, see the rope let go, and then experience an eight-second chiropractic catastrophe.

Some rodeo experts will stress the toll taken not on the back but on the single arm permitted to hold the rigging. If with his free hand the cowboy touches either the horse or himself, he's disqualified. It's that free hand, flying out and up as the horse bucks into the arena, that a spectator's gaze is drawn to. The gesture it makes seems to say, simultaneously, "I'm okay" and "I'm going down, help me." The eight seconds look more like an electrocution than a ride, and even after a successful one the plaintiveness of the waving arm is magnified by the most curiously poignant moment in rodeo, when the dismounting rider throws himself onto the body and horse of a pickup rider. The strangest aspect of the event, and it's the same with saddle-bronc and bull rides, is that even the highest-scoring cowboys, ones who have gone the distance firm in the saddle, appear to be getting rescued.

Whatever the outcome there is little time for pride or wound licking, and certainly, not ever, any McEnrovian tantrums. On Friday night Troy Smithson of Spring Hill, Tennessee, is badly thrown, enough to make one of the clowns go to his rescue. But the next rider is already out of the chute before Smithson can be brought off the field. At the IFR Trade Show a browser finds not only saddles and boots and trucks and buckles, but also a display of Niagara lounge chairs from Joplin, Missouri, "official therapy equipment of the 1980 and 1984 Olympics," relieving muscle spasms and back pain with Radiant Heat and the Rolla-ssage System.

The winner of each bareback-riding round takes a victory lap, and over several nights a few of the leaders develop a modest celebrity. A second Troy, Troy Eaton of Bouton, Iowa, has the unthreateningly pretty looks of a bubble-gum rock star, and during his second victory lap, on Friday, the announcer shouts, "Mamas, grab your daughters!" But remoteness does not seem to follow rising popularity. A fan can go out to the concession stands ringing the arena, and cowboys who've just had a big round will be there drinking beer with everybody else. They're "working" for you, and this is their break.

By the time the steer wrestling begins, a front-row spectator will be used to the particular discomforts of his position: horses slamming into the metal bars in front of his face, clods of dirt striking him on the nose. These are minor matters compared to what the steer wrestlers go through in an event that makes Jerry Todd's talk about working seem close to the literal truth. Twisting a steer's neck until he's down on the ground is hard, sweaty labor. The cowboy seems to be struggling less with a big living creature than with an immense boiler valve. A good time will average about five seconds, but as with most hard jobs, it some-times takes longer than you expect. On Thursday night Jimmy Dale Wisdom walks away tired and disgusted after making an 11.6. The following night Jack Wiseman, a sentimental favorite from Krebs, Oklahoma, who's qualified for all twenty IFRs ("Two generations have seen this cowboy!"), gets pinned to the ground by an upside-down steer but persists for 17.4 seconds. "A lot of men would've given up," says Todd, but Wiseman will prove smart to have stuck with it. He finishes way out of the money in this second go-round, but it's better to have a 17.4 than a no-time factored into your total for the rodeo if you want to preserve a chance of winning the five-round average — which is what Wiseman will have accomplished by Sunday afternoon.

Steer wrestlers tend toward the solid and stocky. They don't have the stringy look of the cowboy stereotype. They're bigger than the rough-stock riders, who, while hardly jockey-sized, usually have the average trim build of the first astronauts, whose vehicles couldn't accommodate six-footers. But even the big-boned ruggedness of the steer wrestlers is giving way to some modern polish. "We've got some pretty smart cowboys," says Todd, referring to Shawn David of McCloud, Oklahoma, who's come out of collegiate rodeo and holds a degree in business.

If any rodeo event can appeal to products of modern education and technocracy, it is probably team roping. Though a timed competition where good scores average around six or seven seconds, this seems the most leisurely of all the events, a matter of balletic precision and teamwork, not brute strength and single combat. The "header" must take the steer by the horns with any of the three approved head catches (figure eights are not allowed), and then the "heeler" goes for the feet. The crowd seems appreciative of the skills displayed, but Todd's assertion that this has become rodeo's most popular event seems a gross overstatement. Tom Bourne of Marietta, Georgia, was the IPRA's 1988 Rookie of the Year, and is touted for his blond good looks ("the blue-eyed wonder!") in the manner of Troy Eaton, but this is not an event that excites the crowd much. (Almost nothing, it might be noted, brings rodeo fans to their feet. Even the most harrowing bull ride going on at a far end of the arena is performed for fans who are shouting and sitting.) Team roping has been around for a long time, but the event wasn't even added to the Sitting Bull Stampede up in Mobridge, South Dakota, until 1984. It may promise too much longevity to its competitors. Saddle-bronc riders last longer than bareback ones, and team ropers can go on much longer still. Team roping is the golf of rodeo.

Rodeo humor is a matter of strictly regulated convention. A clown roams inactive patches of the arena at almost all times, chatting up sections of the crowd between exchanges with the announcer. Cliff ("Hollywood") Harris is IFR 20's funnyman, and the jokes run to the Hee-Hawish: baldness, Preparation H, swishy walking behind a saddle-bronc rider who's just dismounted. Between bursts of bull riding, Hollywood tells Danny Newland that he named his four kids Eenie, Meenie, Miney, and Fred, because he didn't want no mo'. Each night Newland asks him how he feels — the cue for someone to start a tape of James Brown's "I Feel Good," so Hollywood can drop his pants and gyrate in frilly pink underwear.

The crowd expects and gets a precisely formulaic mix of cowardice and bravado: the clown cowers, but imputes effeminacy to the hyper-macho cowboys; he quavers, but quite bravely allows the bull to charge the little barrel he hides in, a one-man shelter reminiscent of a jar in the *Arabian Nights* or an air-raid manhole in Hanoi. Although removed from all the cowboy exertion and animal anger in the ring, Hollywood Harris is not so much a foil to those things as an extension of the audience, an Everyman caught on the wrong side of the bars.

Between the steer wrestling and bull riding, Brother Taylor, the main comedy act this year, alternates his "Government Trapper" and "Matador" routines, each of which leads up to his doing battle with a small dog dressed up as a skunk or bull. Married to a trick rider and himself a former rodeo contestant, Brother Taylor delivers acts that, according to the program, are "family-oriented and keep all ages entertained." The bits are so bad that they generate more laughter each time one sees them, the elements of the cornball cocktail — Taylor's audacity and your own indulgence — growing stronger with each performance.

"Like most government jobs, that was a stinker": this comment from the announcer, after the "Government Trapper" meets up with the skunk, is the only Reaganesque political moment of IFR 20. The kind of solidarity the crowd is worked into has less to do with ideology than with regionalism and way of life. The intermission music goes a little way toward this with numbers like "San Antonio Rose" and "Don't Call Him a Cowboy Until You've Seen Him Ride," which warns people from

New York City that the guy they think is a cowboy may have had his toughest ride in a foreign car. But there's not much musical will to fight homogenization: the themes from *Bonanza* and *Rawhide* are recognizable to anyone in the crowd over thirty, irrespective of geography, and at one point the band resorts to a zippy westernized version of "Frère Jacques." The only musical joke, played before the start of each go-round, is what seems at first, inexplicably, just an old Engelbert Humperdinck number, until — ah, got it: "Release Me."

Aside from Brother Taylor and Hollywood Harris, the only noncompetitive entertainment is provided by S. L. Pemberton, a twenty-one-year-old Roman rider from Tennessee. "Isn't that a pretty sight?" the announcer asks, and it is. Skinny S.L. is a child's fantasy, standing on two horses with another two trotting in front of those, wearing satiny red white and blue, delighting the crowd as his whole team jumps hurdles, together, like the long sine curve of a slow-flying lariat.

After the bareback riding, the Miss Rodeo USA contestants, looking more Bob Mackie than Kitty Wells, line up for a much-complimented appearance. For the next hour or so, until after intermission, spectators will see, aside from a female photographer, only one woman on the field, and that's the wife of Rick Chaffin, a steer wrestler. She acts as his "hazer," racing along on the other side of the steer from the one he's going after, making the animal run in a straight line so the wrestler can get a clean throw of his rope before jumping off his horse to take the animal by the horns. From that point on, spectators have to wait until the cowgirls' barrel racing to see the combination of "fast horses and beautiful women," as Jerry Todd puts it, the first time one's heard the phrase unreversed in a joke-listening lifetime.

Done well, barrel racing is fast, precise, and satisfying to watch. The rider gallops out of the gate, and then she and her horse do hairpin turns around three barrels (oil drums painted red white and blue) set up like a baseball diamond. The barrel occupying the second-base spot is the last one she has to round before charging back to the gate. Times usually fall between fourteen and fifteen seconds and are carried to three decimals on the stopwatch. Knocking down any barrel means a five-second penalty, though the rider is allowed to brush and wobble them in the manner of ski slaloming.

"I want you to make some noise!" shouts Jerry Todd. "She makes the turn, you make some noise!" Listening to this frequent, insistent encouragement, beyond anything asked for the working cowboys, one wonders if this isn't mostly condescension, a little something for the little ladies. There's some truth in that, but the prodding also has a practical side. The louder the audience cheers, the faster the horse will run. If the audience yells about equally for each cowgirl, the playing field stays relatively even.

It's the only elegant event in rodeo, the only one where the competitors' facial expressions seem readable for meaning. Unlike in the rough-stock competitions, the contestant here doesn't draw a horse by lot. She trains and travels with her own animal: Connie Cooper and her two horses, Saw Bucks and Baby Bucks, have gone seventy thousand miles through twenty-one states between the last IFR and this one. The training of the horse is particular and problematic. Dayna Cravens does some barrel racing but, she tells me, the new horse she's working with doesn't really get it yet. On Friday night when Tracy Postrach's horse messes up, you can see her give the animal an angry whack with her crop when she gets it back through the gate. "She's not a happy camper," says Todd, from his announcing booth directly above.

Tracy Postrach gets the cowgirls' Hard Luck Award that evening. There's also a Best Dressed title conferred in this event each night, and those citations tend to downgrade the exertions of the cowgirls — who have been known to require stitches after bad bangs against the barrels — to those made by the Miss Rodeo USA contestants. Next to me in the stands, a teenage boy from Tennessee named Chance, sporting traces of a never-shaved mustache, ogles their program pictures; for all the barrel racers' skill, they suffer from an unspoken sense that the event is the ladies' auxiliary one. Its placement on the program after intermission, and its being the evening's shortest event — no recalcitrant animals to keep rigging up in the chutes — contribute to the feeling that it lies somewhere between being one of the real, statistics-riddled competitions and part of the evening's entertainment, along with the trick riders, the clowns, the pageant.

DeBoraha Akin, a barrel racer with four children between seven and sixteen, is the first black woman to qualify for the IFR finals, and she receives some good-willed attention from the press and crowd. Asked by the *Tulsa Tribune* about other black women in her sport, she says: "There are some tough ones out there . . . The problem is most of them stay mostly in the black rodeos. I go to some of those, but I don't understand why you wouldn't go to the main circuit events." Rodeo has a number of persisting concentric circuits — for blacks, gays, and prisoners — that show little desire or chance to ripple outward into the main ones. IFR 20 has two black cowboys, steer wrestler Clarence LeBlanc and bull rider Larry Mosley, both of whom still seem novel to the almost entirely white crowd. The announcers can exhibit a foot-in-mouth well-meaningness toward them. Danny Newland says that Mosley has a lot of grit even though he doesn't ride with "a lot of class." During a rough ride he's praised because he "keeps on keepin' on," a phrase one doesn't hear applied to anyone else. (Steer wrestling may have been invented by a black cowhand, Bill Pickett. In *Man, Beast, Dust,* the rodeo historian Clifford P. Westermeier wrote: "As the story goes — based on tradition and hearsay, and elaborated upon in repetition — Bill, upon failing to drive a steer into a corral, became angry and leaped from his horse to the steer's head and proceeded to wrestle the animal to the ground.")

What Larry Mosley is keeping on doing is responding to "rodeo's toughest challenge." This is what the announcers like to call the bull riding. It's the event that closes the show, the one most productive of macho anecdote and legendary injury. IFR 20 makes its own contribution here: Rusty Smith of Fort Smith, Arkansas, scores an impressive 81 points in the first round, even though once he's off the bull he has to get back on his crutches: he accidentally shot himself in the foot with a nail gun the other day. By Saturday afternoon it's clear that no one will ride all five head he draws at IFR 20: after three rounds everyone's been thrown at least once.

I ask Lloyd Burk, Sr., the 1965 world champion bull rider and now a rodeo judge, about the worst injury he ever sustained. "This bull hit me in the face at Cooper, Texas," he tells me. "After the whistle I rode him, won the bull ridin'. He knocked all my teeth out, knocked twenty-eight teeth out, cut my lip off, broke my nose, broke my jaws, and, you know, I stayed in the hospital Thursday till Sunday, and I got out of the hospital on Sunday afternoon. Well, we was comin' home. My daddy came and picked me up, and instead of takin' me home, they had a rodeo started on Tuesday . . . Well, he just stopped and entered me in the rodeo, put me up on Saturday night. Well, I had a hundred sixty-four stitches in my mouth where my teeth had cut my lip off, and so, come Saturday night I borrowed me a football helmet off of a friend there who played football, went down to Ada [Oklahoma], got on the bull, and won the bull ridin', and that was the year I won the world. I went to like forty-somethin' head before they ever throwed me off another bull after I got hit in the face."

On Friday night at IFR 20, with his father watching, "Little Lloyd," Lloyd Burk, Jr., gets thrown by Tar Baby, and on Sunday has another tough break, getting thrown just before he can get through all eight seconds of what looked like a great ride. Still, he'll come in third in the average this year and finish fourth in the yearlong contest for the world championship.

Even in this event, rodeo remains significantly different from bullfighting or hockey, in that the audience is not out for blood. They're not waiting for something awful to happen so much as they're waiting to see something *not* happen — come close to happening, but that's it. The "bullfighters" — not the riders, but the cowboys dressed like clowns and charged with diverting a bull's attention from the rider he's just thrown and would now like to charge — are probably the bravest men in the arena. "These are cowboy lifesavers," says Danny Newland, not putting it too strongly. And yet rodeo psychology and protocol require that the bullfighters present themselves as weak. Their mandatory motley is donned not just as red-flag distraction for the bull, but also to emphasize the bullfighter's own position inferior to that of the rider. On the night before the first go-round, one bullfighter tells a Tulsa television reporter that his greatest reward is to be thanked by a bull rider. A knight-page relationship is the rule, with the curious difference that it's the page who is looking out for the knight. According to the program, "Doug Abbiatti has been chosen as the cowboy's protector by the IFR bull riders eight times in his career! . . . Abbiatti has earned that honor more times than any man in the history of the International Finals Rodeo." He is there to provide the audience with the thrill of hairsbreadth avoidance.

"Haven't you guys got anything better to do?" A city cop, mistaking me for major media, asks this question in a friendly way as we watch an animal rights demonstration gather outside the Convention Center on a cold Thursday afternoon. Actually, with five demonstrators present, it's just about already gathered. Five cops, three of them on horseback, are there to keep things in line; a news anchor and one cameraman-interviewer are also present to provide coverage for the evening news. The cop bets that all five demonstrators — whose numbers have not swelled twenty minutes into the event — are from out of state. But he's wrong about that. A little conversation reveals that it is Tulsans who are carrying the signs: "Rodeos Are Shocking (Literally)," a reference to electric cattle prods; "Animal Cruelty Is No Sport"; "What Does It Prove When You Beat Up a Calf?" A woman hands me an article from the Fund for Animals newsletter: "Those Brave Cowboys, Wrestling Baby Steers."

In fact, it is not steer wrestling but calf roping that excites the most revulsion among animal rights defenders, and even if you have an active hostility for the animal rights movement, you're likely to find the calf-roping section of any evening's rodeo program to be the one in which you're rooting for the animal instead of the cowboy. As Martha Brown, a soft-spoken teacher of history at Tulsa Junior College, tells me from what passes for the picket line: "You rope a calf running at fifteen or twenty miles an hour and throw him down. You injure them very easily at that age. If it were done once it wouldn't be so bad, but the same calf is used over and over and over, without medical care usually. They're babies, after all . . . They're in no place that they can understand. So it seems to me it's really pretty brutal for them." The teenage Cyra McFadden, growing estranged from Cy Taillon, was "blandly disengaged" from rodeo, "except when a calf got its neck broken in the calf-roping event. On these occasions, infrequent though they were, I registered moral outrage. Rodeo was cruel, I said. This attitude my father could not tolerate, not from me, not from journalists and most of all, not the self-righteous, lily-livered SPCA."

The calves do appear horribly frightened, and even when their necks remain unbroken, their heads snap around sickeningly. Their eyes run and their mouths shoot drool. The sound they're making isn't lowing, it's screaming, and after their feet are speedily tied they may defecate in panic. If they start struggling, the cowboys lose points, and if they can stagger to their feet within five seconds of being tied, the cowboys get a no-time averaged into their five-round score. So these calves are not going to be gently ribboned.

Tim McKee, who's organized the demonstration, appears to be an all-purpose radical, with his talk about how he came to an anti-rodeo awareness through an anti-fur one, which came in turn from an environmental one — Greenpeace. He finds it interesting that barrel racing, the least objectionable rodeo event, is the only one women are involved with, and mentions that he is a recent student of "eco-feminism." One feels that if, as the song goes, he could talk to the animals, he'd bore them to death. It's not the menagerie but the millennium that's on his mind, whereas Martha Brown of NOAH (Northeastern Oklahoma Animal Helpers) seems to be in this geographically quixotic enterprise for the creatures themselves. Rodeo is not her "big priority," but she objects to more than the calf roping, reminding me that the bulls and broncs are not wild animals who are normally afraid of humans. Rodeo defenders say that the bucking straps that get them to jump and kick are placed more or less where a belt would be on a human, but foes say that the straps are squeezing the genitalia. As Ms. Brown gently puts it to me: "They're around very sensitive parts of the animals' bodies." (Clifford Westermeier found objections to bronc riding dating back to an exhibition held in Cheyenne in 1872.)

It's hard to tell whether the new aggressiveness of the activists is provoking the slightest defensiveness in rodeo people. Almost each evening Danny Newland tells those folks in the audience who may have an intractable horse, one that "wakes up ornery one morning and refuses to go to work," that they shouldn't abuse him but instead contact the IPRA and see about getting him into rodeo, where his life can be extended and made useful. It's doubtful this is just a cynical pitch designed to improve the level of rough stock, but there's probably a certain public relations motive at the heart of it. On Thursday night a calf gets so banged up it can't hobble off the field even after it's been untied. One of the pickup riders has to take up the hind legs and push him back toward the gates the way you would a wheelbarrow. "We do have a veterinarian who is on standby call at all times in case any of our animals is injured," swears Newland to the fans. "We will take care of that."

The cowboys don't see anything wrong with the way the stock get treated. On the contrary, W. Bruce Lehrke, the president of Longhorn Rodeo, is quoted by a *Tulsa Tribune* sports columnist as saying: "You ask just about any cowboy, and he will tell you if there is such a thing as reincarnation, he wants to come back in his next life as a bucking bronc or a bull. They have the 'Life of Riley.' " Even Martha Brown will allow how the cowboys are guilty not of active cruelty so much as a "different perspective": "I think they *like* their animals."

No doubt they do. The sight of a pickup rider gentling his horse with friendly pats, reassuring him against the lights and noise and sudden bursts of activity by various species, is a sweet one. And however off-putting may seem the fate of the calves and steers, any brutality suffered by the rough stock (those straps) seems not very great, and furthermore, it is not so much the result of a cowboy's desire to dominate as his understanding that he and the animal are equal partners in this event. It's not simply the even-steven agreement that the cowboy can hurt the horse because the horse will hurt the cowboy; there's a numerical equality established by the rules. A perfect score in bareback or saddle-bronc riding is 100, with most cowboys who stay on scoring in the 70s, half from each of the two judges on opposite sides of the arena. But 50 of the potential 100 points are earned by the animal. A horse that won't buck is like a dog that won't hunt, and fans will express more displeasure over an animal's poor performance than a rider's. "At least that son of a bitch bucked," said somebody not far from me when an energetic horse followed a more contented one during the first night's saddle-bronc riding.

Bucking stock are listed by name and number in the program, and a spectator can look up their records the same way he can a cowboy's. Marijuana, lot 360 from the Gene Smith Rodeo Co., is a brindle "age 7, wt. 1600; out 8; dis. 8" — which is to say, he's thrown every contestant who's been momentarily atop him. Godfather, a saddle bronc from the JS Pro Rodeo Co., an eight-year-old quarter horse weighing 1,350 pounds, is six for nine. The bull on the cover of the current issue of *Rodeo News* gets to take a special promenade before being auctioned off for over $6,ooo at the bucking-stock sale held the day before IFR 20 opens.

The purpose of that daylong event is to sell broncs and bulls to local rodeo companies, the kind that make up the circuit leading IPRA cowboys to the finals in Tulsa. By the time one reaches the level of the IFR, rodeo, like most things in modern life and art, starts to be about itself. The crowd watching Rocky Top, a five-year-old sorrel gelding, buck up a snorting storm on Wednesday morning is advised that they're watching a "Saturday night ticket seller!"

As they sit in front of advertising banners for Stetson, Ford trucks, and Pepsi, cowboys in the stands videotape the proceedings with hand-held cameras. The older women, permed and teased, wear neatly pressed pantsuits; the younger ones tend toward pink sweatshirts. The auctioneer knows a lot of the bidders by name, and what they're listening to, all day, is a curious blend of hype and understatement. On the stock sheet, lots 3 through 9 are presented by their owner, Bill Moore of the Diamond M Rodeo Co.: "As I have sold my indoor arena, I will sell the remainder of my bulls. All of these bulls are outstanding bulls." The pitch often takes the form of straight-faced humor: "Boys, y'all count your money. I can't stay here all day. Boys, y'all asleep there?" All a young longhorn needs "is some groceries and a little time." After the announcer's laudations, the animal's angry bucking, and the auctioneer's amplified tongue trills, the gavel goes down with a kind of sigh, allowing everyone involved to catch breath and return to modest reality. Then the auctioneer will say nothing more than the simple truth: "I sold a bull."

The stock sale showcases animals less on the basis of their vital, measurable statistics than their personalities and life histories. "Here's an old campaigner," says auctioneer Sam Howry, of Band Wagon, a horse that's seen "about every finals that's been," has in fact "been all over the world." He comes "out of the north country" — Jim Crothers's rodeo company in Gypsum, Kansas — and in his advanced age is recommended as a practice horse. The crossbred bulls being auctioned seem easily the angriest, and anger is a prize virtue. Lot 55, a six-year-old Bradford cross, is "a big stout rodeo rascal." Bidders and spectators in the stands are asked: "Don't you like that crooked-horned bull? Mercy, mercy." The Reverend B. Thomas is on his way to New York after a crowd-pleasingly scary show of stuff. He gives the bullfighters a lot of attention and gouges a piece out of the clown's barrel with his horn. He's as good as lot 23, a brindle modestly described in the list of available animals as a six-year-old who "bails out and bucks hard, hooks a little" and is "hard to ride," but who excites Sam Howry to happy heights of commercial appreciation: "Here's the rodeo-est bull we've had in here! . . . He's a Saturday night bull!"

The clowns and bullfighters work the stock sale for nothing. They, too, are on display for local rodeo companies who might want to hire them. If they do well here, the bullfighters will get their IPRA cards on Friday. When a bull goes after one of them hard, the announcer hardly knows whether to hype the animal or the man, settling for a soft sell of the bull: "He will tend to scoop 'em up."

Martha Brown objects when events she finds cruel are historically justified, as if tradition itself were a reason to sanction them. The first professional rodeo is thought to have been held in Prescott, Arizona, in 1888. In the special 1988 Sitting Bull Stampede issue of the *Mobridge* (South Dakota) *Tribune,* Matt Kohlman wrote that the sport's origins are imprecise, but "the cattle drives of the late 1800s definitely played a major part in its development. When ranch outfits met on the trails or at towns, riding and roping exhibitions would often take place as the cowboys bet their scant wages on the outcome. Usually conducted in the wide open prairie without fences or corrals, the contests provided a welcome relief to the hard life of the trail."

Clifford Westermeier links rodeo to fiesta, noting that the word "rodeo" originally meant "to round up the cattle for branding, or to take them to the cattle market, which was often held during a fiesta." The movement from trail to ranch to city occurred over several decades, and by 1936 the cowboys were beginning to organize themselves into what would eventually become the PRCA. According to Matt Kohlman, "Because they [were] slow in organizing, they called themselves the Cowboys Turtle Association."

If pro rodeo is cut off from the ranching labors that brought it into being, it keeps going by constantly extending its own bloodlines. This is a family sport, not in some PG-rated sense of the term, but literally. It is hard to find anyone competing at the IFR who is unrelated to someone else in rodeo. Tulsa's Connie Cooper, the world champion barrel racer, had an aunt in the same sport and a daddy who rode bulls. DeBoraha Akin jokes to the *Tulsa Tribune* that she took up barrel racing to get on the good side of her rodeoing father-in-law. Tracy Postrach may have taken Friday's Hard Luck Award in the barrel racing, but by Sunday afternoon her brother Terry is the world champion calf roper. Mika John Calico's mother is the arena secretary, and his father is a judge. There are so many Foremans who team rope that on opening night Jerry Todd imagines that, back home, "Poor old Mama Foreman's legs are all scraped up." On a couple of nights, even S. L. Pemberton is joined by his trick-riding ten-year-old sister, Jaclyn, named, one suspects, for a Charlie's Angel.

Lloyd Burk, Sr., did not come out of a rodeoing family. He tells me that back in 1953 his high school basketball coach offered to pay his entry fees for a "little old FFA rodeo" if Lloyd would go ride a bull. "This thing throwed me so high that a bird could've built a nest in my hat before I hit the ground." But the next week he won $165 in merchandise at another rodeo in Sulphur: "Britches, shirts, clothes, boots, hats . . . I got my mama some stuff, my daddy stuff, and I got [the coach] stuff, and I got his wife clothes. Back then, you know, you could buy a lot of clothes and stuff for a hundred sixty-five dollars. And that's how I started ridin' bulls, on a bet."

For Lloyd Burk, Jr., bull riding was a birthright. Little Lloyd was born one day when Lloyd Senior was at a rodeo in Jonesboro, Arkansas, and by the time he was six he was getting up on calves. Five years later he started going to rodeos, and "for lots of years" after that he rode bulls with his father. Lloyd Senior is pretty sure his son will win a world title someday: "He rides real good. He's got a lot better style than I got." But rodeo is "about all he knows." On Tuesdays and Wednesdays Little Lloyd works at the livestock auction in Ada, and by Thursday he's off to a rodeo.

Lloyd Senior says that "a man can make a good living rodeoing today." Entry fees and purses are a lot higher than they were thirty years ago, and the circuit runs year-round, not just the six or seven months it used to. Still, it's clear that very few cowboys are getting rich here. According to Danny Newland, "Downtown" Jason Brown figures he can wait to make $50,000 a year with his marketing degree; right now he can have a better time making $25,000 riding saddle broncs. The championship standings going into IFR 20 had Mika John Calico, the leader in bull riding, with a total of $21,745 for 1989 and Lloyd Burk, Jr., in sixth place, with just $8,653. Four days later, Little Lloyd would be up to $10,603, and Calico, the world champion, would have added less than $200 to his total. To get these sums, IPRA riders may get up on between fifty and seventy animals. The PRCA circuit has more money, more rodeos, and more self-supporting cowboys, but according to Steve Danylo, the regional bareback-riding champion, who's a construction worker during the week: "In rodeo, as long as you break even or a little bit above, you're doing good." Dayna Cravens tells me about the IFR cowboys who work at American Airlines here in Tulsa.

A bull rider can go on until he's thirty-five or so, according to Lloyd Burk, Sr., who, in good health at forty-nine, still gets up on a bull every now and then. But mostly he judges now: in 1990 he's got contracts to work twenty-seven rodeos. Cy Taillon's son, Terry, went in the same way from saddle-bronc riding to judging to announcing. Perhaps the most unexpected thing about rodeo is that it gives the people who work in it a chance to age gracefully.

On Friday afternoon, IFR's "Old Timers" gather at the Park Plaza for their reunion. Dayna Cravens, who grew up with these people, introduces me around before the event gets going. I ask her father, J.O., if the IFR is really leaving Tulsa. He'll tell me only that there are two rumors every year: that they'll have a full house and that they're pulling out of the city.

The women walk with video cameras between tables holding finger food and Lite beer as the event gets under way in the highly structured manner of a rodeo go-round. Even here the master of ceremonies is constantly announcing. The nostalgia is formal: people go up to the mike and compete for a prize in storytelling. They're asked to keep the stories "rodeo-related." A plaque goes to the Most Deserving Old Timer, and another to the oldest clown present — "and I'm sure that pertains to comedy acts and things like that," says the emcee. The Mark Trophy Co., donor of the plaques, is thanked like any other sponsor. Some of the reminiscences involve particular animals, and Buck Crofts takes the storytelling honors after ending with a sentimental monologue about two departed friends — a tale in keeping with the invocation mentioning those who have gone "to ride a much higher range."

The Cowboy Chapter of the Fellowship of Christian Athletes is present not just with their first-into-the-ring banner at each session of the rodeo but with prayer meetings throughout the week and testimonial literature available at the trade show. The Cowboy Chapter was conceived at a 1974 rodeo in Denver by Wilbur Plaugher, a rodeo clown, and Mark Schricker, a contestant. It now claims four thousand members and boasts of having "distributed over 130,000 Cowboy Bibles throughout the world." Allen Bach, a 1979 team-roping champion, writes that for a time he "put roping first instead of my relationship with the Lord. If I had put into my Christian walk what I put into rodeo, and read the Word like I practiced roping, I'd be a better example today. I didn't need to stay a baby Christian for 12 years." A small blue pamphlet asks contenders if they'd rather be a "Rodeo Winner or Soul Winner": "Would you rather lay up a horde of worldly treasures to dust and rust and mold in the short time we are here on earth, or would you lay up a multitude of treasures in heaven by working for God and leading others to do the same?" This seems especially sincere in light of what the figures say about the chance of making any kind of extravagant living through the IFR.

The undisputed king of IFR competition, Dan Dailey, who has qualified in four different events, won seventeen world championships, married a Miss Rodeo USA, and is still competing in IFR 20, is the Cowboy Chapter's most attractive spokesman. He has the good looks and bland dignity that make you think of him as a potential Republican candidate for the Senate, a kind of Steve Garvey who may not be too good to be true. But for all his formidable skills he seems completely lacking in any of the rough-edged, dirt-covered, hot-damn colorfulness that might make Danny Newland shout, as he sometimes does, "Wild and western!" If Dailey's sport were women's tennis, he'd be Chris Evert, a champion for sure but one who has professionalized himself into a higher, stainless-steel order of being. It's no surprise that he's been nicknamed the Bionic Cowboy. One thinks that he — with the addition of one of those college diplomas held by some competitors like "Downtown" Jason Brown — must represent the future of the rodeo cowboy.

Still, one doesn't yet have to look too far to find the tobacco-spitting, shit-kicking rodeo model, the kind who's still going to be given a jolt by the Doubletree's elevators. Greg Wheeler, a bareback rider from Kellyville, Oklahoma, is the son of Earlene Wheeler and Bobby Wheeler, a rodeo veteran who, while feeling no pain at the Old Timers' Reunion, steps up to the mike to tell the story of how maybe twenty or so years ago, out on the circuit with a very young Greg, he spent a night in a Missouri jail after being a little disorderly. The next morning, when both he and Greg were standing in court, the head-shaking magistrate asked the boy his birthday. "September third," replied Greg. "What year?" asked the judge. "Well, shit," answered Greg, "every year."

Like Tulsa's boom-and-bust economy, five days of rodeo expand and contract, stretches of boredom separated by eight-second bursts of excitement. It is, like track and field, a sport of repetitions, one giving rise only sparingly to individual dramas. Before the final, Sunday afternoon round gets started, most of the world championships, dependent on the yearlong money totals, have already been decided; the only suspense, and it's minor, is to see who will win the round and the five-day average. Attendance seems the lowest of any session, and the hoof- and horn-pocked banners give the arena a tired atmosphere. Even the crowning of Miss Rodeo USA, when it finally comes, before the last steer-wrestling round, seems anticlimactic: Miss Nicki Barefoot's new tiara-ringed Stetson doesn't seem much different from what she already had on. Still, the repetitions have their pleasures — even if they only involve catching sight of Brother Taylor's assistant holding the "skunk" she's got to set loose, or hearing someone in the stands, wishing to be the one who brings forth the sound of James Brown, shout: "Hey, Hollywood, how do you *feel?*" Actually, Hollywood, still in his pink underwear, started looking a little tired yesterday.

But the real moment of IFR 20 is about to come. It will last, of course, for eight seconds, and be provided by Justin Rowe of Tulsa, during the last round of saddle-bronc riding.

With his custom-made monogrammed black and white shirt, Rowe seems more dandified than his competition, and he's in the enviable position of being not only the hometown favorite but second only to Dan Dailey himself in the yearlong trail of bank deposits leading to the world championship. Last night he seemed to get a suspiciously lucky break: needing 81 points to stay in first place for the five-day average, he came up with 82, on a ride that seemed less spectacular than Mike Hemann's, though that one earned only a 76 and some boos for the judges. The scoring does at times seem arbitrary. On Thursday night, for example, Tim Smith of Miami, Oklahoma, rode a saddle bronc with an elegance the sport usually makes impossible to display, and came up with only a 69. Maybe it was the forward dismount that kept him low on points. Still, when Rowe comes out of the chute on Sunday afternoon, one is past being blindly faithful toward the judges' abilities.

But there he is, stunning the crowd on a horse that's bucking to high heaven, beating the air with his free arm, mastering all around him with a steady, slicing control. It's a gorgeous, hard ride and he's raising the roof, taking the crowd, which realizes what it's seeing, up into its own roar of pleasure. It's the best thing anyone has watched in five days. In fact, it's the best saddle-bronc ride the Tulsa Convention Center has *ever* seen, an arena record — 90 goddamn points.

And a little while later he's out by the concession stands, just talking to somebody near the beer line, and you want to shake his hand.

The last thing the crowd sees each night is a riderless bull, let out of the chutes not to try and throw a cowboy but just to disport himself as threateningly as he can in the presence of the bullfighters. This little bit of closing business by the best of the bulls — "*Close your rodeo with this bull!*" — seems designed to let the animal have the last word and to prepare the arena for its desertion by the riders.

On Sunday afternoon Steve Danylo told me he planned to hop a plane back to Arkansas before the last round of bull riding was finished, and a couple of hours after that all the living creatures of the IFR were moving on from Tulsa. At around 5:30 you could find a rodeo family in one of the deserted downtown parking lots, packing things into a pickup — garment bag, attaché case, bucking rope. In the back of the Convention Center, lot 360, the brindle called Marijuana, the big stout rodeo rascal ridden in the first round by Mika John Calico, the world champion, was loaded up behind the bars of his truck, ready for his next move with the Gene Smith Rodeo Co.

The IFR, as it happens, was leaving Tulsa for good. The next morning a press release from J. O. Cravens would announce that the twenty-first finals would take place next January in Oklahoma City, partly because of its "20 years experience hosting the PRCA's National Finals Rodeo" — before, that is, the PRCA moved to Vegas. Like the training wheel on a bicycle, the smaller circuit was chasing the larger one.

Rodeo, like country music, is stuck on itself. Both of them have to be, because they depend on a sense of cultural disappearance. Each asserts that it's as strong as ever in these rootless, rushed, and misguided times, but the only way such defiance works, and gives its hearers poignant pleasure, is for them to know the proclaimant *is* embattled, slowly but certainly fading. When the announcer says goodbye each night to the crowd, his valediction is meant to sound robust, but his chosen emblem can't help being elegiac: "Good night, God bless you, and remember, as long as there's a sunset, there'll be a West."

Why, O Why, O Why O, Do They Ever Leave Owosso?

JUNE 1991

On a Tuesday night more than forty years ago the town of Owosso, Michigan, had a date with history, and history stood her up. As the boyhood home of Thomas E. Dewey, Owosso was supposed to take her place between Independence, Missouri, and Abilene, Kansas, in the line of small-town mothers of Presidents, a spot she ended up being accorded for just a brief, false moment on the pages of the *Chicago Tribune*.

The dowry she had ready was the sort of plain, prosperous real estate required by the role. Tom Dewey had been born in 1902 above his grandfather's general store on Main Street, on the west bank of the Shiawassee River. The apartment, though marked, is now boarded up, and a bird sits cheeping on the ledge above the deserted commercial floor, last occupied by a furniture store that couldn't quite make it. Dewey's father, an editor, fared more successfully, and "our Tom," as another marker several blocks away calls him, would do most of his growing up in a big frame house on prosperous West Oliver Street, which, like most of Owosso, could serve as the location for a remake of any Andy Hardy movie. Lined with porch-fronted homes and Protestant churches, the street still belongs to life, not history. The big Dewey house is privately occupied;

on a June afternoon in 1991 some girls are splashing in the backyard pool behind it. A few blocks down the Methodists are planning tonight's Swiss Steak Supper, and thanks to the Baptist Harry S. Truman, nobody coming to it will have to fight for a parking spot with any tourist: whatever cars are riding westward into town, past the corn and soybean fields between Flint and Owosso, will be heading toward something other than the presidential library that never got built here. No, the only library in town is the Owosso Public, a sturdy brick affair built with Carnegie money and opened in 1914, and the framed old Bachrach portrait that hangs inside on the second floor is not of Thomas E. Dewey at all but of the town's true favorite son and local hero: James Oliver Curwood, 1878–1927.

He was not pressed into service as a substitute. While Dewey was still a student at Owosso High, Curwood's adventure novels — many of them set in the Canadian wilderness with titles like *The Gold Hunters* (1909) and *God's Country and the Woman* (1915) — were making him rich and famous, giving him a readership and sales figures, Curwoodians will tell you, comparable to Zane Grey's. After Dewey went off to trap the sharks and slugs of the New York underworld, he was more or less gone for good, but Curwood loved coming home from his northern encounters with wolves and bears to write his stories in Owosso: "I think it is the nicest place in the world. I was born there and I hope to die there. It's American, and it makes you feel at home."

Many of his thirty-three books were turned into hasty movies, some by his own production company. Recently, however, *The Grizzly King* (1916) was filmed, with some seriousness and distinction, as *The Bear,* by Jean-Jacques Annaud, the director of *Quest for Fire.* In the fall of 1989 the movie had its American premiere in Owosso, making Curwood's hometown feel a little as Atlanta did when David O. Selznick unveiled *Gone With the Wind* at the Loew's Grand on Peachtree Street.

The Bear is eager to be both entertainment and art (a friend describes it as "Disney meets German expressionism"), and just as Selznick's achievement far surpassed Margaret Mitchell's, Annaud's rises way above and beyond the nicely realized moral yarn that is Curwood's novel. *The Grizzly King* was a kind of tract, the result of a conversion its author underwent when he was shown mercy by a bear ("Thor" in the novel) that he had just before wounded. He came to realize that

> the greatest thrill of the hunt is not in killing, but in letting live. It is true that in the great open spaces one must kill to live; one must have meat, and meat is life. But killing for food is not the lust of slaughter; it is not the lust which always recalls to me that day in the British Columbia mountains when, in less than two hours, I killed four grizzlies on a mountain slide — a destruction of possibly one hundred and twenty years of life in a hundred and twenty minutes. And that is only one instance of many in which I now regard myself as having been almost a criminal — for killing for the excitement of killing can be little less than murder.

So heartfelt and clear-minded was his recantation that the indiscriminate hunter wound up becoming chairman of the Game, Fish and Wildlife Committee of the Michigan Department of Conservation.

Even if one can follow some of the novel's diction ("cayuse" and "hobble") only by remembering certain lyrics of Cole Porter (another small-town boy), one can't help being affected by *The Grizzly King,* just as one can't help being charmed by Curwood Castle, the folly the author built right in town beside a stretch of the Shiawassee flowing between the two Dewey homes. He used it as a writing studio and a place for entertaining movie people and foreign visitors: all over its main room you can still find the holders needed for displaying their flags.

"She looks a bit like Myrna Loy, doesn't she?" says the woman greeting tourists who have come. She doesn't know who the lookalike in the painting actually is, but the canvases on the castle walls depict scenes from Curwood books made into movies. Going up a winding stair to one of the turrets, you find the author's big black L. C. Smith & Bros. typewriter, and one more turn above that brings you to a circular wall full of display cases containing an assortment of translations, movie posters, and family photographs, including one of Curwood's second wife, Ethel M. Greenwood, who was every bit as pretty as Myrna Loy. The only item really to interest some teenagers wandering through is, of course, the author's driver's license, set out with some other personal effects.

"If he was that famous," says one visitor to another, "how come the whole time we grew up in Holly we didn't hear about him?" They may have forgotten James Oliver Curwood in Holly, Michigan, but when he prematurely departed this world from Owosso, an extra edition of the *Argus-Press* for August 14, 1927, ran a headline so wide that the editors had to resort to periphrasis to get it across eight columns. JAMES OLIVER CURWOOD'S ILLNESS FATAL is the curiously indirect news that Owossoans got. Curwood had been sick with a streptococcal infection for just ten days.

The basement of the castle provides space for the Shiawassee County Genealogical Society and the Owosso Historical Commission, and in a little room tenanted by the latter, one can find Ivan A. Conger, the local historian who has worked mightily to keep Curwood's name and books circulating. There's a little exhibit devoted to Dewey down here, too: old *Life* magazines with the candidate on the cover; a letter on the stationery of the Owosso "Dewey for President Club"; and an old campaign button touting the contender and his running mate, that Californian chosen to balance the ticket, Earl Warren. But it is a small display, and it isn't even permanent. By contrast, James Oliver Curwood will be celebrated this weekend (June 7–9) with square dances, hamburger-eating contests, raft races, brass bands, and a parade expected to attract one hundred thousand people.

The Curwood Festival gets off to a small but determined start at noon on Friday. Splendid in their blue and gold uniforms, the Owosso High School marching band makes its peppy way over the swaying Heritage Footbridge that crosses the Shiawassee to the castle, where it plays "The Star-Spangled Banner" as members of the local VFW post raise the flag. It's a weekday, and most folks, auto-industry recession or not, are working, so the number of red and white T-shirted festival organizers almost matches the number of spectators present for the invocation by a young minister in a suit and tie. Hal Degerstrom, the festival president, introduces the mayor, Christine Mitchell, who looks like a Century 21 representative, and who declares that this year's festival will be a continuation of the celebration the town has been having for the return of two local National Guard units from the Persian Gulf. One of them, the 146th, got back to the States only last Friday, arriving in Owosso, via Philadelphia and a fort in Wisconsin, for a Tuesday night parade. She thanks the marching band for being there on Tuesday, just as they'd been there in the January cold to see the troops off. Now that the soldiers are back home, she tells everyone to have a "fantastic" time, hitting each short vowel with a friendly midwestern rasp.

The Curwood Queen, young Rachel Rodriguez, and her court are introduced. Curly, tiara-topped Rachel thanks God for blessing Owosso with such a beautiful day and urges that the crowd "please don't hesitate to ask my court members or myself" any questions about the festival activities. (Rachel is going to make a *great* Century 21 rep.) Next it's the turn of the 1990 grand marshal to bring on his successor, a public school teacher and small businessman and former state legislator, during whose remarks one of the girls in the band, which has been standing at attention in the sun, quietly faints. The theme of this year's parade honoring the ecology-minded Curwood is "Trees — Guardians of the Earth," and the girl is led off and revived under one of the very environmental wonders that has made Owosso, in the words of a festival pamphlet, "the Bright Spot That's a Shade Better."

A woman down at the local chamber of commerce will joke about Ivan Conger's inclination toward prolixity, and he does hold the microphone in front of the castle longer than any of the other speakers this noon. Standing there with his crew cut and string tie, the local historian marvels over how in 1977 the festival organizers were planning just a modest one-time centenary for Curwood. "Now, as we roll on year after year, we must not forget James Oliver Curwood as we continue to have fun at each Curwood Festival. We must keep his memory alive and ever before us in every way that we can." He recalls the famous 1915 encounter with Thor that left Curwood "a new man," and refers proudly to "Jean-Jacques," the French director who said his trip to Owosso for *The Bear*'s premiere was the highlight of his American stay.

Recalling Curwood's efforts to clean up the polluted Shiawassee, Conger quotes his renunciation of the "overlords of business" to whom no natural beauty is sacred, and one thinks that the silent assent by this gathering of Rotarians and boosters is something the Republican National Committee might be interested to note. He ends by reciting the Curwood credo: "Nature is my religion. It is my desire and my ambition to take my readers with me into the heart of this nature. I love it and I feel that they must love it, if only I can get the two acquainted."

The band strikes up the Owosso High School fight song, and when the little crowd has finished clapping along, it disperses to put the finishing touches on the activities that will be in full swing by tomorrow. A chubby kid in an "Alf" T-shirt rises from the grass; one red-shirted woman tells another, "I got a float to get up and ready"; two VFW members make plans for taking care of the flag over the weekend; and a group of women arrange to be at the Hardee's on Main Street by 6:30 tonight. The sound of hammers and an occasional train whistle floats across the sunshine on a breeze.

Of course the Curwood Festival does not live and grow from year to year on pure devotedness to conservation and literature. Like Christmas and the Fourth of July, James Oliver Curwood is good for business. So mindful is Owosso of what this weekend brings in that the organizers inflict a good-natured insult on those vendors who are taking money *out:* Carpetbaggers Row is the name for the parking lot where they sell the same paraphernalia they'll be selling this summer at another dozen fairs in another dozen venues: T-shirts (heavy metal and Desert Storm), leather knife sheaths, Jesus buttons, pewter Garfields. The only remarkable thing about all this generic stuff, if you're used to seeing it on urban avenues, is the lack of litter that gathers around it by the end of the day.

The midway, going strong by early evening, has its nondescript aspect, too, with name-brand Skee Ball booths and "NASA" rides that offer disclaimers to the pregnant and back-injured — warnings put up not to attract thrill-seeking business, as such signs tried to years ago, but only to stave off lawsuits. The sound of baseballs hitting the tin backboard behind stubbornly upright beer bottles is now produced at 67 cents a pop (three throws for $2), but it still timelessly rides the air with smells of frying food and caramel corn. The barkers in their pink shirts have the kind of anger that proceeds from boredom, and they throw themselves into their work with a surly aggression, with out-of-town faces that can almost make you see them representing leering, luring evil — the seducers in some long-ago Sherwood Anderson story.

But all these franchised operations in the open spaces near City Hall are really exceptions to the one-of-a-kind, authentically Owossoan, nature of the Curwood Festival. Its essence can be found, if you're looking for it early on Friday evening, at the new outdoor amphitheater behind the junior high school. Across the Shiawassee from the castle, it's really just a big outdoor stage with a homage-giving turret motif to its roof. On the lawn in front of it at 6:30 P.M. are spectators ready for a round of the Mr. Owosso contest, which is a matter not of beefcake but of cheerful charity; it is, in fact, one of the festival's big deals. For weeks each contestant has been representing a worthy local cause, and his "campaigners," now working the crowd in identifying T-shirts, have been collecting donations for their candidate's chosen charity. The lighthearted premise tonight is that you'll put money into the cans and mayonnaise jars in proportion to the talents displayed onstage by each of the three finalists and his backup men.

Gale Burke and his beer-bellied group, representing a local hospice, do a lip-synched version of "Sea Cruise" complete with chorus-line kicks. By eschewing the esoteric, they prove altogether more crowd-pleasing than Jeff Smelser and his men, who rather let down the Handicapped Children's Foundation with a drag version of "Send in the Clowns" that somehow segues into an unknown rock number. Say wha? The Association for Retarded Citizens of Shiawassee County is much better served by Tom Thon and his guys, who do an M. C. Hammer number ("U Can't Touch This") with as many acrobatics as a small group of overweight white boys can manage.

The big announcement of the winner will come tomorrow night on the midway, in the Happy Hunting Grounds — the beer tent — and Cheryl Gapinski returns to the mike after "U Can't Touch This" to remind everyone to be there. Meanwhile, they should enjoy this first day of the festival, because "it's a beautiful night in Owosso."

It is, too, although it falls slowly. Here on the western edge of the eastern time zone, plenty of golden light will last well past 9 P.M. — more than enough for the Kids in Curwood Country Parade, a sort of small-scale preview of tomorrow's. By a quarter to eight, it's a few blocks from the Deweys' old house, coming down East Oliver Street, where the "School Slow" sign still features a boy in short pants and a cap, not those bubbleheaded space children in the modern version. There are teeny twirlers and the Owosso sixth-grade band, Brownie troop 538 and Cub Scout pack 78. "Hi, Josh!" scream some girls bent on mortifying a passing, marching Scout. Carrie Senk, the Curwood Princess, comes by on a red convertible with her two-girl court, and you look at her on this lovely June night knowing that three quarters of a century from now, long after this evening has passed out of everyone's memory, it won't be entirely gone from hers. Antique cars glide by every few minutes, and a wine-colored '41 Ford holds the 1991 Beautiful Baby Grand Prize winners, two little blond toddlers, a boy and girl, waving in a somewhat nauseating pre-professional way. And then more than a score of unbelievably orderly dogs are permitted to promenade on leashes.

The parade provides an opportunity not only for parental photography ("Yeah, we're the next one coming up," says a young wife to her videotaping husband) but for parental propaganda as well. The floats and banners bear mildly improving injunctions that the kids are made to endorse as the price of their brief celebrity. Even the American Legion's gone eco-happy: the children of its Junior Auxiliary wear tree-shaped sandwich boards saying (front) "Plant a Tree and . . ." (back) "Let It Grow With Me." Members of the Little Rascals 4-H Club appear to have been tricked. What was no doubt proposed to them as a contribution to environmentalism is really a domestic pacification program: the big paper hands they hold up while riding their tractor-pulled farm wagon say not just "Don't Litter" but also "Turn Off the TV."

Owosso is, if ever the saying was true, a good place to raise children. Here you can overhear boys on their bicycles talking about sliders and fastballs ("I started smashin' 'em in there so hard he started cryin'. Nobody could hit 'em"), perhaps on their way down to Ken's Coin Corner on Main Street for some Desert Storm trading cards. But this is 1991, and the world of the Bundys — Al and Ted — keeps leaking into the Shiawassee Valley. Down near the midway you can find teenage girls wearing I LOVE MY BAD ASS ATTITUDE T-shirts, as well as a contented family whose mom's upper-body message to the world is: COWBOYS ARE BAD LOVERS BECAUSE THEY THINK 8 SECONDS IS A GOOD RIDE. And if you want to gaze at Mr. Curwood's little castle, sit down on a wooden railing near the Heritage Footbridge on the east side of the river; you'll find yourself near some recent graffitied poetry signed by "Arnold D. Hallock 91":

A sovereign soul: despised
Creation damned, psychotic,
American dream: demised,
Assassin embryonic

Through the sniper's scope I see,
This intruder oligarch,
The "perfect" society,
Pray, my bullet finds its mark . . .

Perhaps, after all these years, Owosso will put itself on the map not by sending a President to Washington, but by taking one out.

Both the T-shirts and Arnold D. Hallock are unlikely to do much harm, but the fact is that we've got trouble, right here in River City, and that starts with T and it rhymes with D and that stands for drugs. No more so than in any other place, of course, but the admonitions in tomorrow's grown-up parade will be noticeably stronger than the ones in tonight's. After a day or two in town you feel the subject is never very far from the parental mind, and whenever you think you've stumbled into Grover's Corners, you can just go and buy a soda at the PACE booth (Positive Alternatives through Counseling and Education) behind the armory. Fifteen percent of its Coke-selling operation goes to the festival, and the other 85 percent toward combating "substance abuse" in the county. The PACE banner displays a sunburst-shaped panoply of codependencies and clienteles: DE-PRESSION, EATING DISORDERS, EMOTIONS, ABUSE, WELLNESS, STRESS, COMPULSIVE BEHAVIORS, FAMILIES, PARENTING, STU-DENT PROBLEMS, CHILDREN, TEENS, SENIORS, ADDICTIONS, BEHAVIORAL PROBLEMS, ADULTS. As another graffitist working close to Arnold D. Hallock wrote: "No matter where you go, there you are." Look over toward City Hall and see the ferris wheel prettily dripping its riders and cars through the twilight. Are they going faster than you thought they were an hour ago?

*   *   *

"You must have been in the army," says a man in line to the probable World War II veteran griddling row after row of perfect flapjacks at the Rotary's breakfast in the Owosso Junior High cafeteria. A man behind a piano draped with the blue and gold school banner is banging out "Mona Lisa," "Glow Worm," and a baffling near-ragtime version of "Misty." It's Saturday morning, and this will be the festival's big day, so folks are stoking up. Most take three pancakes to start with (cholesterol-conscious seniors can pass up sausages in favor of fruit cup), and a small corps of efficient young club members are quick to come around with seconds. People are not typically slender in these parts, and the skinny ones seem somehow seedy. This country may not know what to do with the Kurds, but you're reminded once more of how it can feed them and anybody else in a jiffy.

Whether or not you wanted sausage, you're sure to be interested in the African Guinea forest hog. There's one of those, named Arnold, just outside in one of the pens set up on the school's front lawn. There are also some Tennessee goats with startled expressions, a six-year-old royal-palm turkey, a Jacob 4-horn sheep named Ramses, and some unexotic ducks and bunnies. There are no two-headed calves or freakish fauna of any kind, and when the festival advertises a Little People's Place, it's talking not about midgets but the spot where pre-schoolers can fingerpaint.

Actually, the Curwood Dog Contest has drifted perilously close to political correctness. From the amphitheater stage, a woman explaining the Ugliest Dog event detects a murmur of disapproval (lookism!) and asks, a little apologetically: "Is that controversial?" Size — biggest and smallest — is a more acceptable bone of contention, and the competing dogs parade around squares marked off with the yellow tape that in other towns usually indicates a homicide scene. In the Smallest Dog event, little kids carry puppies in their arms and a couple of local women, clearly not apartment dwellers, marvel at the diminutiveness of some chihuahuas. The Biggest Dog prize is taken by Benushka, a St. Bernard complete with neck keg. He's bested a handsome Dalmatian wearing an American-flag scarf who seemed to be shamelessly trying to capitalize on both the movie *Backdraft* and victory in the Gulf.

"Go for it, Geri! You've got to try somethin' besides one thing!" Thus does Edgar, a ringer for Spuds Mackenzie, make a late entry into the Owner Lookalike contest, even though he is registered only for the Ugly Dog event. In the end, however, the lookalike prize goes to Jake, who bears no resemblance at all to his owner, a little girl named Megan.

"How do you make your dog do it?" asks one owner whose animal companion (the PC term for pet) is competing with another's in the Singing Dog event. Actually, no amount of advice seems to help this morning. "I guess the cats must have their tongues today," says the announcer. A man in a gimme cap sings as he imagines his dog might, but it doesn't produce anything from the poor animal, and a big brown Labrador, into whose ear a small blond boy is making a high-pitched howl, succeeds only in looking tormented. Ultimately these two, Chip (the dog) and Clint Simmons (the boy), will be the winners, since no dog in the ring was willing to sing on the first attempt, and Chip was wise enough to howl on the second, no doubt to get his master away from his ear. "The rest of 'em'll go home and talk up a storm," predicts one lady after Clint goes up to claim his ribbon. A bit of philosophy emerges, too: stick to your knitting. Edgar (Spuds), after washing out as an owner lookalike, has walked off with the honors as Ugliest Dog — his original category.

On this second day of fine hot weather, all of the festival's exhibits are up and running. Near Owosso's first house, an 1836 cabin in which this morning some ladies are hammering dulcimers to the tune of "Danny Boy," a Revolutionary War camp has been set up ("Holy! A cannon!"). There's also a pioneer area. Near its tents hang some guns and skins (Mr. Curwood would approve according to the utility principle) and pots and skillets. A boy licks a spoon that's just been removed from what looks like a clear plastic cup of instant pudding. The smell of cinnamon is elsewhere more authentically detectable, and the local YWCA has a pie tent. Just a short stroll south along the river will bring you to the Woodard Paymaster Building, from which folks long ago received their wages from the Owosso Casket Factory. There's a Phunny Phamily Photo booth close by it now, but the Rusty Strings — a mandolin, guitar, and bass — have been a bigger draw for older people this morning.

The riverbanks remain crowded with lazy activity until a little before 2 P.M., when you can feel the whole town being drawn, entranced, away from the river, away from the midway, away from the castle, on bicycle and foot, carrying lawn chairs and sun umbrellas, as if by Professor Harold Hill, toward Main Street. Owosso is about to have the remarkable experience of *doing* something that the rest of the country is watching on television: it is time for a parade.

The National Victory Celebration in Washington, being carried live on CNN, is a bigger affair than what the Curwood organizers have put together, but there's something to be said for knowing the men marching past you as you sit on the curb in front of the Key State Bank. "Mom, you are so!" says a girl whose mother is trying to deny the tears she's wiping from behind her sunglasses while the 146th and 144th, military police who were recently guarding Iraqi POWs, ride by in their Humvees. The only shred of ambivalence that will be expressed today about America's military is a dissent quietly voiced by two boys when the VFW's Patriettes come marching by to much applause: "A little old, aren't they?" says one kid to the other, who replies: "A *little?*"

Congressman Dave Camp, who looks like a college student-body president, elects to run beside his car, as if doing road-work, waving and tacking toward the sidewalks, shaking hands and performing with a manic quality that makes George Bush seem like Coolidge. He generates a polite, and complete, lack of crowd interest. Much more engaging, and dear, are the senior-citizen King and Queen, who drive past in a closed, air-conditioned black Chrysler that's unfortunately reminiscent of a hearse.

Local commerce and culture are responsible for much of what floats by on flatbeds: a huge inflated milk carton from the Michigan Milk Producers; a promotion for the Chesaning production of *Showboat,* starring Bobby Vinton; the Queen of the Montrose Blueberry Festival; and a banner for Yaya's Flame-Broiled Chicken. Charities and good causes abound. The curbside crowd gives its applause to a retarded citizen in a wheelchair and a group of people — walking, not riding — who have had organs replaced. "The Best Plant Is a Transplant," says their sign, which makes good use of the botanical-minded parade theme, reminding everyone of the collection containers in fast-food restaurants around town for Dan Rose's needed bone-marrow operation. A bustle of philanthropy takes place among the spectators as campaigners for the Mr. Owosso title continue collecting for their men. The contestants themselves are parade unit 54, right behind last year's winner, Jim Stechschulte, who sits clutching his trophy in glorious contentment atop a white convertible driven by two fabulous sunglassed babes.

The Shriners, crazy as bedbugs, zip around on little toy cars, shaking up the tassles on their fezes, and Benushka, this morning's victorious St. Bernard, glides along on a Chevy pick-up. But most of what passes by has a clear, didactic message, in accordance with either the conservation thrust ("Trees Supply Our Oxygen") or the local devils: "Get a Kid Hooked on Fishing Instead of Drugs," says the Elks' float, and a grandma under the Hardee's sign applauds vigorously when an ecology/anti-drug combination float ("Make the World a Better Place . . . Be Drug Free") progresses in front of her. It is, however, the students of nearby Baker College who propose the most sweeping synthesis of various new world orders:

SUPPORT OUR GUARDIANS
TREES = EXISTENCE
MILITARY = FREEDOM
EDUCATION = GROWTH

It is a simple-minded algebra, of course, and these universal theorems are offered from a kind of racial and religious Stepford. (Where, by the way, did they ever find a Festival Queen named Rodriguez?) Still, if this town seems a shaky base for big beacons, the parade leaves you feeling you're in a place that does a good job producing its little points of light.

In a couple of hours it's all over (with that almost eerie lack of litter), and the citizens are retracted, like changelings, back toward the festival grounds and their own frame houses. You walk along Oliver and Washington streets and see girls sunning themselves on a rooftop, people eating ham and jelly roll at a picnic table in the driveway. There are still "Support Our Troops" signs in some windows — and in one of them, you notice, a security-alarm decal. Back at the amphitheater a band or two keep going (marimba-ing "New York, New York" after a soft Eagles song), while the crafts booths make a few extra dollars before the castle closes up at seven o'clock.

By that time the crowds are back on the midway and in the beer tent. It's jammed with over-twenty-ones, though they're not over by much. The boys with their dates wear T-shirts from the festival's three-on-three basketball tournament and the *Risky Business* style of sunglasses fashionable several years ago. The three Mr. Owosso hopefuls reprise their performances from last night, and their campaigners keep collecting, up to the last minute, the money that will, according to Cheryl Gapinski, "stay right here in Shiawassee County." After being paraded in their boxer shorts, the finalists retreat to the dressing room of the nearby firehouse, and the contributions are counted. The crown, a little model of Curwood Castle made by a high school student, will be placed on the winner's head by Rachel Rodriguez. By 8:40 the combined take is up to $12,000 and the counters are still going. Gale Burke does not yet know that the crown will be his, and when the three contestants emerge from the firehouse in tuxedos, they look like nervous prom dates from another time.

A time when girls would dress for the prom by humming "I Feel Pretty" and "Tonight." This night, the sparsely attended teen dance, held in the "Wigwam," is a pretty poor spectacle, with a handful of very young people attempting Madonna moves to recorded rap. It's clearly cooler to be hanging outside the tent than in it, but most kids between driving and drinking ages are well away from the whole scene. No doubt, if they're not parked, a few romantic couples are strolling by the river and looking up from there at the lights of the midway, those man-made "suns and moons all over the place." Some of them must even know the words to that song: there were kids from the Owosso High School Choir on a float this afternoon lip-synching what sounded like their own recording of "Lullaby of Broadway." One important function of small towns has always been to make some of their sons and daughters hate them, and there was surely at least one boy and one girl on that float dreaming, even now, of New York. Unless they read the tiny *Detroit Free Press* obituary for Larry Kert, who played the original Tony in *West Side Story,* yesterday morning, they probably don't know who he was, this man who like James Oliver Curwood departed life prematurely, from an infection; in Larry Kert's case it was AIDS. There has to be someone here tonight, a forty-five-year-old mother of somebody in the tent, who long ago fell in love with love to the sound of his wonderful voice coming through the wire-mesh of her hi-fi speaker.

Huck Finn took a raft down the Mississippi to get out of St. Petersburg, Missouri, once and for all, but on Sunday morning the raft traffic on the Shiawassee is headed for the center of town and meant to express the hope that the rafters can forever stay in an Owosso just as green and peaceful as it is now. The River Daze races are the environmentalist climax of the festival.

The rafts are comic and ingenious, as varied as the floats in yesterday's parade, bearing slogans such as "Trees 'R' Us — This Raft Is Totally Recyclable." Swimmers and waders flank their progress, participating in splash battles fought with paddles, buckets, and water balloons ("Incoming!"). The Kelly Temporary Services raft capsizes after being shot with a hose — and then the hosers offer to help in righting it. ("Is that a 'temporary' raft?" someone on the bank calls out.)

The race ends at the Heritage Footbridge as some of the last of the festival's contests, human iron-pumping and canine Frisbee-catching, run their course. There are still some musicians and vocalists going, including one who's softly singing "From a Distance," that surprisingly popular song about how God is watching us, and how to Him, Up There, it all looks the same.

For $15 this morning you can fly over Owosso in an open-sided Bell helicopter, if you're willing to depend on your seatbelt to hold you in as you rise from the community airport over the newer part of town, and then fly right above Tom Dewey's leafy old street. From an aerial perspective like this, a place like New York appears as a marvel of rationality, its clean lines canceling the anger and randomness of all that's scurrying in the elevators and streets below. But Oliver Street looks pretty much the same up here as it does on the ground, a spot on which it's easy to keep your bearings.

During its 1986 sesquicentennial, Owosso buried, right near the castle, a time capsule it intends to open in the year 2036. The vault and its marker were a donation, unsuperstitiously accepted, from the Jennings-Lyon funeral home, an establishment with, after all, a reliable record of burying things. Those homes below your helicopter with subscriptions to *Time* magazine have on their coffee tables this week an issue whose cover inquires: "Evil: Does it really exist — or do bad things just happen?" One is inclined to respond with J. P. Morgan's line: if you have to ask, you can't afford it. But until the truth at last gives itself up, mercy and luck will, for all practical purposes, amount to the same thing. The helicopter that took you up here still has to get down to the same airport where, in 1930, Curwood's son, James Oliver, Jr., was fatally injured in a plane crash. With enough mercy, or luck, you'll make it, and Owosso will too, you hope, past another forty-five summers, to the resurrection of its time capsule, on a June day right in front of Curwood Castle, whose trees will still be green with life.

POSTSCRIPT

Almost fifteen years ago I was teaching college English in west Texas, and one night I went with a colleague (another coastal exile) and her visiting parents to the collegiate rodeo. I've come across the diary entry I made when I got home: "I look down [from the stands] at all the college boys sitting in their cowboy hats and boots atop the gates to the pens with the animals, joking and hooting . . . And what if I had been born into their world? Would I have been different, really? Or would my heart simply have begun to race at odd moments when the light hit the dirt of the arena in a certain way on a Friday night — instead of the way it has raced sometimes when spying the moon from a windowed corner of library stacks built on the earth of New England? I don't know."

All I knew was that I wanted to get back north, home. I never saw another rodeo until I went to the IFR in 1990, and what I recognize as having happened between the time I wrote the passage just above and the essay in this section is a sort of double relaxation. All that unpublished Writerly prose in the diary is right in keeping with the inability to look at the cowboys for more than five seconds without imagining myself on their horses. At some point between twenty-six and thirty-eight I must have come to accept my life as a given, not some random thing I was mailed by mistake.

Curiously enough, however, in the two or three years since I was at IFR, more and more coastal urbanites do seem to be imagining themselves up on those horses and Brahma bulls. The nation is going through a sudden fit of enthusiasm for country music: Garth Brooks is selling like crazy and people wearing Walkmen on Madison Avenue are listening to WYNY and Reba McIntire. The last time this trend came around was the late seventies, with the *Urban Cowboy* craze. Perhaps there's a cyclical connection between it and a sour economy, something that during each recession makes you think there's another life out there with your name on it.

I suppose I haven't entirely gotten over susceptibility to fantasy. Otherwise, living in edgy 1992 New York, I wouldn't still keep a picture of Curwood Castle pushpinned to my office wall.

Stars

_____

Independents Days

JANUARY 1992

The subject is film — more particularly, alternatives to typical studio fare, or as Bérénice Reynaud, the New York correspondent for *Cahiers du Cinema,* puts it, the "men-strim bullsheet" of Hollywood. So French and so filmic is Mlle. Reynaud that, if one cannot quite see her laughing at *The Nutty Professor,* one can certainly imagine her gaga over the on-screen sight of Mickey Rourke. This student of "films by women, people of color and Third World directors in a postcolonialist context," as the program of the 1992 Sundance Film Festival identifies her, has so warmed to the subject of the discussion she is supposed to moderate, "Art and Film: New Directions in Cinema," that she can barely permit the actual panelists to start talking about it. Why, she asks, do we take it for granted that there will always be new content but find ourselves resistant to new forms? We *need* new, experimental forms, since, "as we advance in the discovery of ourselves and our society," there is "no other way of saying what we want to say."

Afraid that there may be no way for the assembled directors to say anything at all unless Reynaud subsides, someone near the back of the auditorium shouts, to general assent, "Let's go to the panel!"

Reynaud's excitement is probably pardonable to the panelists on either side of her, since "exciting" is a word they use liberally in describing how it feels to do what they do, which is, in the words of the documentary filmmaker Trinh T. Minh-ha, making something other than the "arrested film of representation." Still, there is much disagreement, some of it over language. Peter Sellars, who with his tall brush cut, big smile, and little hands looks like a friendly animated cartoon character, has only recently turned to moviemaking after years of directing theater and opera, and he admits to not really caring much for words: "Silent movies were my favorite thing," he says. "I think the words most people say are absolutely trivial." Julie Taymor, a MacArthur Genius who has just filmed a puppeteer's vision of Poe's story "Hopfrogs" (her movie is called *Fool's Fire*), is not so sure. She asks people to think of "the great Shakespeare," reminding them that films are not just visual; the language in them is important, too. Derek Jarman, the English painter who the program says "epitomizes the filmmaker/artiste," has in his new film of *Edward II* gone so far as to let the actors make changes in the words of, if not the great Shakespeare, at least the great Marlowe ("Is it not queer that he is thus bewitched?" sounded stronger than "Is it not strange that he is thus bewitched?" so the original was modified).

The real opponents in this debate over improvisation are Sellars and Taymor. He says that once he'd gotten everyone together to begin making *The Cabinet of Dr. Ramirez,* they "of course" threw away the script, which was obnoxious "hackwork" — and that's a "generous" description, by the way. There was plenty of making up as they went along, and since he felt everyone in the room knew more than he did, that was okay. "I work the opposite way," says Taymor, responding to the merry-faced Sellars as if he's one of her puppets who's gone too far. She may wind up throwing away half the shots, but she decides every facial expression she'll film months in advance. It's the audience, not the filmmaker, who should come in unprepared. She wants the people seeing her films to leave their expectations and knowledge of how to respond at home. Her work has an intellectual level, yes, but she prefers visceral to rational response, and she wants those audience members to arrive at their seats like "raw, open boards."

The audience members who paid $15 to hear "Art and Film" were certainly open, but they couldn't be called raw. Some of their faces were eager and aspirant (what they really want to do is direct), and others were older and more dilettantish, but they all knew what they liked and wanted, and that was film, film, and more film, morning, noon, and night for ten January days in five theaters in the mountain town of Park City, Utah.

When the demand for silver gave out several decades ago, the town decided to prosper from the snow on top of the Wasatch Mountains instead of the metal underneath, and the Sundance Film Festival always conducts itself near the height of the ski season. All along Main Street, restored to a boutique frontier look, out-of-towners stroll with tags, either lift tickets or press passes, dangling from their jacket zippers, passing demi-stars like Spalding Gray and trading "Don't I know who you are?" looks for "Don't you know who I am?" ones. Festival participants introduce themselves to one another, responding to bits of résumé and life history by saying "great" to mean what people once meant when they said "I see." The availability of tickets to the various screenings, and how much one has packed into the day, are matters discussed in the same way as ski conditions and mishaps. At a 10:15 show on a Friday night, one man tells a woman near him that this will be his fifth film today. "Awesome," she replies.

Halfway through the 1992 festival I sit down with Lawrence ("Lory") Smith for lunch in the Wasatch Brew Pub, whose restaurant is one floor above its beer-making operation. Lory tells me about his long association with Sundance. Back in the late seventies he had a political science degree and no film industry ambitions; he was then working as a "junk sculptor." But somebody told him about a film festival that was getting going, and he wound up being hired by Sterling van Wagener, the man more or less responsible for starting the U.S. Film Festival, which in those days was held in Salt Lake City, in the fall, and was mostly a retrospective. Nobody really knew what "independent films" were, says Lory, and at the first festival only eight of them were shown in a single competition. But as it happened, the retrospective films were not very well attended, and the new ones had long lines.

What really kept things going beyond the first year, according to Lory, "was the forty-thousand-dollar deficit the organizers managed to run up. The only way to pay it off was to have another festival." Still, financial difficulties aside, he and the others realized that they were on to something. The event's crucial transformation came a few years later from an idea offered casually by the director Sydney Pollack: move the festival from Salt Lake in the fall to Park City in the winter, and you'll attract Hollywood types who'll realize they can ski and scout all in the same week. In the Salt Lake years Lory and his colleagues had to plead with people to send films; this year he's personally looked at about seventy-five of nearly two hundred films submitted for the competitions.

Robert Redford's Sundance Institute, founded in 1981, is "dedicated to the support and development of emerging screenwriters and directors of vision, and to the national and international exhibition of new, independent dramatic and documentary films." According to Lory, the institute really grew out of the festival, and not vice versa, despite what most people think and what the institute doesn't mind their believing. In any event, what in 1978 was the U.S. Film Festival is now the Fourteenth Annual Sundance Film Festival, run by the institute. In attracting over four thousand participants, it is too important for the state of Utah not to have a piece of. So the enormous printed program, along with greetings from the activist Redford, articles like "Out on the Screen: Gay and Lesbian Cinema Arrives," and biographies of some avant-garde jurors ("Beth B has independently produced and directed both short and feature-length films since 1978, including *Salvation! Vortex, Belledonna,* and the controversial music video, *The Dominatrix Sleeps Tonight"*), contains greetings from the Republican governor of this Mormon state and a record of the Utah Film Commission's active support. If the National Endowment for the Arts were as good for the economy as Sundance has been, one suspects that a lot of its political problems would dissolve. Throughout the program, activism and commerce mingle peaceably (Carlos Fuentes and Mike Ovitz are both on the institute's board of trustees), like any happy, heterogeneous movie audience, politely sitting in the dark and waiting for the show to get started.

The independent filmmakers themselves approach the market as a teenager does a parent: with grudging respect and strategic attempts to get away with as much as possible. Their goal is the cinematic equivalent of getting the keys to the family car — a distribution deal. "The Sundance Film Festival," according to Geoffrey Gilmore, its director of programming,

> will continue to be an equilibrium between commerce and experimentation. Illustrating the nature of that balancing act is an incident which occurred last year. A distributor for an independent company came up to me at the start of the Festival and stated that if we continued in the direction we were headed, interest would evaporate, as we would no longer be able to provide companies with films worthy and accessible enough to warrant broad theatrical release. Given that last year's Competition saw over a dozen features ultimately find distribution, we feel that instead we're managing to help expand the sense of the possible in the market without sacrificing either our standards or our efforts at diversity and scope.

What everyone wants most is another *sex, lies, and videotape,* the biggest movie that ever "broke out" of Sundance, according to Lory Smith, who doesn't know if there will ever be another one to sit so profitably upon Geoffrey Gilmore's "equilibrium." But there's really no need to wait for such a heavenly situation when, according to Robert Redford, it's already arrived up here at seven thousand feet: "It has become the festival I had hoped it would be," he says at an opening press conference. "I mean skiing and watching films is a kind of nirvana."

Onto one of the Wasatch Mountains overlooking Park City, some boosters have placed two giant letters — PC — and there are times during Sundance when, looking up at them, a nonresident might forget that these are the town's initials and take them as a reminder to remain Politically Correct at all times during the festival. Redford has said that beyond anything else he is proud of the event's "diversity," but as with college curricula these days, the festival's demographic variety is held together with a fairly uniform ideological glue.

Some Divine Wind, which plays one Wednesday morning at the Holiday Village Cinema, is summarized in the program:

> Ben, the restless central character in Roddy Bogawa's first feature, is a young man of mixed parentage whose father was part of a World War II American bombing mission that destroyed his Japanese mother's village, killing her entire family. His father has kept this information a secret for twenty years; in finally confessing it, he suffers a breakdown at the same time that Ben is struggling to reconcile his own conflicting loyalties. Played with minimalist cool by Benjamin Tu, Ben is aloof and diffident with the accommodating Helen, whose fascination with Japanese literature and culture has either prompted, or been prompted by, their involvement.

The audience that half fills the theater gets to watch Ben as he lies in the bathtub until turning pruny; walks past graffiti saying "Piss on the Patriarchy"; sits in an empty auditorium watching cartoons of anti-Japanese World War II propaganda; and experiences nightmares featuring Allied bombing and the voice of Franklin Roosevelt. Ben, we learn, dislikes maps, let alone actual travel; the maps remind him of how huge the world is, and how small he is.

This is the kind of movie that grips you by the eyelids and won't let go until you've fallen asleep. Helen can't act, and Ben can barely breathe. We have somehow been trapped in a seventy-two-minute Warhol film set in San Diego and possessed of what it thinks is a political consciousness. The production values have a willful, ascetic shoddiness: this is the kind of movie in which you can't make out the dialogue, but in which the movement of a piece of silverware is deafening. As for the scenery, one wishes the actors *would* chew it.

The film is minimalist propaganda, full of propaganda's comic obviousness but devoid of its heart-quickening Day-Glo effects. Nonetheless, *Some Divine Wind* would claim that it is really an attack on the stereotypes of American propaganda from fifty years ago: a modern-day Japan basher and a misinformed Valley Girl who studied World War II one week in high school are held up for scorn, and there is the suggestion, made through references to his old plane ("Barbara"), that George Bush was singlehandedly responsible for a large portion of Japanese civilian casualties a half century ago. The movie likes to repeat fragments of its own dialogue and voice-overs, underlining their significance, and it of course points out that the United States is the only country in world history to have used nuclear weapons — a fact that is supposed to leave one struck dumb with its incomprehensibility. When poor neglected Helen goes and gets her stomach tattooed with the Japanese ideogram for "excess," the film cuts to shots of the names and pictures American bomber pilots painted on their planes' noses. Just as there are distinctions without differences, there are connections without content, and this is one of them.

There are probably few more satisfying, if pointless, experiences than preaching to the converted. If *Some Divine Wind* goes about that business in a grindingly obvious way, then *Swoon,* an eighty-five-minute film by the very young Tom Kalin, accomplishes a similar piece-of-cake mission with hugely more talent and power than the job requires. Shot in just fourteen days, the film retells the Leopold and Loeb thrill-killing story of the 1920s, which has come to the screen at least twice before — obliquely in Hitchcock's *Rope* (1948) and more directly, if a bit reticently, in Richard Fleischer's *Compulsion* (1959), starring the young Dean Stockwell. The Sundance program notes explain: "Portrayed in court as depraved, Leopold and Loeb paradoxically became heroes to the public." Exactly what part of the Coolidge-era public the writer has in mind is unclear, but certainly to the public filling the Holiday Village Cinema on the second Saturday of the festival, the two young murderers *are* heroes of a kind: gay martyrs. When little Bobby Franks, the killers' almost theoretical victim, is bludgeoned to death in a car, the audience reacts with nothing more than an ordinary movie-watching wince, but later, during their trial, when Nathan Leopold and Richard Loeb are on the receiving end of some slurs (imagine, their being called perverts in 1920s Chicago), the reaction in the theater is a sort of collective gasp, an audible expression of horror and moral superiority. On the meter of historical revisionism, this is a true ten.

The beautiful grainy look of the film was achieved, its makers explain during a postscreening question-and-answer session, by blowing up the 16-mm stock on which the entire production, except for the archival footage, was shot. The film is so lush and elegant as to seem like an homage, which in essence it is. Tom Kalin says he grew up in Chicago with his grandmother's scrapbook on the case, and there is a sort of reverence to what he says about his historical subjects. After regretting how, in his autobiography, Leopold apologized for his relationship with Loeb, the young director himself apologizes to Leopold's memory, saying he knows the murderer wouldn't want to be described as contrite.

The film has a number of deliberate anachronisms — pushbutton telephones, tape recorders during an interrogation session — that add nothing, indeed only distract from the otherwise excellent period re-creation. Kalin says they are there to "rupture" the narrative so that contemporary "resonances" are "amplified." In fact, they're just about the only things in this superb, repellent movie that don't work. Neither does the director's explanation of them ("I still don't understand that," says someone in the row behind me). The film can't make up its mind about history, because to do so would close off the chance to have things both ways. It wants to dazzle its viewers with "periodicity," but it doesn't want to be cluttered with so many old things that the audience won't decide that little has changed since 1924 and that what drove these boys to their unfortunate actions is still very much oppressively around today. The actor who plays Leopold says it was the "maddening isolation" of being gay back then that added to Nathan's obsession with Richard and his willingness to do anything to keep him. Basically, it was/is society's fault, and putting in too much of all the Nietzsche business that was fairly central to the killers' obsessions would have made history less serviceable. Kalin admits that in the twenties Nietzsche was very "vanguard and empowering," but this is clearly not one of the elements he was most interested in dealing with. So it is treated as an inconvenience, something easily set aside, like plausible passages in the Warren Report.

The audience was primed for *Swoon*'s sexual politics by a short that preceded it: "Thanksgiving Prayer," a "cinematic collage of cities, breadlines, burning buildings, the Lincoln Memorial, astronauts in space and the American flag, scored to William Burroughs reading his [poem] 'Thanksgiving Prayer.' " O irony! The audience got to whoop its approval as Burroughs's filmy face deadpanned through a litany of objects of thanks that went right up through "laboratory AIDS." After this appetizer, made by Gus Van Sant, director of the overpraised *My Own Private Idaho,* any manipulations of history by the makers of *Swoon* were bound to seem trivial.

Sundance repeatedly contends that gay cinema has "arrived," and the work of Tom Kalin (somebody to watch out for in every sense of the term) is proof enough of that. Each year the festival gives a send-off to in-your-face films like *Poison,* to truly eye-opening ones like *Paris Is Burning,* and to good-willed, culturally accommodating ones like *Longtime Companion.* A touching, less glossy version of the last, shown this year, is Laurie

Lynd's *RSVP,* a twenty-three-minute film about an AIDS widower who hears his recently dead lover's radio request (mailed in before he died) of "Le Spectre de la rose" from *Les Nuits d'été.* The film shows a series of people who knew, or didn't know, the dead man, all of them listening to the radio station after the announcer mentions whose request he's playing. Among them are the young man's parents (phoned by his lover) and his sister, whose quiet sobbing, as she stands alone in her house, is shatteringly well acted. This is a very different short from *Thanksgiving Prayer* — one that doesn't believe AIDS was made in a laboratory, just tries to hope it will be cured there. The audience viewing it made no sound until the credits had run their course.

Characters in books are just stews of letters, available to be set in motion or frozen at the individual reader's will, and usually pictured, despite authorial description, any way the reader pleases. Movie characters (at least in the pre-VCR era) have always been more remote and intractable, going at their own speeds in their literally larger-than-life sizes; and while the print characters had no life beyond their cloth covers, the movie actors, one knew, had real lives somewhere else. Their otherness was the point. One might go looking for oneself, or someone very like oneself, in a book, but up on screen? To find him there would be to feel one hadn't gotten one's money's worth.

At this festival, where the stars are usually no bigger than life, all the actor-audience mingling winds up poking a sort of hole in the screen. A few hours after seeing *Some Divine Wind,* I run into Helen Molesworth, who plays "Helen," on the Park City bus that shuttles among the hotels, Main Street, and the ski areas. I ask her if the tattoo she got in the movie is real, and she says yes — making me feel that the saddest thing about *Some Divine Wind* is that the actors were playing themselves.

Most nights during the festival there is a cash bar and music down at Z Place on Main Street, where actor-audience separations are further narrowed. On Wednesday a soft-rocking band, racially and sexually integrated in a Sundance-diverse sort of way, is playing, but Mammon is showing the flag, too: *Entertainment Weekly,* one of the festival's big sponsors, has its banners and blowups and free issues everywhere. A guy who looks as if he might or should or wants to be one of the Baldwin brothers, struts around in leopard shorts, cowboy boots, and a T-shirt saying (front) YOU KILL ME and (back) NO MEANS NO. Deborah Harry, who blew the first puffs into Madonna's Zeitgeist fifteen years ago, sits with her choppy reddish-brown hair (no longer a blondie), chatting and smoking with three or four other people, the only ones to be taking any real notice of her. Wendi Tush is at the bar looking for cable-TV news stories, and just before 10:00 Derek Jarman and some of the *Edward II* crowd come in, fresh from their premiere across the street at the Egyptian Theater.

The Egyptian is Park City's restored movie palace. Stained-glass pharaohs cover its wall lights, and a little old-fashioned piano sits off to the side of the stage. Displayed in the lobby are memorabilia of the theater's first incarnation, which lasted from Hollywood's golden era until the early 1970s, when protests over the showing of *Last Tango in Paris* (a film that would be very tame at Sundance 14) probably helped the owner decide that keeping the place going was more trouble than it was worth. A decade later, by which time Park City had turned hip and prosperous (in at least a small measure because of Sundance), the Egyptian reopened for movies and live theater.

Jo-Jo at the Gate of Lions has two of its four showings there, an incongruous setting of old-time Hollywood-worship for such a deliberately un-Hollywood film. And yet *Jo-Jo,* for all its disdain of flash and success, all its pride in the now, arrives on a history nearly as long as Hollywood's. There is, after all, no more stable or definable cinema style than the "experimental." Film school students probably have as clear an idea of what still constitutes the avant-garde, decades after it started marching, as the Thalbergs and DeMilles did of what would set hearts beating in the darkness of the Egyptian during Park City's unpaved, pre-ski days.

Like most other films of its kind, *Jo-Jo* is in black-and-white. Its narrative is carried through vignettes that are announced by titles and concluded with dissolves. The heroine is a beautiful young woman who receives a prophecy: she will develop four lines on her face and will meet disaster unless she has "taken a new path" and changed her life by the time the fourth one appears. The program declares that this voice-receiving "modern-day Joan of Arc" begins a relationship with "a young astronomer" named Jon (he actually seems more like a listless low-level observatory worker) but is "slowly drawn into the orbit of Luke, a shadowy phone-sex entrepreneur who relentlessly pursues her and oddly entices her with promises of good pay and flexible hours." Like a lot of men in films at this year's festival, Luke is a rapist in the making.

As the film chronicles Jo-Jo's gradual farewell to reality, it has a number of humorous moments, some seemingly unintentional (Jo-Jo telling her friend why she's not calling Jon: "If I don't take what I want, maybe I can prevent nuclear war") and others improvisational: Jon asks Jo-Jo, when she's become severely disengaged, to think of her future: "What kind of job are you going to be able to get as a catatonic?" One can imagine the same material in the hands of Pedro Almodóvar, who would let lines like the last one run the show, which would be renamed *Jo-Jo on the Verge of a Nervous Breakdown.*

When the lights in the Egyptian have come back up, the director, Britta Sjogren, who can't be any older than Tom Kalin, won't say exactly what her film means — "I don't want to answer that. You can interpret it any way you want" — but will admit to having been inspired by Christa Wolf's novel *Cassandra* and by the work of Jean-Luc Godard. One factor adding to *Jo-Jo*'s enigmatic nature is the sound quality. I doubt that I was the only member of the audience to hear "taken a new path" as "taken a bath."

Later, across the street at Z Place, Britta Sjogren and her cast talk to me about their film. The director is philosophical about those audience members who walked out ("If they're looking for a slick Hollywood film, I can't blame them for leaving"), even if she did finance her project mainly with loans, and work on it for more than two years. She tells me she assembled her cast by auditioning "easily a hundred people" over an entire summer, and through connections. Chris Shearer (Jon) recommended David Schultz (Luke), and Lorie Marino (Jo-Jo) was a friend of a friend of a friend of one of the director's collaborators. The main shooting was done over about two and a half weeks, followed by a series of pickups over the next couple of years.

"Sometimes we'd come to shoot," says Chris, "and it would be like we wouldn't have read anything. They would have written the scenes the night before or whatever, and said, 'Okay, this is your scene.' I mean, it was a technique, I guess, to keep it fresh?" He and Lorie Marino describe a degree of improvisation lying somewhere between the storyboarding of Julie Taymor and the here-goes-anything of Peter Sellars. The director's scope "is so gigantic," says Lorie, "and you're like in the moment kind of thing." The very deliberate-appearing Britta Sjogren sometimes had to adjust her serious vision to spontaneous fun. For one scene she had a melancholy voice-over ready, but "we got to the beach, and I had to put them in the car, and my brother was doing the sound in the back seat, so I couldn't see what they were doing, right? I decided to let them do it, and they came back and said, 'Oh, it was great, it was so funny.' And I said, 'Funny? What are you talking about, funny? Have you read the voice-over?' I was so mad at them, and I made them do it over really serious, you know, and then when we watched the rushes, you know, everybody was watching that scene and everybody was cracking up, and I thought, well, it's obviously better this way, and so we chose that take instead of the other one, and I rewrote the voice-over to match that mood."

Britta's cast have just seen the whole film for the first time, because she finished the mix only last week: "The lab got the first print here on Saturday," she says. Sitting in the Egyptian just half an hour ago, Chris Shearer finally understood what "Jon" is really about: "I look at the whole thing and I think, 'God, the guy doesn't know what he wants.' I didn't know I was that character until I saw it." In a case like this, the film process seems one step away from live television, but for all its appealing freshness, there are considerable risks involved. Lory Smith, who has looked at prospective entries while they were still on the editing bench, without music or dissolves or optical effects, says that some filmmakers have regretted playing Sundance in a rushed fashion, wished they'd held off until they were really ready.

One of the attractive things about the young people who made *Jo-Jo* is that they would rather not wait for much. Britta Sjogren was at Sundance for a couple of days last year with her ex-boyfriend, but this time she's here looking for a distribution deal: "Definitely I want to try for a European [one]. I think that it would probably play really well in Europe." Lorie Marino, the member of the project whom one can most easily imagine on some future talk show, says that this film "will hopefully give me the credibility I need to get over the hump of legitimacy in order to land other parts, other roles where the competition has more credibility than I do, or studios behind them." Meanwhile, the festival gives her a "great audience" for a "labor of love" that was made while working from "grant to grant." David Schultz and Chris Shearer are hoping to get some work and representation out of *Jo-Jo*'s exhibition in Park City.

The immediate future for each of them is problematic. From here Britta must look for a job and a new apartment and buy a car. She's thinking of making a movie about a dating service, so she might try to get hired as a videographer at such a place. Lorie goes back to an advanced acting class in New York, and David will be doing "whatever I can to make money: carpentry, design, auto mechanics, anything I can do. In the meantime I'm trying to develop some projects with a director and writer, so I can finally get arrested in this town, or actually Hollywood, not this town." And goofy-handsome Chris Shearer, who seems afraid of becoming the lackadaisical character he just played, says he's going to make "a big push" after Sundance, following up on the various leads and connections he's acquired here: "I did another film, and I didn't do all that. I sat and waited for the calls to come in, and it never happened. So now I'm really gonna jump on this. I'm very hopeful."

Some films land a distribution deal as soon as they've been picked to play at Sundance, and some of those in the competition have one even before that. These movies that show up for the dance with dates are no doubt the focus of some secret envy from those independent projects afraid of becoming wallflowers, and the latter wait for the former to betray the first signs of sellout gaucherie. A few of the films seem already to have traveled so far down the road toward Hollywood that it's hard to find any resemblance they might still bear to downtown would-bes. They even have Hollywood stars in them, ones willing to work cheap for the chance to be associated with a "prestige project."

Fathers and Sons has Jeff Goldblum playing a former film director and bad husband who has been taken down a peg (a sure Hollywood sign of impending regeneration) by the sudden death of his wife. He has moved himself and his son to a seaside town where he runs a bookstore and participates in a local theatrical adaptation of *Don Quixote*. His son, Ed, is hard to reach these days, threatened by drugs and the wrong crowd and a serial killer. Serial killers are as common in today's movies as the boy next door used to be, and the one in this film by Paul Mones has supposedly written a weird vanity-press book called *Cats and Dogs*. "Mones' work as a director is," according to the program, "quite straightforward here, but he also includes elements which lend an atmosphere of suspense to the film and cryptically hint at its outcome. *Fathers and Sons* is alternately quirky and comic, dramatically powerful and elusive." These quirky, cryptic elements are worn like the tenured professor's folk-art earrings, a token badge of solidarity with her bohemian past. Cryptic is artful, so the slickly made *Fathers and Sons* throws in a preposterous fortune teller (Rosanna Arquette!) and some dolphins being mysteriously poisoned by pollution (elusive ecological motifs show up in a number of films at the festival). Still, despite drugs, serial murder, and pollution, the town in which this film is set seems to be a model of racial integration and peace, something that goes beyond movie fantasy and over the border into television.

The Jeff Goldblum character is able to rescue young Ed from the serial killer because of some telepathic connection between father and son, and when, the morning after, near the end of the film, he comfortingly tells the boy, "We've all been through a horrible thing," he has said a mouthful. And yet, with the exception of two snickering people behind me, the Friday morning audience seems to like what it's seen, and director and star are happy to take their questions.

"I feel that a lot of people can relate to what's in this flick," says Paul Mones, meaning the "environmental" stuff, the "drug thing," and "if you've ever lost a parent." One definition of an experimental film might be a movie to which the audience can *not* relate. Indeed, what makes *Jo-Jo* rather fun to watch during even its most somnolent moments is that one can't relate to *any* of it: it is entertaining, even intriguing — to an extent never possible with a print equivalent — because it is so willfully beside one's own point. *Fathers and Sons,* on the other hand, hopes its audience will relate to the parent-child troubles but also be dazzled by the spooky off-the-wall stuff. It wants to be two kinds of movie. This is, after all, an independent film that has a credit for "Mr. Goldblum's Tanning Facilities."

Mr. Goldblum puffs the movie with the kind of affable phoniness he might use with Arsenio. The first time he saw the film straight through he "was like very emotional," and on the day that last scene between father and son was shot — a scene he prepared for with a lot of improvisation — he tried not to put too much pressure on himself. Mones says Jeff is great to work with because he really lets himself go "with the energy." The director/writer also notes that he started the whole thing with just one sentence ("Max and Ed on the front porch"), not knowing where he would go with it. But, hey, that's the thing about writing: you don't know where it's going. The audience gasps when it hears the whole film took only twenty-four days to shoot, but if they'd seen *Swoon,* they might be wondering what took Mones so long. Nonetheless, the information that *Fathers and Sons* cost only $1.8 million might make a studio head, if not gasp, at least cock an eyebrow, since the only difference between this and a bad studio film is about $20 million.

At the extreme commercial end of Sundance lies *Poison Ivy,* which actually looks less like a studio-made theatrical release than a TV movie of the week. Even its cost — $3 million — approaches that form's ballpark, and its presence at this festival seems a little like Rob Lowe doing two weeks as Coriolanus. Its genre is Beverly Hills Gothic: a glamorous bad-girl teenager (Ivy), the "throwaway" daughter of a dead coke addict, makes friends with the malcontented, bookish, but very prosperous Sylvie and proceeds to destroy her plain patron's family by seducing Sylvie's father and, after becoming a companion to Sylvie's beautiful invalid mother, pushing her off a balcony so that she can have Mom's dresses as well as Dad's body.

This is a vixenish nineties version of *The Bad Seed,* and even more risible, but *Poison Ivy* has its surprising little pleasures, chief among them Drew Barrymore, who is no longer just the cross-addicted little girl down the lane but a luscious, rotten peach, a sort of satanic Brooke Shields. The program describes her performance as "layered," and the truth is it's better than that; she is *wonderful,* a gaudy, fearless camera swallower. In addition to her, about all the movie has going for it is a great car crash and a great fall (Ivy, needless to say, ends up going over the same balcony as Sylvie's mother). As the father, Tom Skerritt does succeed in looking terrified to realize just how horny he is.

As men-strim bullsheet goes, this is a straight cruise down

the lazy river, but don't tell director Katt Shea Ruben that. During the q-and-a, she describes the movie as a "suspense drama," which is why she's gotten over worrying about the success of *The Hand That Rocks the Cradle:* that's closer to a horror movie. *Poison Ivy,* insists Ruben, is more on the order of *Rebecca* and — fasten your seatbelts — *All About Eve.* When a man in the audience asks her to explain how the Tom Skerritt character made his money — was it real estate? (a good question, since the film is unclear about this) — Ruben responds: "You should see the movie again, and listen better."

To be an artist, and to be surrounded by pygmies!

A number of full-blown press conferences, not just audience q-and-a's, take place in the resort hotels during Sundance, and in all respects but one they are like any other press conference touting any other endeavor.

On Thursday afternoon one of them has been set up in connection with the presentation of the Piper-Heidsieck Tribute to Independent Vision, to John Turturro, who has performed in such independent films as *Miller's Crossing, State of Grace,* and *Jungle Fever.* Sundance's closest thing to a Life Achievement Award, the Piper-Heidsieck Tribute, being given for the first time this year, is sponsored by the champagne company, whose banners adorn the dais and walls of the meeting room in the Yarrow Hotel.

Before reading a letter from Robert Redford, Geoffrey Gilmore, the director of programming, tells the assembled reporters that the American independent cinema is mostly known for directors and writers, whereas with this award, actors will be getting their due. Certainly John Turturro, the star of this event, is more a vaguely familiar face than a household name. A bit of a mumbler (not always a handicap in independent films), he has an appealing self-deprecation ("I thought I was a little young for an *hommage*") as he recollects his career to date and appraises the directors he's worked with. "Spike's a really good person," despite some of the negative impressions one may have formed from his public manner, and as for the Coen brothers, "they're great, too," quite sensitive with real senses of humor. Turturro is so in love with his work that in musing on those occasions when he might feel prostituted as an actor, the example he selects involves a director who yells "Cut!" after an actor accidentally falls down.

A couple of days later, the morning after the world premiere of *Light Sleeper,* Paul Schrader's film about "a forty-year-old drug dealer at a crossroads," the director and some of his cast, including Willem Dafoe and Dana Delany, meet the press at the Prospector Square Hotel. Schrader, best known for *American Gigolo* and the screenplay for *Taxi Driver,* says he made his new film for $6 million and it looks better than *Frankie and Johnny,* which cost about $28 million. His remarks run the gamut from the informatively specific (most night scenes in Hollywood movies are overlit) to the sort of cinema verities ("Everything on screen is a choice") that can compete with the curiously meaningless way in which writers talk (always too much) about writing.

He declares that "the drug culture is a very good metaphor for a lot of things about this decade," you know, the kind of "outrageous S & L world" we live in now, and when the press conference is over, the reporters do the one thing you never find them doing at a press conference about anything else. Just as they did after John Turturro's meeting with them, as if the experience of sitting in the presence of movie people precludes them from functioning as anything but an audience, they applaud.

Sitting in the Wasatch Brew Pub, Lory Smith and Nan Chalat (a mutual friend) talk with me about how *dark* so much of what's playing at the festival is. Lory says that he's tried to splash a little sun into Alberto García's "bleak vision," but there's certainly a lot of resolutely grim fare on screen. García, the competition director, says in this year's program that "for those of us immersed in this event, the rest of the world will fade away during the ten days of the Sundance Film Festival. SO BE IT! GOOD RIDDANCE!!!"

Actually, an assiduous attendee, spending most of his hours inside in the dark instead of on the gleaming slopes, might be pardoned for feeling that the world was never more with him. A viewer from New York can easily, during the ten days of the festival, wind up riding the subway and paying more visits to the Bronx and East Village than he might in many a month back home. Some of this vicarious experience, that on-screen grimness, is strong and well presented. *Jumpin at the Boneyard,* Jeff Stanzler's film about two Bronx brothers, one who is unaddicted but unemployed, and the other who is strung out on crack, is perhaps the most powerful film at the festival. Manny, the clean but angry brother (played by Tim Roth, who looks and acts like a young De Niro), tries desperately, in the course of a night and a day, to straighten out Danny, partly by dragging him through the past of their "changed" white ethnic neighborhood: they pay visits to their father's grave, an old gym, and, harrowingly, to their living mother, who hasn't seen the addicted brother in ages and refuses to see him now. The film is full of loud, agonizing futility and is so uncompromisingly depressing that the rumor heard at one Sundance party made perfect sense: Twentieth Century–Fox, which has agreed to distribute the picture, was said to be backing away from it.

Black and White concerns the interracial romance of a young black Lower East Side super and a pretty Soviet immigrant. Made in New York by Boris Frumin, himself an émigré, the film was completed back in the director's homeland, thanks to glasnost. As the program says, "this quintessentially rude, independent New York production was edited in Leningrad." In trying to love Lisa, Roy (played by Gilbert Giles, who is to Denzel Washington what Tim Roth is to De Niro) must compete with his boss and Lisa's landlord, Atkins, another okay-guy-evolving-into-a-rapist. *Black and White* is a "little" movie, smaller than *Jumpin at the Boneyard* and without its technical smoothness, but it, too, has believability, as well as an unsentimental love for New York, whose craziness and squalor it straightforwardly shows. Like *Jumpin, Black and White* is in color: both films have enough confidence in their material to avoid "authenticating" it with the sober treatment so many of the serious, small films at the festival seem compelled to embrace.

Anthony Drazan's *Zebrahead* is another film of interracial romance, set among high school students in Detroit ("I think we all went there with a little bit of trepidation," says the director during q-and-a). Despite some good performances, this one, unlike *Black and White,* is very polished, and never lets you forget it's a movie. This last trait arises not from some self-referential aesthetic but from the film's constantly evident desire to be liked and admired, something the smaller film with so much less of a chance seems unconcerned with. It comes as little surprise to see, in the credits, that one of *Zebrahead*'s producers is Oliver Stone.

Comedy is not absent from Sundance, but it often gets short-subject shrift, confined to a few minutes before the features. Some of these comic shorts are genuinely funny and memorable, like "Complaints," in which people sing their twenty-words-or-less peeves to piano accompaniment. (The director, David Weissman, was able to make this first 35 mm work after being given "free short-end film left over from *Barton Fink,*" a movie starring John Turturro.) "That Sinking Feeling," a two-and-a-half-minute amalgam of cel and 3-D computer-animation techniques, "is the very short story of a man who, on seeing his old girl in a bar, shrinks so small he falls into his own glass, which she then drinks by mistake and swallows him whole." The funding credits take up a good portion of the total running time: the Film Arts Foundation Grants Program, the Advanced Computer Imaging Center, the Western States Regional Media Arts Fellowship . . .

The one full-length animated feature at the festival is *The Tune,* a seventy-two-minute film by Bill Plympton. It is so replete with invention that it exhausts both eye and brain. This merry movie full of "morfing" (the seamless change of one face or image into another) comes complete with a flossing albatross and a mustache that turns into dancing shoes. *The Tune* is also a musical, full of enough memorable, silly songs ("Flooby Nooby") to fill an album — and there probably will be one if Plympton and his collaborator Maureen McElheron get a distribution deal. Though two assistants colored in the cels, Plympton did every one of the thirty thousand drawings in the film: he'd just put on his Walkman and listen to Emmylou Harris tapes and draw until midnight and have a ball. The film contains a huge measure of cartoon violence in the form of two men trying to top each other by doing violent things to each other's heads, but after each mashing and bashing, the figures revert to exactly the same state and appearance they had before. There is, in fact, a sweet, pure inventiveness to *The Tune* that reaches beyond anything else at Sundance, and Plympton, a graying, plump man with an amused air, is different from any other filmmaker on the scene. At the Z Place party on Friday night (the featured band is Taj Mahal, who did the music for *Zebrahead*), a distributor from Los Angeles comes up to him, and before she can say what she does, he jokes: "Hi, are you anybody important? What can you do for my career?"

The Tune's plot involves Del, a mild-mannered songwriter trying to come up with a number that will please his angry boss, Mr. Mega, and his coworker, Didi (Mr. Mega's secretary). As plots go, it is really not so different from that of *In the Soup,* a full-length feature that itself resembles a lot of other films here in Park City by being in black-and-white and set on the Lower East Side. Technique and locale aside, however, *In the Soup* is an independent version of what reviewers still like to call a "romp." It is the story of a young man living in hapless squalor who's energized only by the hope of getting his huge white elephant of a screenplay made into a movie. He must survive a pair of rent-demanding Mafia brothers, the indifference of the beautiful Hispanic woman who lives in the next apartment, and finally the criminal adventures into which he's enticed by Joe, a crazy, life-loving crook who bucks the kid up and promises him the money for his movie.

In the Soup is the independent movement's funny Valentine to itself. Starring two "veteran actors in American independent film — one from the Cassavetes era (Seymour Cassel), and one from the Jarmusch generation (Steve Buscemi)," it plays at the Egyptian one afternoon in the middle of the festival. "Some of these things happened to me," says the director, Alexandre Rockwell, "but not all of them." His press release talks about how, years ago, Homer, "a small time gangster who took a shine" to him, gave him $7,000 to make his first movie. "He seemed to trust me completely (although it was pretty clear I wasn't going to mess with a guy who carried a .45 in his belt). Homer became my first 'producer,' " someone who "took me out of a world of theories and made me a filmmaker." Whatever experiences he may have had a decade ago, the thirty-five-year-old Rockwell is no longer anything like the ineffectual dweeb played by Buscemi. (Gelded dweebs are the safest male heroes these days, and one finds them all over Sundance movies.) Standing handsomely on the stage of the Egyptian in his jeans and leather jacket, Rockwell admits to an "incredible feeling" — sort of like the one his wife, Jennifer Beals, danced to (sort of) in *Flashdance* several years ago. She plays the beautiful neighbor, and she's here as well; the two of them are the glamour couple of Sundance, poised on the crossover horizon.

Appropriately enough, *In the Soup*'s financing fell through two days before shooting began, but according to Rockwell, one of the producers, Jim Stark, got it going again. The Egyptian viewers, many of whom are traveling the same route from theory that Rockwell did, applaud. If ever there was an independent movie inviting audience identification, it's this one. "I guess you could say I got bitten by the bug," says Seymour Cassel's character, meaning the filmmaking bug, at the movie's disastrous close, and the real-life Cassel, on stage later with Rockwell and Beals, cheerleads: "Independent film is where it's at."

After the screening, on the Park City bus, I hear a woman summarizing the plot of *In the Soup* for someone who didn't see it. Told that it's about a starving guy who's trying to get his screenplay made, the listener says, sarcastically, "That's original." But told that he tries to do it by placing an ad in the paper, offering his screenplay for sale, the same listener, sincerely excited, says, "Oh, that sounds wild!" Straight up with a twist: a good movie is like the perfect martini, and everybody at Sundance can tell you how to make one.

The polite movie-star demurral that "it's an honor just to have been nominated" has a sort of practical truth at Sundance. When Lory Smith says that "all the films here are already, in a sense, winning films," he's talking about the selection-process hurdles they have already cleared, and he might be alluding to their improved distribution prospects, too. Still, winning is winning, and the independent-film industry is perhaps most derivative of its studio forebears in the practice of bestowing lots of awards upon itself, with one important difference. The Sundance jurors, according to Lory, tend to ask themselves, as they deliberate: "What film can we help the most?"

This year's awards ceremony is held on Saturday night at Z Place, which is jammed. It's time to thank those who put the festival together, and what better way to do that than to roll some credits? An expertly produced clip is run to enthusiastic applause. And the jurors are named. Bérénice Reynaud cannot be here, alas, because she had to go off to Rotterdam, but Beth B is thanked for rearranging her schedule so that *she* can be here instead of in Amsterdam. The competition director, the young, ponytailed Alberto García, says it's been "thoroughly, totally, excellently exciting," before he lets Geoffrey Gilmore throw things over to "one of the most intelligent men you're ever going to meet," the monologist Spalding Gray.

Like independent film, Gray is an acquired taste, but as a downtown version of Billy Crystal he's a good choice, starting things off by describing Park City (which he keeps wanting to call Park Slope) as a "tacky, tacky frontier town," a combination of Alaska, Austria, and Poland instead of the manicured Aspen he was expecting. For its wild inaccuracy the description is crowd-pleasing, as is his story of once meeting Robert Redford, which was "like meeting the Immaculate Conception."

Though the awards don't proliferate to quite the extent they do each March in the Dorothy Chandler Pavilion, there are still plenty of them. Shortly after announcing a special jury prize for a work outside the Documentary Competition — the recipient is a film about Samoan street gangs in Los Angeles — Gray bestows an Outstanding Performance Award on Seymour Cassel, a likably emotional presence with his great pudding face and suspiciously blond hair. He tells the crowd, and means it, that it's a wonderful thing "to do something with your heart, for nothing." Neal Jimenez, who wrote *The Waterdance,* a film about paraplegics, is wheeled up to the podium to accept the Waldo Salt Screenwriting Award, which he does by good-humoredly acknowledging all the actors who "screwed with every single word on this script." The presentation of the cinematography prizes (one of which goes to the deserving *Swoon*) is slightly marred by a faulty projector, which renders these film-quality winners fuzzy, jerky, and finally immobile.

The evening's biggest award is the Grand Jury Prize for Dramatic Competition, and it goes to *In the Soup.* Alexandre Rockwell accepts this honor for a movie about moviemaking by thanking all those independent filmmakers who "go into debt and put their asses on the line." Afterward, one can hear a few grumbles about how the festival must be losing some of its progressive edge if it can honor as amiable a film as this one (Monday's *New York Times* article about the awards will be headlined "For a Change, Popular Films Win Top Prizes at Sundance"), but the self-congratulatory choice meets with general approval, and Alexandre Rockwell and Jennifer Beals provide the cameras with an approximation of Hollywood dazzle.

(*The Deseret News* reports the frustration of photographers, throughout the festival, with the number of participants wearing black.)

Later, over at the Park Meadows Racquet Club, guests at the enormous awards-night party (is that Deborah Harry out on the dance floor?) are not unduly gotten up, as if that might be bad form. About the only fur jackets one can spot are draped over the backs of chairs at the American Express sponsorship table. The decorations include some huge white balloons that rest on the floor like small planets. There's a prom-like air to the mingling: most of the people here are ones you've already spent a lot of time with, going from theater to theater, like classrooms.

A film distributor who's been looking for documentaries complains to me that he's watched a lot of "visual masturbation" this week, a lot of "film for film's sake." The trouble with a lot of these films is that they "*don't make sense.*" But he wouldn't be able to convince one wide-eyed connection-seeking young man across the room of any such thing. "I'm living off my savings and writing screenplays," the young man tells me. The only real complaint of somebody like this is against time itself. Will he have enough of it to get lucky? Enough to take off, or too little before he finds himself deflated, like those shrinking balloons in the corner, and has to give up?

The day after the awards is Super Bowl Sunday, a warm, sunny day in Park City. Melting snow drips from the roofs of hotels and condos, as a lot of skiers stay inside to watch the game. By now some of the festival participants have been looking at movies for a week and a half. But there is still more to see. Each year, on the day after the awards, the winners screen at the Egyptian. (After so many days of film watching, one also starts thinking of "screen" and "show" as intransitive verbs.)

Among these winners is *The Waterdance,* which received the Audience Award in the Dramatic Competition, a prize sponsored by *Entertainment Weekly* and based on the ballots filled out by people leaving the theaters after each screening at the festival. *In the Soup* (the juried winner) is certainly a film audiences can warm up to, but it is probably still too much of an in-joke for the general viewing public, to the extent that the audiences at Sundance can be said to constitute one. So instead they gave their prize to *The Waterdance,* which already has a distribution deal from Samuel Goldwyn Films, and at 5 P.M. on Sunday I am back at the Egyptian, watching it through the frizzy gray hair of Spalding Gray in the seat in front of me.

Based on the aftermath of Neal Jimenez's own accident (the hero of the film is "young novelist Joel Garcia," played by Eric Stoltz), *The Waterdance* shows a wardful of paraplegics trying to cope with what has happened to them. The conflicts among these men desperately thrown together are the same that have engrossed moviegoers from *Lifeboat* to *Airport '75.* "In a perfect world, those two would be lovers," says Joel to his girl-friend about the warring Raymond (a black street dude) and Bloss (the redneck motorcyclist). As sure as you know that light will follow darkness once the projector is turned off, you know that Raymond and Bloss will bond after a furious fight. The movie is full of wisecracking and insult humor, but is at bottom, for all its graphic representation of the problems caused by the characters' injuries, very sentimental. And that's just fine: one has seen more than enough hopeless stuff this week. The performances are uniformly good, and the film ends with a small moment of such power — a brilliant emotional mugging I wouldn't dream of revealing here — that it takes a moment to realize, after the lights are up, that like a lot of people shuffling out toward Main Street, you're having one old-time sure-fire studio-film experience that you haven't had all week: you're crying.

Rex Harrison: Bidding Goodbye

DECEMBER 1990

The man at the lectern looks out over his half-glasses and asks the audience who among them will give $275 for Richard Nixon. Actually, it is an autographed copy of *The Real War* that's being auctioned, and the $600 it eventually fetches has to do not just with the book's author but also with the single copy's owner, the late Sir Rex Harrison (1908–1990), whose effects are being sold off this afternoon, December 13, 1990, at the William Doyle Galleries on the Upper East Side of Manhattan, the proceeds to benefit the scholarship fund bearing Sir Rex's name at Boston University.

Nixon's boilerplate inscription ("To Rex Harrison with appreciation for his incomparable contribution to excellence in the theater and motion pictures") tells people something about the very quality that has to one degree or another brought them all here: style. You either have it or you don't.

People have also come in search of clever Christmas presents, and a few holiday touches — poinsettias near the lectern, a Christmas tree behind a pegboard screen — further encourage the sentimental commerce. It will take less than three hours to sell more than two hundred lots, and if you lose track, you can find which item is whizzing its way from Harrison's possession to that of someone here by consulting the red digital light attached to a pillar at the front. On a wall to the right of the auctioneer hangs a huge photographic portrait of Sir Rex, looking down upon the proceedings — slightly scandalized but rather more amused.

People took their seats early, the way they might for a hit play or a prominent man's wake. This is, of course, a bit of both, though two days ago, when one could "preview" the items for sale, the feeling was even more theatrical. Set out under the flashlight-shaped lamps of the gallery, Rex Harrison's possessions looked as if they had been acquired not in the course of somebody's long life but during a set decorator's afternoon shopping spree. (An absence of squeamishness helped a potential bidder in his survey: he could flip through a rack of the departed's suits as if he were on the second floor of Macy's.)

The bidders are an entirely civilized group: well-dressed older women; pretty younger ones no doubt chatting ironically about the romantic impulse that brought them up here; stylish gay men calmly alert to the procedures of bidding. I sit with my all-day-sucker-shaped paddle, number 302, recalling how a year ago this week I saw Rex Harrison do Somerset Maugham's *The Circle,* and was startled, alas, by his seeming in more urgent need of revival than the play. He had aged into something shuffling and simian, and yet, determined to keep his limited energies focused entirely on the props and people right in front of him — the audience was a distant irrelevance — he created a more forceful illusion of actually being his character than he probably did in many other productions, when just being Rex Harrison was more than enough to give the crowd their money's worth.

Along with his opening instructions about the state sales tax, the establishment of provenance, and so forth, the auctioneer offered a disclaimer: all items have "been used." It was spectacularly beside the point because, of course, it *is* the point. The first real bidding war — the auctioneer's pen pointing back and forth, like a metronome, between the potential purchasers —

was over a shaving mug, manufactured by Mug Makers of Hollywood and inscribed "Rex." The catalogue suggested $10 to $15. The successful bidder paid $325. Lot 50, even more intimately tactile, some makeup and a hairpiece, went for $125. This toupee, held up high by one of the green-shirted porters who keep pace with the auctioneer, looked like something pulled up from a drain, but it's been the only thing bid upon by the young man in front of me, who wears a punkish black hat throughout the proceedings — a theater student (a bald one?), perhaps. He fruitlessly offered $75.

In life, possessions give their owner status. In death, it's more like the reverse, the owner's celebrity, if he had it, electrifying the object with a personal history. Some objects in this auction, beneath that luster, have clear intrinsic worth, too: the "Provincial Louis XVI style fruitwood swivel armchair, used by Rex Harrison in his dressing room at every performance for make-up," combines handsomeness with hallowedness in a way that makes the final bid for it — $3,100, from someone in the audience competing with someone on the telephone — no surprise. One would like to know more about some pretty but less imposing items, such as a "Cartier sterling silver bookmark, inscribed 'Rex.' " Did he actually use it to keep his place in the works of Shaw and Nixon, or was it a Christmas present *he* once received and promptly put in a drawer? One or two objects even become instruments of revenge. Surely Julie Andrews would be pleased to know that the framed stage bill for the London production of *My Fair Lady* is commanding $125 more than a poster for the movie version with Audrey Hepburn.

The paintings Harrison did late in life — Corsican and West Indian landscapes, mostly — prove to be the biggest disappointment of the day, the only class of items to bring consistently less than the gallery suggested. It's true that they're pretty awful: in this geriatric field Harrison was no Winston Churchill. "It's upside down," the auctioneer has to tell the porter holding up lot 119, *Beach Scene,* before musing that it might bring more money that way. But, bad as they are, shouldn't these paintings' close contact with their owner — their maker — endow them with even higher sentimental value than, say, the shaving mug? Does their failure come from their seeming full of effort, things this man of ultimate insouciance had to worry over rather than just deign to use? Is that why they seem uncharacteristic, of doubtful psychological provenance? They aren't *him*.

Whereas, surely, wool hats and cardigan sweaters were. These signature items are presented late in the auction, one by one. The catalogue shows that the original plan was to offer bunches of them in a few lots (the way the ties and shoes are disposed of), but someone has decided to split them up, a move that proves commercially shrewd. Lot 158, a box of fourteen sweaters, was estimated at $200 to $400. In the end, the new lot 158C, a single camel-hair cardigan, sells for $450. A year ago the same gallery sold the possessions of Bette Davis. At that auction it was the ashtrays, of course.

By five o'clock I am on the bus heading back downtown, having purchased, for $75 plus tax, Rex Harrison's Victorian oak-and-silver-plate wine bucket. My sister had adored him, and this would be just right for her Christmas present. She will later tell me that at her New Year's party it leaked all over the place, turning her dining room table into a soggy plain. But she knew that that, too, was beside the point.

POSTSCRIPT

After my return from Park City, weeks passed before I wanted to see another film, and when I did go out to the local Cineplex Odeon it was to *The Addams Family,* something quite deliberately picked for its being a *movie,* a word that never appears in Sundance programs and brochures. Over the next few months I continued to follow the progress of some of the exhibits, noting for instance how later in the winter the Forty-second Berlin International Film Festival gave one of its International Film Critics' prizes to *Edward II* and the Caligari Film Prize to *Swoon.* For some films without a major studio deal, the festival circuit can become a kind of distributor in itself.

During the same post-Utah period Rex Harrison showed up on television, wearing one of the sweaters I couldn't afford at the auction; I came in on him while he was telling Mrs. Pearce to take Audrey Hepburn away and give her a bath. "Biographies," wrote Mark Twain, "are but the clothes and buttons of the man — the biography of the man himself cannot be written." In Sir Rex's case, the clothes and buttons were gone after the auction at William Doyle, but a year and a half later, the undeterred Nicholas Wapshott was readying a biography, the "first truly revealing one," its publisher promised, which would depict Rex Harrison as "an *homme fatal* who married six times, divorced four, and drove the women in his life to desperation and — more than once — to suicide." But never, at least, in front of the audience. R.I.P.